Making the World Safe for Capitali~

D1433049

MAKING THE WORLD SAFE FOR CAPITALISM

How Iraq Threatened the US Economic Empire and had to be Destroyed

Christopher Doran

PlutoPress
www.plutobooks.com

First published 2012 by Pluto Press
345 Archway Road, London N6 5AA

www.plutobooks.com

Distributed in the United States of America exclusively by
Palgrave Macmillan, a division of St. Martin's Press LLC,
175 Fifth Avenue, New York, NY 10010

British Library Cataloguing in Publication Data
A catalogue record for this book is available from the British Library

ISBN   978 0 7453 3223 9   Hardback
ISBN   978 0 7453 3222 2   Paperback
ISBN   978 1 84964 667 3   PDF
ISBN   978 1 84964 669 7   Kindle
ISBN   978 1 84964 668 0   ePub

Library of Congress Cataloging in Publication Data applied for

This book is printed on paper suitable for recycling and made from fully managed
and sustained forest sources. Logging, pulping and manufacturing processes are
expected to conform to the environmental standards of the country of origin.

10   9   8   7   6   5   4   3   2   1

Designed and produced for Pluto Press by Chase Publishing Services Ltd
Typeset from disk by Stanford DTP Services, Northampton, England
Simultaneously printed digitally by CPI Antony Rowe, Chippenham, UK and
Edwards Bros in the United States of America

This book is dedicated to the memory of Peter Gray.

Contents

Part I

Making Sense of the Invasion and Occupation of Iraq

1
Introduction: Making Sense of Iraq

> If you thought the army
> Was here protecting people like yourself
> I've some news for you
> We're here to defend wealth
> ... We're making the world safe for capitalism
>
> Billy Bragg, 'Marching Song of the Covert Battalions'

In April 1917, Woodrow Wilson told the people of the United States that they had to join the carnage of the First World War in order 'to make the world safe for democracy'. He lied. Wilson's desire to have America enter the war was in large part to protect American corporate investments in Britain and France, and to ensure that bankers like JP Morgan would get the money back they had loaned those countries.[1] The war was not to make the world safe for democracy; it was to make it safe for capitalism.

Eighty-six years later, in 2003, the US would enter another controversial war to make the world safe for capitalism: Iraq. And like the First World War, an American president would deliberately lie about the real reasons the country needed to wage war, a mainstream media would follow blindly, and in the war's aftermath people would still be trying to make sense of what had happened, and why.

The 2003 American-led invasion and subsequent occupation of Iraq has arguably received the most media attention and analysis of any event in recent history. Yet a decade after the 9/11 attack that launched the US War on Terror and the subsequent Iraq invasion that fundamentally changed the course of US history, there is still a shortage of credible explanations. The key arguments put forward by the Bush, Blair (UK) and Howard (Australia) administrations were proven to be false, and Iraq proved to be the political downfall of all three leaders and their reputations.

What has resulted is a decade of national soul-searching, and a deep divide between left and right, progressive and conservative. Few agendas have been more divisive in American history than

Bush's self-proclaimed global War on Terror. This agenda has continued under the Obama administration, which despite being elected on a platform and promise of change, has continued much of the War on Terror policies of the Bush administration, which it had roundly condemned. Unfortunately, this has included Iraq. Ensuring that Iraq remains a US client state will continue to be American foreign policy regardless of who is in the White House, because a truly free and independent Iraq, unlike the vast majority of the world's 195 nations, could actually challenge the key underpinnings of America's global dominance.

Which is the point of this book: that the motivation for the US-led invasion and subsequent occupation of Iraq in March 2003 was to eliminate the threats a post-UN sanctions Iraq posed to American economic hegemony. This hegemony, rooted in Third World debt and corporate market access, has seen trillions of dollars flow from the Third World to the First via the World Bank, the International Monetary Fund (IMF), the World Trade Organization (WTO), and free trade agreements. An independent Iraq, free to develop its own oil resources unimpeded, would have had the potential to challenge Saudi Arabia's petrodollar financing of the US economy, and directly challenge the Saudi state's capacity to serve American interests via its dominant oil producer status.

The war has been an extension, and protection, of the same free market neoliberal policies which have driven successive American, British, and Australian governments over the past three decades. It was market access and control of the global economy that motivated the US to invade Iraq, not weapons of mass destruction, or ties to Al Qaeda, or a simplistic desire to seize Iraq's oil. While consistent with those policies, invasion by military force was also an important – and frightening – new phase of US willingness to guarantee the survival of its global power.

Neoliberalism is the supercharged form of capitalism which emerged as a concerted American corporate response to the anti-Vietnam war, pro-consumer and environmental movements of the 1960s and 1970s, to become the dominant government ideology from the early 1980s onwards. Along with Austrian Friedrich Hayek, American economist Milton Friedman is one of neoliberalism's most famous, and enthusiastic, founding champions. In *Capitalism and Freedom* (1962), Friedman outlines the three key cornerstones of neoliberal policy:

1. Governments must remove all rules and regulations standing in the way of the accumulation of profits.
2. Governments should sell off any assets they own that corporations could be running at a profit.
3. Governments should dramatically cut back funding of social programmes.

These can be succinctly summarised as deregulation, privatisation of public entities, and cutbacks of government services: capitalism on crack cocaine.

Better known in the United States in its various guises of free market ideology, Reaganism, trickle-down economics, or corporate globalisation, neoliberalism, in its most recent ideological incarnation under the Tea Party, is also the fundamental belief that the individual in society is best served by as little government as possible.

Friedman's formula was applied domestically in the US beginning with the 'Reagan Revolution' in the early 1980s and, slightly earlier in the UK, under Margaret Thatcher. It was then applied internationally via the debt control and market mechanisations of the World Bank, IMF, WTO and free trade agreements. Neoliberalism has continued through successive administrations and congresses, including the 'Yes We Can' Obama presidency. Fuelled by ever-increasing corporate donations, lobbying and media concentration, the era of free market neoliberalism has seen a massive transfer of wealth from the world's working class and poor to the wealthiest of the wealthy. Neoliberal policies and their effective implementation have been the basis of US global economic dominance from at least 1982 onwards, when the first World Bank/IMF Structural Adjustment Programmes were instituted under Reagan. Ironically, it has perhaps brought about its own potential downfall through massive unsustainable spending on Wall Street bailouts and military outlay to guarantee its survival.

The election of Barack Obama, the financial markets meltdown and bailouts to Wall Street amidst significant public anger, and the subsequent rise of the Tea Party – at few other times in US history has there been the intense mobilisation of political forces regarding the role of government in the economy: a quintessential question of neoliberal ideology and reality.

The ultimate beneficiaries of free market neoliberalism have been corporations and their shareholders. The ideology of neoliberalism emphasises the right of the individual to be free from government interference. Because corporations are legally recognised as individuals, it is these 'rights' of the individual as protected by the US Constitution's Bill of Rights and under common law provisions in the UK and Australia that have given the corporation as an 'individual' the ultimate power and benefits under neoliberalism. Understanding this connection is key to understanding US motivation not only in Iraq, but in any number of other crucial policy crises, such as national health care, climate change, or environmental protection.

This book's following five parts examine the five areas of how a post-UN sanctions Iraq either directly threatened the ongoing success of American economic power, or provided enormous opportunities to extend it.

IRAQ'S POTENTIAL THREAT TO SAUDI ARABIA AS A US CLIENT STATE

Part II examines the crucial underpinning that Saudi Arabia and Middle Eastern oil revenues have provided for US global hegemony from at least 1973 onwards in the aftermath of the OPEC oil embargo, in both its direct funding of the American neoliberal agenda, domestically and internationally, and via Saudi Arabia's capacity to control oil supply and price concerns for American interests. The Saudis and other Arab oil-producing states have been reinvesting the bulk of their oil revenues back into the US economy. This had resulted in an estimated $1 trillion in petrodollars being invested in primarily the United States from 1973 to 2000.[2] The American economy had become increasingly dependent on these petrodollar investments as a means of addressing its own debt and budget deficits.

A post-sanctions Iraq would also have been in position to use revenue from its oil reserves – second only to Saudi Arabia's – and offer its internal development model as an alternative to the neoliberal US-dominated World Bank, IMF, WTO and regional free trade agreements. This is what Iraq had done prior to the first Gulf War, when it advocated that other Arab states should reinvest their oil revenues back into their own economies for internal development. In contrast, Saudi Arabia and Kuwait sent their oil profits to be invested in US banks and government securities, money which had provided the backbone of Third World loans via the World Bank and IMF. This arrangement had been instrumental in developing countries paying an estimated $4.6 trillion from 1980 to 2004 to creditors in First World countries, in particular the United States.[3]

It was, and is, Iraq's oil-producing potential to directly rival Saudi Arabia that made it imperative that Iraq either be contained (increasingly more difficult under the UN sanctions), or directly placed in the US client-state orbit. Direct control of Iraq via 'regime change' meant not only removing these impediments to American global economic dominance, it also meant potential control of Iraq's oil production as a complement to, or even potential direct replacement of, Saudi Arabia.

Within this context, the 2003 invasion was not the start of a war on Iraq, but a long continuation from when Iraq invaded Kuwait in 1990 and the UN Security Council, under US leadership, passed UN Resolution 687, which placed economic sanctions on Iraq. Despite the US and its allies driving Iraq from Kuwait, the sanctions remained in place for 13 years. The sanctions officially were to ensure Iraq eliminated its weapons of mass destruction programmes. The sanctions were actually intended to remove Saddam Hussein from power and remove the substantial obstacles, as well as open up new opportunities, for the free market neoliberal agenda by having control over Iraq. That the sanctions had failed in their purpose and were nearing the end of their vitality as an ongoing strategy due to increased international pressure regarding their humanitarian effect, meant that the US and its allies went to the next phase: regime change.

DOLLAR DOMINANCE: CONTROLLING THE DOLLAR, CONTROLLING IRAQ

Part III looks at how American economic power was also directly threatened by Iraq's 2000 decision to switch from accepting dollars for its oil sales to only accepting euros. Up to that time, all oil had been sold exclusively in dollars, which was a key factor underpinning the US's dominant role in the global economy since the new world financial order was established by the Bretton Woods agreements in 1944. If other Middle East oil producers switched from dollars to euros, trillions would be taken out of the US economy, as countries would need to move from having dollars in reserve to pay for oil, to having euros on hand. The tremendous advantage for the US of having trade exclusively denominated in American dollars is little explored in neoliberal literature, yet it is arguably as vital a component of US economic hegemony as any other. In particular, the Nixon administration's decision to no longer require the dollar to be backed up by gold reserves, combined with the near-simultaneous decision to remove capital constraints on US banks, created a new economic paradigm for the United States.

The 2003 invasion of Iraq is just one instance, albeit a significant one, of nearly one hundred years of US and British attempts to subjugate Iraq for market control of its oil. Part III also addresses the post-First World War British imperialist founding of and subsequent domination of the nation state of Iraq, through Iraqi independence and the post-Second World War American support for coups in Iran and Iraq. In particular, it addresses American support for Saddam Hussein during the Iran–Iraq War of the 1980s, including assistance in developing chemical weapon infrastructure.

LOSING OUT: US ELIMINATED FROM OIL AND OTHER IRAQI MARKETS POST SANCTIONS

The United States had also been eliminated from any participation in the Iraqi economy once the sanctions were lifted. Saddam Hussein's regime had signed huge post-sanctions contracts with European and Russian firms to develop its oil resources, at the direct prohibition of American companies. The US was thus eliminated from playing any role, let alone a controlling one, with regard to the world's second largest oil reserves. Access to markets is a fundamental tenet of free market, neoliberal ideology and policy.

In 1995, the *Wall Street Journal* summarised: '… the European companies will have grabbed the best deals … Indeed, the companies that win the rights to develop Iraqi oil fields could be on the road to becoming the most powerful multinationals of the next century.'[4] Iraq post-sanctions had also eliminated the US and its corporations' access to every other Iraqi market: agriculture, electronics, vehicles, manufacturing, and so on.

Over nine years after the invasion, actual control of Iraq's oil remains elusive due to the ongoing militancy of the resistance and the questionable legal authority of the central government. However, despite lacking the clear legislative authority to do so, the Iraqi government has in recent years signed oil contracts that, if fully realised, could see Iraq pumping enough oil to far outstrip Saudi Arabian production, and as a result destabilise if not outright eliminate OPEC. This in turn would solidify US hegemony for the foreseeable future.

The US does have *de facto* control of the Iraqi government, control which it believes will continue regardless of troop levels thanks to the ensnaring of Iraq in the World Bank, IMF, and the WTO. Even if Iraq descends into all-out civil war and no oil is pumped, it would mean no other nation state or their companies would have control either. Had Saddam Hussein remained in power post-sanctions and honoured the European companies' access to Iraq's oil at the expense of American ones, he would also have further strengthened Iraq's commitment to selling its oil in euros, and influenced others to do the same. Preventing the rise of any potential rival to its superpower dominance is implicit in the Bush administration's 2002 National Security Strategy, and is even more emphatically declared in previous documents written by Bush administration officials before taking office, as examined throughout this book.

REGIME CHANGE: THE OPPORTUNITY TO CREATE A BRAND NEW, NEOLIBERAL, FREE MARKET STATE

As well as eliminating these threats, seizing direct control of Iraq presented a number of opportunities. Part V examines American efforts to impose a new free market, neoliberal US client state where one had not previously existed. Such a client state would open up a new market to US capital of 28 million well-educated people, affluent from oil revenues. The head of the Coalition Provisional Authority, Paul Bremer, was blunt about American intentions: 'It's a full scale economic overhaul. We're going to create the first real free market economy in the Arab world.'[5]

According to free market neoliberal theory, it is the state's responsibility to create markets where they did not exist before. As examined in Chapter 13, in the face of a diminished ability to continue to expand free market neoliberalism in the face of hostile global resistance, the United States moved to the next level of invading Iraq.

The enforced economic orders under the Coalition Provisional Authority are examined in detail in Chapter 17. Chapter 21 addresses ongoing American efforts to control Iraq's oil, including pressure for the Iraqi Parliament to pass legislation that would have given western oil companies unprecedented access to the country's nationalised oil industry, and the inspiring story of Iraqi civil society successfully resisting its passage.

The United States, along with Australia and the United Kingdom, the other key members overseeing the occupation, laid the institutional framework to ensure that Iraq's economic future would be tied to the World Trade Organization, and to the neoliberal structural adjustment programmes of the World Bank and IMF. Chapter 20 also relates how the CPA established the political and legislative framework to ensure that these laws would be embedded in any future elections, constitution, or legislative context.

EXPANDING THE EMPIRE: A NEOLIBERAL FREE TRADE AREA FOR THE MIDDLE EAST

As examined in Part VI (Chapters 22–25), the United States now has established the basis for a free market, neoliberal policy expansion to the largely closed-off markets of the Middle East via the US Middle East Free Trade Area (US-MEFTA). In May 2003, Bush announced the US's intention to create the MEFTA. Despite the open hostility of much of the Arab populations, the US has made progress in ensuring US capital has access to the last bastion of the world not penetrated by free market corporate globalisation, aka neoliberalism. Saudi Arabia, as well as Iraq, is now locked into the WTO market liberalisation of its economy; as a result, Saudi Arabia, the world's dominant oil producer, has had to open up its oil services market to US and other companies.

However, while it may be construed as progress for the US neoliberal free trade agenda, it has not been progress for the countries involved. The twin standards of free trade agreements – lowering tariffs and reducing impediments to trade, combined with liberalising a country's economy to facilitate direct investment by US and western corporations – directly contributed to destabilising food security for a number of Middle East and North African countries. Record-high food prices were a major factor in the 2011 Arab Spring protests and uprisings. This leap in global food costs was a direct result of the US deregulating commodities markets, and allowing the purchase and sale of food to be indexed like any other stock market entity. Countries which had reduced their tariffs had little protection or recourse when the cost of imported food skyrocketed. The Middle East free trade agreements signed thus far have also resulted in horrific sweatshop working conditions and further repression.

Part VII, 'Sowing the Seeds of Democracy: A Case Study of Iraqi Agriculture', examines how the US has put great effort into creating the conditions for large-scale corporate agriculture, at the direct expense and devastation of Iraqi food sovereignty. By eliminating tariffs and other protections, the US instantly created a billion-dollar annual market for its own agricultural exports, a market which did not exist in 2002 under the sanctions. Combined with allowing Wall

Street to speculate on food for new opportunities of exploitation and profit, American corporations are literally making a killing.

American efforts in Iraq are part of a larger and more sinister story of how US agribusiness is attempting to control the entire world food market for profit, from growing, transporting, through to eating. Via the WTO and free trade agreements, the United States profits from forcing its own highly subsidised food onto countries that have agreed to tariff reductions and to slash or outright eliminate their farm and price support systems. The type of agriculture that the US is pushing in Iraq is the same large-scale monocrop production that has devastated small farmers around the world, including in America itself. Crucially, the US is attempting to create genetically modified crop dependency on Iraqis as a launching pad to forcing genetically modified crops and food onto the rest of the highly resistant Middle East and North Africa.

In outlining these areas, this book argues that free market neoliberalism and corporate market control provide the best understanding for American motivation regarding the invasion and occupation of Iraq. The first three areas were vital to guaranteeing the ongoing viability of American power via neoliberalism, in particular the debt restructuring mechanisms of the World Bank and International Monetary Fund and *de facto* control of oil markets. The latter two, plus potential control of Iraqi agriculture, facilitated a significant expansion of that power. In particular, critics who say it was simply 'all about oil' miss the larger story regarding how oil, or rather control of oil, is a key to US power, and how a post-sanctions Iraq could have impinged on American ability to maintain its global economic and political supremacy.

In fact, once one understands the basics of market access and control, it becomes self-evident that this has been the overwhelming reason the US has intervened in so many countries, whether by coup or direct invasion, and is the same reason they invaded Iraq: that the country had restricted American corporate access to its markets. The US has not hesitated to take whatever action it deems necessary to create or protect market access for its corporations since the 1880s, when the US Supreme Court recognised that corporations had the same 'rights' as flesh-and-blood citizens, and where this book traces the origins of the modern corporation and its subsequent dominance of American foreign policy. The United States has directly intervened in more countries, and more often, than any other country – by far – since that time.

Contrary to the widespread view that Iraq has been a disaster for the United States, the book argues the opposite: that the invasion and subsequent occupation have been a success. Not only has the United States eliminated potential threats to its global dominance, it has also succeeded in expanding it. By invading Iraq, the US sent a strong message to other countries, a message also made clear by the unsuccessful US-supported coup in Venezuela in 2002 to remove Hugo Chavez, a vehement critic of US neoliberal economic and foreign policy. It was also made clear when the Obama administration, along with British and French allies, launched air strikes against the Libyan government in its dubious support of the Arab peoples' uprisings in 2011.

Any recognition of American and Coalition 'success' regarding Iraq must be placed in the context of the tremendous cost to the US nation state in terms of financial outlay. Brown University's Eisenhower Study Group now estimates the cost of the Iraq and Afghanistan wars to be between at least $3.7 and 4.4 trillion dollars.[6] But the ultimate cost has been to Iraq itself.

2
Iraq: A Devastated Country

Regarding the past eight years of the occupation of Iraq, I would like to press that the occupation brought nothing but destruction and devastation ... and the alleged democracy brought by the occupation is nothing but the destruction of the Iraqi people.

Iraqi Federation of Oil Unions (IFOU) President Hassan Juma'a Awad, 2011[1]

We are going to fight them and impose our will on them and we will capture or ... kill them until we have imposed law and order on this country. We dominate the scene and we will continue to impose our will on this country.

Coalition Provisional Authority head Paul Bremer, 2004[2]

The extraordinary financial outlay for the Iraq War must also be placed in the context of the tremendous devastation and suffering of the Iraqi people. Their suffering originated in the first Gulf War, was institutionalised during the sanctions period, and was then significantly accelerated through the invasion and subsequent occupation.

Bremer and the Coalition Provisional Authority's focus on establishing the Middle East's first neoliberal free market economy via a 'full scale economic overhaul' meant that it was economics and opportunities for the US and its allies' investors that took precedent over the welfare and chronic immediate humanitarian needs of the Iraqi people. This was blatantly evident to Iraqis when the American military prioritised the protection of the Oil Ministry while Iraq's cultural heritage was looted; equally evident when the CPA announced the country's entire economy apart from oil was for sale; and also obvious when the US gave priority to its own agricultural exports over ensuring Iraqi's food security.

American efforts to portray their Iraq experience as positive and in the best interests of Iraqis are belied by the overwhelming evidence to the contrary. 'Shock and Awe', Abu Ghraib, Fallujah, the brutal house-to-house searches and detaining of suspects, often innocent and often never to be seen again, are the enduring hallmarks of the invasion and occupation, just as napalm, Agent

Orange, and 'destroying the village to save it' are the lasting legacies of US involvement in Vietnam.

In Iraq, the horrific bloodletting and sectarian-based violence which peaked in 2008 was the direct result of a flawed political and constitutional process established under the US that framed political parties – and hence political power – in terms of Iraq's ethnic and religious identities of Shias, Sunnis and Kurds. These political parties were then dependent on the US for keeping power; power framed in the context of occupation under (until recently) 150,000 Coalition troops, and power based on a weak and non-inclusive constitutional process that a large and crucial segment of the population, Iraqi Sunnis, refused to participate in.

As examined in Chapter 20, the US trained militias for those parties it needed for political control, which in turn led to the sectarian violence that sought to control parts of Iraq under Sunni, Shia and Kurdish power. It was the American military, not Iraqis, who formed and trained the Special Police Commandos, replicating the hated *mukhabarat* secret police of Saddam Hussein. This divide-and-rule strategy created a system of repression and terror with the intent to suppress any and all resistance, and to ensure Iraqis fought each other rather than unite against the US occupation. The training of death squads is not, unfortunately, a unique element of US policy. It was widely deployed in Vietnam, and more infamously as the 'Salvador option' in El Salvador and Nicaragua in the 1980s, among others. The latter two programmes were overseen by John Negroponte, who was US Ambassador to Iraq in 2004 when the Special Police Commandos were formed. Further evidence of US responsibility for the carnage was laid bare in the massive release of documents from Wikileaks in 2010.

The intent is clear: to create a level of sheer terror that the population has no recourse but to accept the US imposed neoliberal, free trade system where corporate investors and the predatory right to profit take all precedence. This 'Shock Doctrine', made famous by Naomi Klein's 2007 book by the same title, means that the Iraqi population has had to focus purely on survival, rather than opposing an economic system which they had no say in creating. The system rewards its collaborators, and these collaborators then have the political and economic power to further entrench it. Those foolish enough to oppose it will end up as one of the many thousands of unidentified bodies which have inundated Baghdad's morgues since the invasion.

Chapter 17 also details how the entrenched neoliberal free trade economic laws have directly contributed to Iraq's present pitiable state of affairs, such as the elimination of tariffs and other protections of the Iraqi economy, thus facilitating the flooding of the economy with cheap foreign products and sabotaging any chance of Iraqi economic or food sovereignty. In addition, the CPA established a constitutional framework that entrenched these laws for future Iraqi governments, and tethered the oil-rich Iraqi economy to the US-dominated IMF, World Bank, and WTO. Equally as important, the US-directed constitutional process instituted a political system based on ethnic religious denomination representation which in turn inflamed previously dormant sectarian allegiances, leading directly to the sectarian bloodbaths of 2005–08, and which still plagues any attempts at Iraqi national unity.

The utter callousness of the US's approach has been stunning, particularly given the fact that the eyes of the world have been on it and its actions in Iraq. Through either outright fraud, sensational incompetence, or, most likely, theft, over $12 billion of Iraqi money for which the US was responsible for overseeing is simply unaccounted for.

The result is that, as of 2011, Iraq is a devastated country. According to the Iraqi Ministry of Planning, the official poverty rate was 23 per cent in April 2011[3] and is undoubtedly much higher. Similarly, official statistics state unemployment to be approximately 13–15 per cent; but in 2009, Ali Baban, Iraqi Minister of Planning and Development, stated it to be 35–40 per cent,[4] and even higher in rural areas. Despite billions allocated by the US for reconstruction and repairs, much of the country still only has electricity for a few hours a day. As detailed in Chapters 26–29, Iraq is not able to feed itself and now imports an incredible 80 per cent of its food despite its proud and ancient tradition of agriculture.

As many as 1.2 million deaths have been directly attributed to the invasion.[5] In 2008, the United Nations High Commission on Refugees estimated that nearly 5 million Iraqis had been displaced, including many teachers, doctors, engineers and other professionals crucial to the rebuilding of the country's civil society.[6] Many professionals are dead, intentionally targeted in the bloodletting. It is a country now plagued with horrific birth defects and cancers thanks in large part to the millions of tons of depleted uranium and other toxins used by US forces.

After eight years of having been liberated from Saddam Hussein and eight years of US occupation and ascendancy to representative democracy, Iraq ranked second only to Somalia as the most violent and least peaceful country in the world in the 2011 Global Peace Index.[7] The *Economist* magazine's 2010 Democracy Index classifies Iraq as a 'hybrid regime' placed between flawed democracy and outright authoritarianism, and ranked it 111 out of 167 countries.[8] Transparency International lists Iraq as the most corrupt country in the Middle East, and gave it a corruption score of 1.5 out of 10 in 2010.[9] US based global watchdog Freedom House flatly states that Iraq is not an electoral democracy: 'Although it has conducted meaningful elections, political participation and decision making in the country remain seriously impaired by sectarian and insurgent violence, widespread corruption, and the influence of foreign powers.[10]

While it would seem that the near-total breakdown of Iraqi society in the midst of carnage and reprisals would not be in the best interests of American intentions to convert Iraq into a privatised, free market paradise, the collapse has benefited the US. And while the ground may not be fertile as yet for a thousand McDonald's to bloom, and a lack of a clear legal system has stymied efforts to allow multinational unfettered corporate control over Iraq's oil, it has also meant that the country cannot function without US support.

But as devastating as the US intervention has been, Iraq is also a cause for hope. Ordinary Iraqis, representing a vast composite of grass-roots civil society, have exemplified incredible courage and dignity in their steadfast resistance to the occupation and to the seriously flawed constitutional and legislative process imposed upon them. This resistance transcends Arabs or Kurds, or Shias or Sunnis. As we shall see in Chapters 11 and 12, it is a resistance that has defined the Iraqi people since the artificial creation of Iraq by British diplomats in the aftermath of the First World War. Whether the story of Sanaa Abdul Wahab Al Sheick's attempt to save Iraq's national seed bank by hiding seed germplasms in her backyard during the invasion (as described in Chapter 28), or the successful mass civil society opposition to the passage of the US-sponsored oil legislation, ordinary Iraqis are at the forefront of global movements for a just and equitable future. Much of what the US assumed it could accomplish – such as the wholesale privatisation of the entire Iraqi economy (apart from its oil) – has not been achieved. Iraqi resistance, both violent and non-violent, has meant that the invasion has not been the cakewalk strewn with flowers that Dick Cheney and others predicted. And the US would never have agreed to withdraw its troops if not for Iraqi society demanding it, and translating it into political capital.

Iraq is also the story of global resistance to tyranny. As horrific and unjust, not to mention illegal, the actual invasion was, one can only imagine how much worse it would have been if not for the tens of millions who marched and protested, and the thousands who dedicated their lives to try and stop the invasion.

As a result, much of what the US has done in Iraq has had to be covert. The invasion occurred not because of democracy, but in spite of it. Public opposition to the war in America, exceeded only by the sheer will and determination of the Iraqi people to see their occupiers gone, greatly contributed to the Bush administration agreeing to the total withdrawal of US combat troops as part of the Status of Forces Agreement. The last of these technically departed at the end of 2011, although with military bases, the world's largest embassy, and several thousand private security forces remaining, just how much of a withdrawal will occur remains to be seen. The sheer brutality as exemplified by Abu Ghraib, Fallujah, and seemingly daily reports of US troops' torture and callous disregard for Iraqis as highlighted by Wikileaks, and the lack of accountability or punishment for those responsible, has even more fully exposed the emperor as having no clothes.

3
A Full-Scale Economic Overhaul: The Rise of Free Market Neoliberalism

In order to understand why the US invaded Iraq, we first need to understand how the application of free market neoliberal ideology was responsible for US economic power. While the US has been an economic superpower since at least the end of the Second World War, its government and economy went through a profound change beginning in the 1970s, when there was a unified and wildly successful attempt by American corporations to institute neoliberalism as the guiding economic – and of equal and crucial importance, social – ideology governing American society. Bremer's 'full scale economic overhaul' in Iraq, examined in Chapter 17, is a replica of what the United States has done domestically beginning with the neoliberal 'Reagan Revolution' in the early 1980s. The difference is that what the US attempted in Iraq was without the Iraqi people's consent, and was instituted illegally and as a result of horrific violence and destruction resulting from a full scale military invasion. Whereas in the US itself, it was done with the democratic acquiescence of its own people, and with little resistance.

It is also the same model, often with violence equivalent to what it unleashed in Iraq, that the US has successfully forced onto the rest of the world. When America's nemesis and superpower rival, the Soviet Union, began to disintegrate in the late 1980s, the US was able to force free market neoliberalism onto the rest of the world. The rest of the world, however, has been much more resistant to American insistence that market freedom for corporations is the equivalent of human freedom, or that the devastation and social dislocation wrought by free market corporate globalisation has been worth the cost.

In the year 2011, uprisings and mass protests raged from Greece to London and throughout North Africa and the Middle East against the relentless neoliberal cutbacks to government services, privatisation of any and all public entities belonging to the people themselves, and deregulation which has seen the banks responsible for creating the global financial crisis being bailed out while millions have had their homes foreclosed. All in the name of national debt restructuring, which has so very obviously made the rich who created the crisis much richer, and the poor who had nothing to do with it much poorer. In America itself, as of October 2011 the 'Occupy Wall Street' movement had exploded into a nationwide protest against the 1 per cent of the population having wealth and income well beyond any reasonable amount of the other 99 per cent.

But for the most part, the majority of Americans seem to be content with their country's embarrassing income inequality, now worse than Egypt's, with wages that in real terms haven't increased since the 1970s, with upwards of 50 million of its people with no health care coverage, and with unemployment and poverty at record levels. Few equate any problem with the economic system itself, or that these problems have steadily worsened since the advent of neoliberalism under Reagan when the free market neoliberal assault began on American society. The US is after all a democracy, albeit a feeble one, and it has been freely elected officials who have pursued massive deregulation, who regularly bail out and subsidise large corporations while punishing the people who have become poor as a result, and who keep getting re-elected. That's not to say there isn't resistance; the mass civil disobedience shutdown of the 1999 Seattle WTO Meeting a major case in point. But compared to the social upheaval of the 1960s and early '70s which openly challenged the American way of life and resulted in real and substantial social justice change, there has been no equivalent opposition to the last 30 years of neoliberalism which has eroded much of the victories of that period.

Yet, as this book argues, America invaded Iraq to ensure the status quo continues, both domestically, and globally. And while there certainly was American public opposition to the war itself, there has been relatively little awareness or criticism of American economic policy in Iraq despite its radical anti-democratic and devastating reality. The majority of Americans are apparently so accepting of capitalism, and so approving of the predatory early twentieth-century neoliberal version of it, that they are comfortable with the idea that once a country is invaded, it is completely acceptable to transform it into a capitalist, free market neoliberal version of America itself.

But capitalism and neoliberalism have not occurred in vacuums. Capitalism has come about due to centuries of wars and violence and the intentional displacement of millions upon millions of people. No one has ever willingly given up their communal land to have it sold off as private property, or to have their food that had previously been grown and shared by the community for free to be commodified and sold for profit, and then agreed to compete with countless other displaced people for work in a factory for wages.

How neoliberalism became the dominant ideological reality of the late twentieth century, and how an ideology that elevates corporate profit and markets as holy and government regulation and services to protect a country's own people as evil, needs to be understood if we are fully to understand why the US felt it had to invade and destroy Iraq.

PROFIT IS SACRED: A BRIEF INTRODUCTION TO NEOLIBERAL IDEOLOGY

The founding of neoliberalism as an official ideology can be traced to 1947 and the first meeting of, among others, Friedrich Hayek and Milton Friedman at the Mount Pelerin spa in Austria; they subsequently referred to themselves as the 'Mont Pelerin Society'. They believed that the world order was threatened because wider society had started to question the concepts of private property and the competitive market. They took on the name of 'new liberals' – that is, neoliberals – as they believed themselves to be in the firm tradition of the liberal European commitment to individual freedom. They were intent on providing an antidote to the Keynesian economic prescriptions and government-funded social programmes which had taken hold in western governments dealing with the Great Depression. These policies had become entrenched in the post-Second World War international policy framework, including the World Bank and International Monetary Fund.[1]

Friedman would advocate in *Capitalism and Freedom* (1962) that taxes should be at the same flat rate for both rich and poor. Corporations should be free to sell their products anywhere in the world, and governments should not protect any local industries or ownership. Labour costs and prices should be determined exclusively by market forces. National parks, health care, education, pensions, the postal service – any and all government services – should be privatised.

Neoliberalism as a political theory calls for the sanctity of the individual and individual freedom, and states that it is individuals, operating in an open market economy, that can best decide what is good and bad for them. Markets are the best and most efficient means of providing goods and services to society, as dictated by the freedom of individual choice, and therefore are the best means of maximising a just society. Therefore, government interference in markets must be kept to a minimum. The hallmarks of neoliberalism are the privatisation of state-owned entities and public services, deregulation of business activities and limits on corporate power, deregulation of labour markets, removal of trade barriers such as tariffs, the free flow of foreign investment and technology, and a general commodification and marketisation of all aspects of life. Markets, not governments, should determine the distribution of essential services such as education and health care. These are all key tools to increase economic growth, which will increase wealth and the individual's ability to participate in – and influence – the market. The role of government is primarily to provide security and the rule of law.

Neoliberalism as an ideology states that the individual should be as free as possible from all government intrusion, and that the best way for the individual to express his or her freedom is via their participation in the market. This is the 'signal' of what the individual desires; the market will then respond and set prices accordingly, as per neoliberal ideology. This 'invisible hand of the market', first envisioned by Adam Smith in the eighteenth century, is rooted in the European liberal tradition which established the primacy of the individual over the community. This has justified the expulsion of people living communally from their land in order to establish private property rights, has been the basis for commodification and profit from what had previously been grown and distributed for free, and was identified by Karl Marx as the 'primitive accumulation' stage of capitalism.

In the last 30 years, this mania for the 'invisible hand of the market' has extended to an erosion of services which governments traditionally provided their citizens, such as retirement pensions, health care, education and social security. As neoliberal theory dictates, all should be subject to market forces and free to generate private profit, regardless of the social consequences. It has also extended to the protection of patents on genetically modified crops and intellectual property rights.

David Harvey is arguably the most influential theorist examining neoliberalism and its application as a crucial underpinning of US hegemony. Harvey states:

> The role of the state is to guarantee the integrity of money, to administer its monopoly of violence via police and military to

ensure equity, ensure courts are available to solve disputes within the market and to protect and administer property rights. Also, where markets do not exist, the state has a duty to create them – pollution rights, education, etc. The state should not interfere beyond that, because it will otherwise interfere in market signals.[2]

As we shall see, both CPA Order 39 in Iraq and the individual free trade agreements the US has signed with Middle Eastern countries have an 'investor state' provision, which means that any disputes will be settled by an international third-party dispute court. It also means that investors, that is, corporations, can directly sue the government in question, and that a nation's laws and courts cannot have any jurisdiction. Removing a country's ability to put the welfare of its people above any so-called 'barrier to free trade' has been a relentless goal of US free trade policy.

Hayek, Friedman, and neoliberalism as a credible policy prescription remained on the fringe of economic theory in the face of Keynesian economic prescriptions and government-provided social programmes, which dominated economic planning and theory from the Great Depression until the mid-1970s. Neoliberalism did, however, find an intellectual home at the University of Chicago, where Friedman taught for over 30 years beginning in 1946, and where Hayek was the university's Professor of the History of Thought from 1950 until he returned to Europe in 1961. Other prominent members identifying as neoliberals included Arnold Harberger. Known as the 'Chicago School', they advocated pro-corporate views such as abolishing the minimum wage, lowering corporate taxes, and Friedman's three-part formula of deregulation, privatisation and cutbacks. This academic legitimacy attracted corporate funding to promulgate the Chicago School's neoliberal ideology.[3]

THE 1970s RISE OF CORPORATE-DRIVEN FREE MARKET NEOLIBERALISM

Keynesian policies and government spending on social programmes were so ingrained in the United States that President Richard Nixon famously declared in the early 1970s that 'we are all Keynesians now.'[4] This was reflected in an embedded regulatory framework in the form of environmental, health, civil rights, public safety, and consumer protection that had come out of the civil unrest and social movements of the 1960s. Corporate activities were restrained by legislative and regulatory restrictions. This is 'embedded liberalism', what neoliberals identify as restrictive to individual freedoms and market choice, and what is referred to in the United States as 'big government'.[5] Friedman is most famous in America not so much as an architect of neoliberalism, but as an outspoken critic of 'big government', which, unique to the United States, is commonly referred to as 'liberalism', and should not be confused with the new, or neo, liberalism advocated by Friedman and Hayek.

What resulted was a remarkably unified and well-resourced push by American corporations to ensure the acceptance of neoliberalism as both an ideology and appropriate guiding government policy prescription. The result would be a fundamental change in the role of government, and the ideological and policy grounding for the dominance of the United States as a global superpower from the early 1980s onwards.

David Yogel, in *Fluctuating Fortunes: The Political Power of Business in America*, summarises the anti-business agenda from that time:

> ... from 1969 through 1972 virtually the entire American business community experienced a series of political setbacks without parallel in the post-war period. In the space of only four years, Congress enacted a significant tax reform bill, four major environmental laws, an occupational safety and health act, and a series of additional consumer protection statutes. The government also created a number of important new regulatory agencies, including the Environmental Protection Agency, Occupational Safety and Health Administration, and the Consumer Product Safety Commission, investing them with broad powers over a wide range of business decisions.[6]

Polls conducted in 1967 found that 55 per cent of Americans had 'great confidence' in major companies; in 1977, that figure had fallen to 16 per cent.[7] Wilson Johnson, president of the National Federation of Independent Business, said in 1977 that 'we're losing the war against government usurpation of our economic freedom.'[8] Clearly, America's large-scale corporate business community viewed this public mistrust of their activities, and the resulting restrictive regulatory framework that ensued, as direct threats to its long-term survival. Their reaction would ensure the enshrinement of neoliberalism as the dominant ideological and policy framework from the early 1980s onward.

In 1971, Lewis Powell, about to be appointed a US Supreme Court judge by Nixon, wrote the 'Powell Memorandum' to the US Chamber of Commerce. Powell called 'for the wisdom, ingenuity, and resources of American business to be marshaled against those who would destroy it.'[9] Powell outlined a plan of unified attack and long-range planning. The Chamber of Commerce, he advised, should lead and coordinate a long-term strategy targeting the major institutions that influenced society's thinking – universities, schools, media, publishing, the courts, and especially government – to change social views

> ... about the corporation, the law, culture, and the individual ... The day is long past when the chief executive officer of a major corporation discharges his responsibility by maintaining a satisfactory growth of profits ... If our system is to survive, top management must be equally concerned with protecting and preserving the system itself.[10]

Powell's specific inclusion of the individual is a *de facto* recognition and inclusion of the corporation as a legally recognised and protected individual (person).

In response to Powell's call to action, coordinated lobby groups such as the Business Roundtable (BRT) were founded. Formed in 1972, the BRT's membership included most of the Fortune 100 companies, which produced almost half of the US gross national product. As of 2005, its combined membership produced nearly $4 trillion in annual revenues – larger than the GDP of most countries.[11] *Suiting Themselves* author Sharon Beder summarises that the BRT's agenda was to 'promote the idea that everyone's welfare was dependent upon the health of US businesses', and has been 'credited with thwarting or watering down anti-trust, environmental, pro-labor, pro-consumer and tax reform measures'.[12]

Other industries formed their own lobby groups, and along with mega-groups like the BRT and National Association of Manufacturers, there followed the formation of think tanks, financing of university departments, and a coordinated and consolidated attack against any and all legislation that hindered business and protected consumers. Soon American university economics departments were focused on neoliberal principles and ensuring that low inflation, rather than overall social well-being, should be regarded as the cornerstone of economic policy.[13]

Think tanks are the public policy arm of both the right and the left. They publish papers, write opinion and editorial pieces, and provide media copy and counterpoints on issues of public debate. They also organise conferences, and publish their own books, briefing papers, and journals, and directly lobby policy makers and elected officials. The corporate funding of conservative Washington, DC-based think tanks provided the ideological engine for neoliberalism, and a consistent research and media voice for the freedom of the individual unfettered by the oppression and restrictions of 'big government'. The Heritage Foundation, Hoover Institute, American Enterprise Institute and Cato Institute were all founded with substantial corporate money to influence public debate and make neoliberalism acceptable to the broader populace. These voices have now been combined with an expansion of commercial right-wing talk radio and the founding of Fox News.

These all went into warp-speed overdrive to promote the invasion of Iraq after the 9/11 terrorist attacks, and provided the Bush administration with a credible and very loud 'independent' voice of support.

The 1907 Tillman Act banned corporations in the United States from giving direct contributions to election campaigns. In 1947, labour unions were also banned from contributing to election campaigns under the Taft-Hartley Act. These prohibitions are still in place, but corporations have found ways around the ban. As part of their united response to the Powell memo, corporations began organising Political Action Committees (PACs). PACs allow a company or union to pool their employees' or members' donations together. In 1974, the Federal Election Committee granted permission for companies to directly solicit PAC contributions from their employees.[14]

The big business focus on overturning 'embedded liberalism' and its threat to the free enterprise system was given a significant boost in the 1976 *Buckley* vs. *Valeo* US Supreme Court decision that recognised spending money to influence elections was a form of constitutionally protected free speech. This included the corporate PACs' direct funding of candidates, political parties and campaigns.[15] Further guarantees of the right of corporations to participate in the political system came in the 1978 *First National Bank of Boston* vs. *Bellotti* Supreme Court decision. It recognised the free-speech right of a corporation to spend money in order to influence the outcome of a state ballot initiative. The result was a substantial increase of corporate funds to both Republicans and Democrats in return for pursuing a neoliberal policy agenda.[16]

In its January 2010 *Citizens' United* vs. *Federal Election Commission* ruling, the Supreme Court struck down previous limitations on corporate spending on elections. This was the latest in a long line of pro-corporate decisions, all of which had their roots in the 1886 *Santa Clara* vs. *Pacific Railway* decision, which recognised corporations as having the same protections and rights as flesh-and-blood citizens under the US Constitution and Bill of Rights. Crucially, the *Santa Clara* decision enabled corporations to directly participate in the political system, and as we shall see, gave rise to the multinational corporation as the most powerful institution of the twentieth century. It also ushered in the era of corporate dominance of US foreign policy, a dominance which continued to grow to the point that it was largely predictable that the US would invade when Iraq had so rebelliously blocked American corporate access to its markets.

Neoliberalism gained further credibility when Hayek was awarded the Nobel Prize for Economics in 1974, and with the same prize awarded to Milton Friedman two years later.[17]

As well as this united corporate front to establish neoliberalism, the 2003 invasion of Iraq had its origins in a series of other events from the early 1970s that provided the crucial underpinnings for American neoliberal hegemony. The first was the 1973 US-supported military coup in Chile, and the violent and ruthless creation of a neoliberal state. The second was the Nixon administration's manipulation of the 1973 OPEC oil crisis, and its near-simultaneous elimination of international capital constraints on American investment banks. As a result, the United States was able to gain *de facto* control over OPEC via Saudi Arabia, and also attain tremendous economic hegemony from the increased dollar value which resulted from a quadrupling of global oil prices, as detailed in subsequent chapters. But it was Chile in the early 1970s that provided the neoliberal blueprint for all future US interventions, whether they be actual physical invasions as in Iraq, or economic invasions via the World Bank and IMF. We will look at Chile in the next chapter.

4
Chile and the Blueprint for Iraq

It might have been Nixon's view that 'we are all Keynesians now', but it certainly was not his foreign policy. At the same time that the most powerful corporations on the planet were uniting to radically transform American government and society to a neoliberal ideological and policy prescription that would be to their ultimate benefit, the Nixon administration was orchestrating the direct application of Friedman's neoliberal rulebook to Chile. This was where Friedman's neoliberal ideology was first implemented; his three-part formula of privatisation, cutbacks and deregulation was established via extreme violence and repression and would provide the ideological vision for the invasion of Iraq 30 years later.

By the late 1960s, Latin America, the safe haven for American corporate investment, was undergoing substantial change. In particular, the Southern Cone countries of Chile, Argentina and Uruguay had by the mid-1960s started their own economic programme: developmentalism. Developmentalism saw government-sponsored protection of key industries via tariffs and subsidies, and state money invested in infrastructure projects. These countries saw a noticeable reduction in poverty and a subsequent creation of and rise in a middle class.[1]

The American government had been funding the education of Chilean economists at the University of Chicago since the 1950s as a direct counter to developmentalism. When they returned to Chile, these 'Chicago Boys' became academics, economists, and business leaders with a firm grounding of the neoliberal precepts taught by Friedman and other neoliberal ideologues.[2]

Developmentalism hit its peak with the 1970 election of socialist Salvador Allende in Chile, who ran on a platform of land reform, wealth redistribution, and nationalisation of large sectors of the Chilean economy controlled by foreign corporations, including a number of American ones. Allende had promised fair compensation to any corporations or individuals losing property.[3] When he became president of Chile in September 1970, Nixon told CIA chief Richard Helms to 'make the economy scream'.[4] The clear intent was to create an economic situation of such suffering that the Chilean people would overthrow any regime that prohibited US capital penetration. As will be seen in Chapter 8, it would also be the same tactic the US would use with extreme force in Iraq, beginning with sanctions, and for the exact same reason.

Copper was the mainstay of the Chilean economy, and had produced huge profits for foreign mining companies. Allende not only nationalised the copper companies, his government refused to pay compensation, citing the exorbitant profits those companies had been receiving. Nixon promptly cut off all aid, as well as any World Bank or other multilateral development bank loans.[5] Nixon and the CIA's efforts failed; Allende's party gained even more support in the 1973 elections. Nearly all social indicators had improved under Allende – employment, health, housing, education, and access to land.[6]

Orlando Letelier served as Allende's ambassador to the United States (1971) and as foreign minister (1973). After the coup, he was arrested and held in a concentration camp for over a year, and then was released and lived in exile in Washington, DC. One of the most outspoken critics of the Pinochet dictatorship, in 1976, he was assassinated by a car bomb in Washington, along with his assistant, Ronni Moffitt, by Chilean agents of the Pinochet government.[7]

Letelier states that the broad popular support Allende enjoyed convinced his neoliberal opponents that it would not be possible to overturn him via the democratic process:

> Reactionary forces, supported feverishly by their friends abroad, developed a broad and systematic campaign of sabotage and terror, which was intensified when the government gained in the March Congressional elections. This included the illegal hoarding of goods by the rich; creation of a vast black market; blowing up industrial plants, electrical installations and pipe lines; paralysis of the transportation system and, in general, attempts to disrupt the entire economy in such a way as to create the conditions needed to justify the military coup.[8]

Similarly, American efforts to create such economic suffering in Iraq via the sanctions that Iraqis would overthrow Saddam Hussein also failed. In both countries, the US moved to the next level: regime change.

On 11 September 1973, Allende was overthrown in a US-supported coup that ended with Chilean troops firing on the presidential palace and Allende being killed. Coup leader Augusto Pinochet took control, and the Pinochet dictatorship quickly adapted the wholesale neoliberal policies of its key economic advisers, Friedman's Chicago School-trained 'Chicago Boys'. Pinochet accomplished this with ruthless torture and repression, and with direct American support.

Pinochet opened up Chile's fisheries, timber and other natural resources to foreign corporations, and guaranteed those corporations the right to repatriate profits. Public schools were replaced by charters and vouchers, and health care became a pay-as-you-go system. Cemeteries, kindergartens and social security were all privatised. Copper remained under government ownership, providing a guaranteed revenue base.[9] Similarly, oil was not included in the neoliberal Bremer orders in Iraq, although for more complex political reasons.

Letelier highlighted the effects:

> ... during the last three years several billions of dollars were taken from ... pockets of wage earners and placed in those of capitalists and landowners. These are the economic results of the application in Chile of the prescription proposed by Friedman and his group ... .[10]

Letelier continues

> ... they have succeeded, at least temporarily, in their broader purpose: to secure the economic and political power of a small dominant class by effecting a massive transfer of wealth from the lower and middle classes to a select group of monopolists and financial speculators.[11]

Letelier emphasised that this could only be accomplished via massive violence and terror:

> [Friedman's] economic plan has had to be enforced, and in the Chilean context that could be done only by the killing of thousands, the establishment of concentration camps all over the country, the jailing of more than 100,000 persons in three years, the closing of trade unions and neighbourhood organizations, and the prohibition of all political activities and all forms of free expression.[12]

Almost identical words could be written to summarise the first three years of the American-led occupation of Iraq. Similarly, the 1976 US-supported military coup in Argentina saw a wave of terror, repression and torture occur hand-in-hand with establishing the neoliberal reforms that had just begun the year before in Chile. The coups in Chile and Argentina meant that other countries were compliant to American demands of keeping their markets and economies open to US capital, and to instigating similar Chicago School neoliberal policies.

Naomi Klein writes that the

> ... vast majority of victims of the Southern Cone's terror apparatus were not member of armed groups but non-violent activists working in factories, farms, shantytowns, and universities. They were economists, artists, psychologists, and left wing party loyalists. They were killed not because of their weapons (which most did not have) but because of their beliefs. In the Southern Cone, where contemporary capitalism was born, the 'War on Terror' was a war against all obstacles to the new order.[13]

Similarly in Iraq, most victims of US initiated violence have been ordinary Iraqis, not terrorists. Klein's 'contemporary capitalism' is simply another term for neoliberalism. Her point is that the supercharged profits of neoliberalism cannot exist without substantial amounts of state-sanctioned violence. This is true in terms of its initial implementation by brutal force in the Southern Cone countries, it is true of the Washington Consensus established in the early 1980s of the Reagan years, and it is overwhelmingly true of the US military occupation in Iraq.

The CIA's own assessment of Chile was that the US 'had no vital interests within Chile, the world military balance of power would not be significantly altered by an Allende regime, and an Allende victory in Chile would not pose any likely threat to the peace of the region.'[14] Similarly, Iraq had no weapons of mass destruction and no ties to Al Qaeda, and posed no military threat to the United States.

Neoliberalism in the Southern Cone is not a success story. Chile collapsed in the Latin American debt crisis of 1982 when the economy crashed and unemployment hit 30 per cent, ten times higher than under Allende. The loans that Pinochet had negotiated with the IMF exploded to $14 billion, thanks to deregulation and speculation. By 1988, 45 per cent of Chileans lived below the poverty line, while the richest 10 per cent saw their wealth increase by 83 per cent.[15] Similarly, Argentina had been renowned for its egalitarian society, with low poverty and unemployment rates of only 4.2 per cent. Within a year of the coup, wages had lost 40 per cent of their value, factories closed, and poverty increased markedly.[16] Similar statistics exist for Iraq, which like Chile had to be utterly destroyed for US-style neoliberal capitalism to succeed.

Chile and the Southern Cone countries were the testing ground and laboratory for the wider-scale adoption of neoliberalism about to be heralded by the Reagan administration and the Washington Consensus of the World Bank and IMF in the 1980s. This in turn led to trillions being paid back to the US and rich countries by implementing Friedman's neoliberal formula of cutbacks to government services, privatisation of public assets, and deregulation of corporate power, in return for bailout loans to save these countries from bankruptcy.

The point is that the Iraq invasion did not occur simply because neoliberalism rose to the top of all possible economic programmes due to some democratic process or its obvious superiority, or because some ludicrous 'invisible hand of the market' meant that it was inevitable. The hegemony of the United States of the last 30 years has been accomplished via intense violence and the ruthless and predatory application of neoliberalism regardless of the social, environmental, or cultural consequences. The blueprint was Chile. Its ultimate expression would be just over 30 years later in Iraq.

NEOLIBERALISM, FREE TRADE AND AMERICAN CORPORATE POWER

As we shall see, the Chilean blueprint would soon be imposed on countries faced with economic collapse and, needing bailout loans from the World Bank/IMF, have had to agree to structurally readjust their economies as a condition. Similar to what Pinochet imposed in Chile, these Friedman-inspired conditions usually include deregulating limitations to foreign capital and opening up their markets, including labour, to foreign corporations. Privatisation of state enterprises is the immediate means to pay down debt, as is allowing multinational corporate access to natural resources and commodities. Cutbacks on government services like health care, education, welfare and environmental protection are also imposed. Thus multinational corporations are given access to cheap labour, natural resources and agricultural products, which had previously been denied to them. These policies also result in driving people away from community-based agricultural autonomy and food production, and pushing the price of labour down, thus providing a cheap workforce for the sweatshop factories which then abound due to labour deregulation.

These policies have displaced millions of people throughout Asia, Africa and Latin America as economic, government and military pressure is applied to open up land for large-scale mono-crop exports like coffee or soybeans for American and European markets. These neoliberal policies have also opened up pristine ecosystems like the Amazon and Indonesian forests for large-scale resource extraction for multinational mining, timber and oil companies. Meanwhile, millions of blue-collar jobs in America and other First World countries go overseas where companies are able to relocate at greatly reduced costs.

This is what is referred to by opponents of neoliberalism as the 'race to the bottom'. Countries are forced to compete with other countries that have also had to structurally adjust their economies, thus driving down the price of natural resources, agricultural products and the price of labour.

And it was (and continues to be) American and other western corporations that acquired the newly privatised state-owned entities. IMF and World Bank bailouts and the subsequent opening-up of economies has meant that multinational corporations gained assets at artificially low prices, automatically sending up their share prices, without needing to produce anything.

Joseph Stiglitz, former World Bank chief economic adviser and Nobel Prize laureate for economics, summarised on the eve of the Iraq invasion:

> If, in too many instances, the benefits of [neoliberal] globalization have been less than its advocates claim, the price paid has been greater, as the environment has been destroyed, as political processes have been corrupted, and as the rapid pace of change has not allowed countries time for cultural adaptation. The crises that have brought in their wake massive unemployment have, in turn, been followed by longer-term problems of social dissolution – from urban violence in Latin America to ethnic conflicts in other parts of the world … .[17]

Through the World Bank and IMF's forced debt restructuring, trillions of dollars have flowed from the Third World to the United States and rich creditors. Most of these countries have repaid their debt many times over due to interest. Initiating, implementing and controlling this system has rendered the United States as the most powerful, richest and most far-reaching empire in the history of the world. The following chapters examine how a post-sanctions Iraq was a direct and dire threat to the continuation of this empire. Chapter 17 examines how the invasion of Iraq was an extension of these same neoliberal policies. The Coalition Provisional Authority would institute these in Iraq, as if Friedman had written the blueprint. That these policies could only be accomplished via a military invasion displays the degrees to which the United States (and its allies) are willing to go for not only its stable continuation, but also for its expansion.

The rise of neoliberalism at the domestic and international levels has coincided with the rise of the US as the world's dominant military power. The two are directly linked. *New York Times* columnist and free market globalisation advocate Thomas Friedman famously summarised this:

> ... The hidden hand of the market will never work without the hidden fist. McDonalds cannot flourish without McDonnel Douglas ... and the hidden fist that keeps the world safe for Silicon Valley's technologies to flourish is called the US Army, Air Force, Navy, and Marine Corps.[18]

Throughout this book, the connection between neoliberalism and state violence and repression is obvious; the most blatant and lamentable example is Iraq. The connection of how corporations have been the ultimate beneficiaries is also obvious. Because corporations are recognised as legal persons, or individuals, under the US Constitution's Bill of Rights, they are included in the neoliberal emphasis that individuals should be free of government interference and regulation. Ludicrous as it may seem that a multinational corporation has the same ability to influence market signals as a school teacher, none the less that is the ideology that is now accepted as sacrosanct. Government provision of health care is an evil interference in the market, but Goldman Sachs and other banks creating a global financial crisis rivalling the Great Depression is completely acceptable market behaviour. Corporate profit and economic growth, not social well-being, is the global paradigm by which the United States judges itself and which in turn, other countries judge themselves, lest they end up overthrown in a coup like Chile, or militarily invaded like Iraq.

The legally protected right of corporations to give campaign donations, to lobby, to fund think tanks and run advocacy campaigns on issues not directly related to their product, and the fact that mass media in the western world is a connected corporate oligarchy, has meant a largely unimpeded rise and subsequent entrenchment of neoliberalism as an accepted government ideology and policy prescription.

In providing an analysis regarding how the need for market access for powerful corporations inevitably results in such unpopular and seemingly undemocratic decisions as invading Iraq, the deeper issue of how that motivation is driven by guaranteed and protected corporate access to the political system is revealed. This then provides a unique and important means of predicting future actions of the United States as long as it retains its superpower economic status. It was corporate individuals who were the most vociferous, and who had the most to gain, from the 2003 invasion of Iraq, and it is American multinational corporations who are the ultimate beneficiaries of US neoliberal dominance. It certainly is not the American people, nor the world at large, which increasingly appears to be unlikely to survive such dominance.

Rather than a diatribe against concentrated corporate power and abuse, the conclusion of this book (Chapter 30) provides a means of addressing this hugely dangerous and undemocratic concentration of power: roll back, if not outright rescind, the 'rights' wrongly granted to corporations in the 1886 *Santa Clara* vs. *Pacific Railway* US Supreme Court decision, which recognised corporations as individuals entitled to the same protections as flesh-and-blood people under the US Constitution and its Bill of Rights.

Part II

Iraq's Potential Threat to Saudi Arabia as a US Client State

5
Nixon, Saudi Arabia and the Geopolitical Roots of the Iraq Invasion

While the corporate onslaught to establish neoliberalism as America's guiding ideology was wildly successful, and the test case of Chile saw its ruthless application on a countrywide scale, it was the Nixon administration's manipulation of the 1973 OPEC oil crisis and the subsequent *de facto* control gained over OPEC via Saudi Arabia that would provide the foundation for the imminent era of American free market neoliberal dominance. The United States was then able to achieve economic hegemony via the increased dollar value as a result of the escalation of oil prices, as well as the ability to capture the World Bank and IMF programmes via Saudi petrodollars flowing to US investment banks. This, combined with Nixon removing the dollar from the gold standard and the near-simultaneous dismantling of capital restraints on American banks, led to the structural implementation of neoliberalism at the international level and the underpinnings of American global dominance that continues to the present day. This series of events led inevitably to the 2003 invasion of Iraq in order to remove the threat that a potentially resurgent Iraq, the only country with the oil capacity to rival the Saudis, posed to these underpinnings.

On 15 October 1973, the Organisation of Arab Petroleum Exporting Countries, consisting of the Arab members of OPEC plus Egypt and Syria, declared they would embargo oil sales to any country that supplied arms to Israel during the Yom Kippur War. As a result of the embargo, the price of oil quadrupled to nearly US$12 per barrel by 1974.[1] The United States was embargoed, and the crisis impacted on the US economy, but less so than it did other countries. The US was a domestic producer of oil, and therefore less dependent on OPEC and the Middle East. The how and why of Nixon colluding with the Saudis to quadruple the price of oil as a result of the embargo is examined in more detail in Chapter 9.

The OPEC oil crisis followed the October 1971 decision by the Nixon administration to remove the US from the gold standard, which had been one of the major planks of the 1944 Bretton Woods

Accord, which had established the World Bank and the International Monetary Fund. Under its chief architects, British economist John Maynard Keynes and American Dexter White, Bretton Woods was intended to provide a stable international financial regime which would ensure that the type of economic collapses that had led to the Great Depression, and the subsequent rise of fascism and the carnage of the Second World War, did not occur again. This meant establishing a rule-based system that could not be manipulated by more powerful states for their own advantage.[2]

Keynes and White set gold as the anchor of the new system. The US dollar was established as the *de facto* global currency for trade and commerce, but the price of the dollar was pegged directly to actual gold reserves, and gold was set at $35 an ounce. Other countries' currencies were then fixed against the dollar; changes in currency rates could only occur via the International Monetary Fund. The criterion for a change in a country's currency exchange relative to the dollar was if the country needed to address a 'fundamental disequilibrium' in its current account. While the dollar served as the main currency for international trade, its exchange rate was similarly fixed to any other country's currency because it was fixed against gold.

The system encouraged states to stay in surplus; they could then demand that their surplus dollars be exchanged for gold. By the late 1960s, under the strain of financing the Vietnam War, the US was running out of gold reserves sufficient to exchange other country's surplus dollars for gold.[3]

The United States had a number of options to address this predicament. These included bringing its own deficit under control by cutting back on the tremendous military costs from the Vietnam War, by reducing imports, or by attempting to devalue the dollar against gold, which would have meant countries received less gold for their surplus dollars. Instead, Nixon pulled the United States out of the gold standard system altogether. By removing the need to have enough gold reserves relative to the amount of dollars it printed, the US gained a major leverage over other countries, in particular regarding oil.[4]

Because oil was and continues to be denominated in dollars, the United States was able to manipulate the dollar to guarantee a financial windfall for itself; higher oil prices meant countries purchasing oil had to have more dollars in reserve to purchase that oil. When the OPEC crisis quadrupled the price of oil, countries suddenly needed four times as many American dollar reserves to purchase oil supplies. These increased dollar reserves did not, and do not, lie dormant. Because they are in US dollars, they are invested in US economic instruments that provide a rate of return, but can also be easily converted when necessary to purchase dollar-priced commodities like oil. A substantial increase in the price of oil benefited OPEC producers, who reaped a huge windfall. The largest OPEC producer was, and is, Saudi Arabia.

As well as dismantling the gold standard as the backbone of a stable international financial and currency regime, the Nixon administration forced another key change in the Bretton Woods Agreement. It succeeded in eliminating the previous limitations on private banks as a source of direct capital for international finance. Under Bretton Woods, international finance and loans were under the direct control of government-controlled central banks. Private banks and investment firms were prohibited from moving their funds freely to other countries, although there were some exceptions for financing trade and specific foreign development investment. The idea was that money would stay in that country and contribute to the country's economic and social development goals and thus contribute to internal financial and theoretically, social, stability, rather than seek profit opportunities elsewhere.[5]

The American proposals to eliminate limits on capital restraints were opposed by all other member countries of the IMF, and by the IMF itself. However, in 1974, the US simply eliminated its own limits on external and internal capital flows. By dropping the capital constraints previously placed on private financial institutions, the increased and considerable OPEC oil revenue was available to be invested directly into New York banks and investment firms. This was a crucial element of the Nixon administration's secret agreement with Saudi Arabia regarding the embargo. American private banks and investment firms then became the dominant international financial force, largely replacing the Bretton Woods government-controlled central banks.[6]

By the year 2000 and the advent of the Bush Junior presidency, Saudi Arabia had recycled as much as $1 trillion abroad since 1973, primarily in the United States. Kuwait and the United Arab Emirates recycled $200–300 billion.[7] This recycling of oil revenues is known as 'petrodollar' recycling. It is a key underpinning of the US economy, and a benefit not available to other countries. As we shall see in Chapter 9, Nixon and Secretary of State Henry Kissinger were also able to guarantee that the Saudis would ensure that OPEC would only accept dollars, thus cementing the petrodollar arrangement that has been the bedrock of American economic power ever since.

John Perkins worked as a consultant for a private firm that helped the US government negotiate trade deals. In his *Confessions of an Economic Hit Man* (2004), Perkins details how he directly worked on the initial post-OPEC oil crisis deal between the United States and Saudi Arabia. Perkins writes, 'I understood, of course, that the primary objective here was not the usual – to burden this country with debts it could never repay – but rather to find ways that would assure that a large portion of petrodollars found their way back to the United States.'[8]

Perkins said of the plan he helped develop:

> Under this evolving plan, Washington wanted the Saudis to guarantee to maintain oil supplies and prices at levels that could fluctuate but that would always remain acceptable to the United States and our allies. If other countries such as Iran, Iraq, Indonesia, or Venezuela threatened embargoes, Saudi Arabia, with its vast petroleum supplies, would step in to fill the gap; simply the knowledge that they might do so would, in the long run, discourage other countries from even considering an embargo. In exchange for this guarantee, Washington would offer the House of Saud an amazingly attractive deal; a commitment to provide total and unequivocal US political and – if necessary – military support, thereby ensuring their continued existence as the rulers of their country ... The condition was that Saudi Arabia would use its petrodollars to purchase US government securities ... .[9]

The interest from those securities was then spent on creating the modern-day infrastructure of Saudi Arabia, using American firms and technology. Much of this had to be built from scratch – the kingdom had no sanitation system, and was lacking in electricity-generating capacity, roads, and much of the critical infrastructure needed to further develop its oil supplies. Perkins says he was aware of two crucial objectives as he worked on developing the overall plan to modernise Saudi Arabia: 'maximising payouts to U.S. firms and making Saudi Arabia increasingly dependent on the United States'.[10]

And the US, in turn, became increasingly dependent on the Saudis. As well as the reinvestment of petrodollars back into a US economy that, from 1981 onwards under Reagan, was relying heavily on credit and deficit military spending, Saudi Arabia had also become a US surrogate in terms of countering other countries in OPEC and any future price hikes or crises. Saudi Arabia is the only country in the world with enough producing capacity to dictate, or at least strongly influence, oil supply and price.

It was Saudi collusion with the United States for geopolitical gain that contributed to the ultimate demise of the Soviet Union and set the groundwork for the collapse of the debt-ridden Soviet economy. In the mid-1980s, as the Soviet Union's oil industry was attempting to expand, Saudi Arabia used its spare capacity to drive down the global price of oil to $10 a barrel, a drop of over 50 per cent. Leading energy industry analysts Edward Morse and James Richard state:

> The aforementioned Saudi-engineered price collapse of 1985–86 led to the implosion of the Soviet oil industry – which, in turn, hastened the Soviet Union's demise ... Saudi spare capacity is the energy equivalent of nuclear weapons ... It is also the centrepiece of the US Saudi relationship. The United States relies on that capacity as the cornerstone of its oil policy.[11]

The exception to this arrangement was Iraq. As further detailed in Chapter 14, it is one of the few, if not the only, country with enough oil to challenge this arrangement. Just as the Saudis could influence and determine global oil price and supply availability, so, potentially, could a post-sanctions Iraq. Invading Iraq and having control over its copious oil supplies could actually allow the US to end its dependence on Saudi Arabia. It would also potentially provide the US with the opportunity to have more direct control over, or even eliminate, OPEC. It is in OPEC's interest to keep prices as high as possible to maximise profits. But when other countries within OPEC have advocated raising the price per barrel, the Saudis have been able to counter with the threat of releasing more oil of their own, driving the price down. Saudi Arabia has been the only country in the world with enough oil capacity to utilise this threat – a threat which as long as it remained a strong and steadfast ally, was a major asset to the United States. The US could not allow a post-sanctions Iraq under Saddam Hussein to be free to develop this potential rivalry to Saudi Arabia.

These crucial underpinnings of both neoliberalism and US hegemony were directly threatened when Iraq invaded Kuwait in 1990 and had an army of 1 million in position to invade, or influence via the threat of invasion, Saudi Arabia. The stated reason for the

1991 Gulf War was to liberate Kuwait. A deeper analysis, however, recognises that Iraq, well resourced with the world's second largest oil reserves and advocating a pan-Arab nationalism that promoted investment back into the region rather than recycling petrodollars back into the United States, directly threatened Saudi Arabia as a crucial pillar of American dominance.

The huge influx of Saudi petrodollar funds from 1973 onwards into the United States was then available for international loans to other countries. Many of these states desperately needed loans because of the sudden trade deficits they had accrued, somewhat ironically, as a result of the price of oil quadrupling due to the OPEC embargo. According to the International Monetary Fund, 'the foreign debts of 100 developing countries (excluding oil exporters) increased 150 percent between 1973 and 1977.'[12]

The manipulation of the dollar as the world's *de facto* currency has been little explored in the context of US neoliberal hegemony. But it is arguably the most powerful, and consistent, tool available to ensure American economic hegemony. The term 'seigniorage' refers to the tremendous advantage that having trade denominated in dollars has given the United States. As well as the obvious leverage it achieved via dropping the gold standard and instigating the OPEC price rise, the US could almost single-handedly dictate international currency rates via lowering or raising its domestic interest rates via the Federal Reserve. A rise in domestic US interest rates would mean that countries which had taken out loans from US banks or the IMF/World Bank would now be faced with a sudden increase in their debt, and an almost automatic increase in dollars going back to the United States.

This is what happened when the ticking debt timebomb exploded in the 'Third World debt crisis' of the early 1980s, when fiscal policy under the Reagan administration saw US interest rates rise to 21 per cent. This in turn skyrocketed Third World debt, which had to be repaid in dollars. This crisis led to the crucial neoliberal, Friedman-inspired conditions imposed as structural adjustment programmes in return for financial bailouts, with significant financial flows to the United States and the developed world occurring as a result. It also foreshadowed the inevitable conflict between countries which acquiesced to this new global paradigm – like Saudi Arabia – and those who did not – like Iraq.

6
Petrodollar Recycling, Third World Debt and the Washington Consensus

By 1980, the full might of American free enterprise, and its united policy prescription outlined under the Powell memo, had resulted in the neoliberal free market presidency of Ronald Reagan. Reagan came to office with a troubled national economy, and inflation stood at 13.5 per cent in large part due to the turbulence unleashed by Nixon's decoupling the dollar from the gold standard. Reagan accelerated the significant shift in monetary policy which started in 1979 under the Carter administration and Federal Reserve Bank Chairman Paul Volcker. Reagan embraced neoliberalism and promised to reduce the role of government. He pursued a programme of tax cuts and deregulation, and communicated the consistent neoliberal message that government and its burdensome and stifling regulation of all aspects of society was the ultimate problem facing America. This was a particularly receptive message to working- and middle-class whites who felt their jobs and affluence had been taken away by affirmative action programmes for blacks and other historically marginalised groups.[1] Embedded liberalism had, according to Reagan and the neoliberal ascendancy, gone way too far.

In his first year in office, the national union of air traffic controllers, PATCO, went on strike. Reagan responded by firing them en masse and was hailed for taking on greedy unions who had gone too far in taking their share of the economy at other's expense. In an economic climate of 10 per cent unemployment, in part induced by Volcker's attack on inflation, national sentiment was not on the union's side.[2] This was the first of a series of Reagan administration-supported attacks on unions. Attacking unions is part and parcel of the neoliberal agenda, as they are seen to be artificial impediments to the market's ability to 'freely' determine wages. Reducing their effectiveness is also one of the most effective means of distributing income to the wealthy, as money saved in wages and benefits automatically accrues to management and corporate shareholders.

One of the only laws the Coalition Provisional Authority retained from Saddam Hussein's era was his prohibition on unions.

Friedman was a member of Reagan's Economic Policy Advisory Board, and he also served as an official adviser and consultant for Reagan's 1980 election. Friedman had a very high public profile, in part because of Reagan's outspoken admiration and his administration's direct policy application of Friedman's neoliberal theories. Friedman also received significant national media attention due to a major corporate-funded ten-part documentary series on his work, *Free to Choose*, which aired on national public television in 1980. Friedman co-authored with his wife Rose a book based on the series, also called *Free to Choose*, and it was the number one non-fiction bestseller in 1980. In 1988, Reagan awarded Friedman the Presidential Medal of Freedom, one of the highest honours bestowed by the US government.[3]

The conservative think tanks that had been established and funded as a result of the Powell memo were instrumental in the election of Reagan and played a key role in disseminating the idea that big government in Washington was the reason, not the solution, for America's problems, particularly its perceived economic decline. The Heritage Foundation's policy agenda, 'Mandate for Change', was largely adopted by Reagan as the cornerstone of his conservative agenda, and was based on Friedman's theories. The American Enterprise Institute (AEI) also advocated deregulation as a solution, and one that became part of the Reagan neoliberal agenda.[4] One hundred and fifty Reagan administration appointees were hired directly from the ranks of the American Enterprise Institute, Hoover Institute, and Heritage Foundation.[5] These and other think tanks were instrumental in the Bush Jr administration's post-9/11 propaganda offensive for the need to invade Iraq.

US HEGEMONY: NEOLIBERALISM, DEBT AND THE WORLD BANK/IMF

The International Monetary Fund's 'Monetary Matters' (2008) provides an excellent history of how Third World debt grew substantially from 1973 onwards, when oil-importing countries had to borrow funds to cover the whopping 400 per cent sudden increase in global oil prices as a result of the OPEC crisis. Saudi and Gulf States' petrodollars that had been invested in the US were then available as loans, either directly or via the World Bank and IMF, to these countries. These loans became the primary core of Third World debt, and would be the basis for further US political, cultural and economic control. The foreign debts of a hundred developing countries (excluding oil exporters) increased 150 per cent between 1973 and 1977 to cover the quadrupled cost of oil.[6]

Many of these same countries then faced severe economic crises in the aftermath of the first round of the debt crisis brought on by Volcker's high interest rates. The debt was owed primarily to the World Bank, the IMF, and the New York private banks that had been liberated under Nixon from the capital restraints built into the original Bretton Woods structure. As detailed below, bailout packages from the World Bank and IMF came with stringent conditions: Friedman's neoliberal prescription of privatisation, deregulation and cutbacks on government spending. The structural adjustment programmes became the ultimate means of American control over a soon-to-be-neoliberalised global economy. By 2004, the year after the US invaded Iraq, this arrangement had seen the world's poorest countries pay an estimated $4.6 trillion in debt repayments to the world's richest countries, in particular the United States itself.[7]

The World Bank and the International Monetary Fund were both established in 1944, as part of the Bretton Woods Agreement, and were intended to ensure that the type of economic collapse that had given rise to the Nazis in Germany did not happen again. The World Bank would provide loans to poor countries to help with development, and the IMF would try to ensure international currency stability. As detailed earlier, the Nixon administration also successfully changed the capital limitations initially imposed under the original Bretton Woods arrangements. The US has had *de facto* control of the World Bank and IMF, as both institutions have voting and decision-making structures based on how much money individual countries contributed.[8]

The World Bank is the world's largest multilateral development bank (MDB) and is technically owned by its 180 member nations, who directly provide the bank's funding. It lends about $25 billion a year to member nations, guarantees credit for countries to access other loans, and directly finances country-specific projects. Voting is determined by the amount of money a country contributes. Major decisions require an 85 per cent majority to pass; but since the US is the biggest donor and has at least 17 per cent of the votes, it has an effective veto power over major decisions. The IMF has traditionally had a similar decision-making structure, with the same dominance by the United States.[9]

The institutions were steeped in controversy long before neoliberal structural adjustment programmes came along. As part of its mandate to address poverty, the World Bank focused on lifting economic growth via large-scale development programmes. It had a particular enthusiasm for big hydroelectric projects, which could provide both irrigation for large-scale monocrop production and electricity generation. These projects often required the forced removal of indigenous or traditional peoples who were practising lower-scale subsistence agriculture, and also coincided with the so-called 'green revolution' of increased productivity from new seeds and fertilisers. While these often did increase production, they also created a dependency on the resource-intensive agriculture employed in the West, which involved fertilisers, high-yield seeds and crops, tractors and fuel, and so on. Increased productivity lasted usually for a few years before insects and other pests adapted to the new crops, and then countries were in debt for the tractors, fertilisers, and irrigation systems. This debt was compounded in the early 1970s with the sudden and rapid quadrupling in the price of oil resulting from the OPEC oil embargo. Countries had to take out further loans to pay for the increased cost of fertilisers, fuel for tractors, insecticides, and other resources. As we shall see in the examination of Iraqi agriculture, this American agribusiness model has been further compounded with the introduction of genetically modified crops and, more recently, allowing global food prices to be subject to the casino capitalism of Wall Street speculation. This is the agricultural model the US has pushed onto Iraq.

THE WASHINGTON CONSENSUS

It was Ronald Reagan who transformed the World Bank and IMF into neoliberal institutions. Reagan secured the appointment of William Klausen as the World Bank's president. Klausen, together with chief economist Ann Krueger, brought in what Nobel Prize-winning economist Joseph Stiglitz calls an 'ideological fervor' for free market, neoliberal policies. Government was viewed as the problem and free markets the solution to developing countries' debt and other financial crises. The bank was then stacked with similar neoliberal ideologues.[10]

The Mexican peso crisis of 1982 provided new opportunities for US capital to expand via the imposition of Friedman's formula, so recently implemented under terror and repression in Chile and Argentina, and to usher in a new era of ultimate American hegemony.

The first World Bank/IMF structural adjustment programme was in direct response to Mexico defaulting on its loans in 1982, in large part because of Volcker's 21 per cent interest rate rise and a US recession which had reduced demand for Mexican products. This was compounded by a slump in oil prices, of which Mexico was an important producer. In 1972, Mexican debt was US$6.8 billion; by 1982, it had ballooned to US$58 billion.[11]

When the Mexican government went to the World Bank to negotiate an emergency bailout, the World Bank, in concert with the Reagan administration and US Treasury Secretary James Baker, set stringent repayment conditions requiring 'structural adjustment' of the Mexican economy and finance regulation. Mexico had to impose deep cuts on government spending on welfare programmes for the poor, including health care, deregulate corporate restrictions on many of its industries, and privatise large chunks of its public assets.[12]

This 'structural adjustment programme' (SAP) was the first of many that the World Bank/IMF would impose as neoliberal conditions for any further loans to heavily indebted countries. The money for these and subsequent loans was available in large part thanks to the huge revenues flowing to the US from Saudi Arabian petrodollars.

The consequences were the exact opposite of the World Bank's stated mandate to alleviate poverty:

> From 1983 to 1988 Mexico's per capita income fell at a rate of 5 percent per year; the value of workers' real wages fell between 40 percent and 50 percent; inflation, which had oscillated between 2 and 4 percent per year in the 1960s, had gone up to the mid teens after 1976, and surpassed 100 percent in several of those years ... At the same time, due to government fiscal problems and the re-orientation of the country's governing economic model, state expenditure on public goods declined. Food subsidies were restricted to the poorest segments of the population, and the quality of public education and health care stagnated or declined.[13]

The Mexican bailout became the model for the World Bank's and IMF's list of policies deemed essential for economic health. Broadly referred to as the 'Washington Consensus', as articulated by economist John Williamson who had worked for the World

Bank, IMF and the UK Treasury. Williamson listed ten key points summarising the shared policy views of the IMF, World Bank and the US Treasury Department.[14] They are an expanded version of Friedman's three-part neoliberal formula of deregulation, privatisation and cutbacks:

- Fiscal discipline: reduced budget deficits at all levels of government (after taking account of debt);
- Public expenditure priorities: redirecting government expenditure from areas of public demand that provide little economic return to areas with high economic returns and the potential to improve income distribution, such as primary health and education, and infrastructure;
- Tax reform: broadening the tax base and cutting marginal tax rates to provide more incentive to high-income earners to invest their money;
- Financial liberalisation: aiming toward market-determined interest rates and the abolition of preferential interest rates for privileged borrowers;
- Exchange rates: setting exchange to induce a rapid growth in non-traditional exports, as well as to ensure exporters remain competitive;
- Trade liberalisation: reduction of tariffs and trade restrictions;
- Foreign direct investment: abolition of barriers to investment by foreign firms and foreign firms to be treated on the same basis as local firms;
- Privatisation: of government businesses and assets;
- Deregulation: abolition of regulations that impede investment or restrict competition, and requirements that all regulations be justified by such criteria as safety, environmental protection, or prudential oversight of financial institutions, and
- Property rights: securing property rights without excessive costs.

These conditions cut to the core of a nation's economic sovereignty, and impose a *de facto* colonial subservience. Often accompanied with military aid and other incentives, they were imposed via structural adjustment programmes, which, as in the case of Mexico, required the government to cut spending on welfare, health care and environmental protection and to open the economy via neoliberal pro-corporate policies, deregulation, and liberalisation of international credit and financial markets. In other words, Friedman's neoliberal formula of cutbacks on government spending, privatisation of public assets, and deregulation of limits on a corporation's ability to generate profit.

Privatisation is the selling off of state, that is, public, assets. These could be services like sanitation, water, telephone, or electricity provision, and the physical infrastructure that goes with them, such as buildings, pipes, towers, wires, and so on. Government-owned banks and public transportation are other examples. They are sold off to the highest bidder – often international companies – and usually with no protection for local industries or employment. In Iraq, the US attempted to privatise the entirety of the country's semi-socialist economy, apart from the oil industry, within a few months of the occupation.

In 2000, for example, privatisation was a core requirement in 70 per cent of the World Bank's structural adjustment loans. Privatisation quadrupled in Latin America and tripled in Asia between 1992 and 2002, and was a requirement for over 30 per cent of World Bank-funded water supply projects. Over 10,000 entities were privatised between 1988 and 1998.[15] By the early 1990s, structural adjustment programmes had been introduced into nearly 80 developing countries by the World Bank.[16]

Davison Budhoo, former senior IMF economist, said, 'everything we did from 1983 onward was based on our new sense of mission to have the south "privatised or die"; towards the end we ignominiously created economic bedlam in Latin America and Africa in 1983–88.'[17] Countries entered into negotiations with the World Bank/IMF neoliberal structural adjustment programmes with US-supported and initiated coups to establish authoritarian neoliberal regimes in Chile, Argentina and other countries still fresh in the geopolitical landscape. Other countries which openly opposed the now-dominant US neoliberal agenda – like the democratically elected Sandinista government in Nicaragua in the 1980s – were targeted with US-supported civil wars.

Budhoo's self-described mission to have the South 'privatised or die' created immense opportunities for foreign corporations to obtain almost instantaneous profits for their shareholders. Three years into the Pinochet regime in Chile, Letelier wrote:

> It may also seem grotesque to speak of the market as the most effective instrument for allocating resources when it is widely

known that there are practically no productive investments in the economy because the most profitable *investment* is speculation.[18]

Selling off state assets as an alternative to bankruptcy meant those state resources were available to US capital at greatly reduced prices, and under conditions vastly favourable to the buyer. The buyer was usually an American or other First World corporation, whose investors would receive almost instant increases in their share price.

7
Neoliberalism, Debt and American Empire

Throughout Latin America, the military dictatorships which had come to power via US support, and which had seized power under the guise of economic order and responsibility, had massively driven up their countries' debts. In *The Shock Doctrine*, Naomi Klein (2007) summarises:

> In 1983 when Argentina returned to representative democracy, Washington granted approval in return for the new government to pay off the debt amassed by the military junta – a military junta the US was directly responsible for installing. This debt had gone from $7.9 billion in 1975, the year before the US supported coup, to $45 billion in 1983. The debt was owed to the IMF, World Bank, US Export Import Bank and US private banks. Argentina's Central Bank announced just before the transition to democracy that the state would take over the debts of large multinational and domestic companies, including Ford, Chase Manhattan Bank, Citibank, IBM, and Mercedes Benz, that had borrowed themselves to the brink of bankruptcy. These debts came to $15–20 billion, to be paid on top of the government debt. In Uruguay, a country of 3 million people, the debt went from $500 million when the coup began to $5 billion. Brazil's $3 billion debt at the time of its military coup in 1964 had skyrocketed to $103 billion by 1985.[1]

Klein also highlights the substantial corruption associated with Argentina's debt. The World Bank found that $19 billion out of $35 billion in foreign loans had been moved to Swiss bank accounts and other offshore tax havens. The US Federal Reserve found that Argentina's debt went up in 1980 alone by $9 billion. Argentinian citizens deposited $6.7 billion abroad in the same year. University of Chicago professor and neoliberal policy advocate Larry Sjaastad called these missing billions 'the greatest fraud of the 20th century'.[2]

The twentieth century still had enough years remaining for Russia's transition to neoliberal capitalism to far eclipse the Argentinian generals' efforts. Fraud and corruption is also a lasting and distinguishing feature of the Coalition Provisional Authority's tenure in Iraq, as detailed in Chapter 18, where at least $12 billion of the Iraqi people's money has vanished. This figure is just the tip of the iceberg regarding the additional fraud, corruption and outright theft of American contractors operating in Iraq.

As well as substantially and almost instantly increasing the amount of debt, Volcker's high interest rates also created a 'price shock' for those countries which had followed World Bank and IMF prescriptions to adapt their economies to export-oriented growth. A price drop in an export commodity like coffee was increasingly likely, as under the encouragement of the IMF and World Bank, more countries were growing export commodity crops like coffee to pay back their debt. Increased competition would naturally drive the price down globally. Buyers of coffee would simply switch to whatever supplier, or country, could provide the cheapest supply. The drop in price would provide the country's economy with a price shock. Even moderate changes – intentional or otherwise – in currency rates, interest rates, or commodity prices can severely destabilise a country's economy. This is yet another aspect of the 'race to the bottom', as countries have little choice but to reduce labour costs, or environmental constraints, or some other input to compete in the international market.

Returning to Mexico, the 1982 structural adjustment programme bailout led to additional neoliberal reforms and structural adjustments in the 1989 US-initiated Brady plan, in return for a portion of Mexico's debt to be forgiven. This provided the conditions for Mexico's entry to the controversial North American Free Trade Agreement (NAFTA) and further privatisation and opening-up of the Mexican economy. To gain entry to NAFTA, the Salinas government overrode the Mexican Constitution which granted communal use of lands (*ejidos*) to indigenous Mexicans.[3] This led to the Zapatista uprising in Chiapas, declared on 1 January 1994, when NAFTA came into full effect. NAFTA is the appalling model for the US Middle East Free Trade Area, discussed in Chapter 13.

Despite its consistent adherence to the neoliberal prescriptions demanded of it, Mexico faced bankruptcy yet again a few years later. In 1995, the US Clinton administration initiated a major bailout programme to rescue not only Mexico but also NAFTA and, more crucially, the integrity of neoliberalism itself.[4]

Whether intentional or not, speculative profit opportunities for US and other foreign multinationals, as identified by Letelier regarding Chile, were rife in the series of Mexican financial collapses and subsequent neoliberal structural adjustment bailouts. In 1990, there had been only one Mexican bank in foreign hands; in 2000, 20 out of 30 were foreign owned.[5]

First World corporations also benefit from having their overseas activities guaranteed by their own governments. For example, the US government's Overseas Private Investment Corporation (OPIC) provides insurance for US corporate projects overseas. If the host government cannot pay for the project, or refuses to pay, due to incompetence, fraud, or cost overruns, OPIC will pay the company directly. The American government will then take on the responsibility of collecting the debt directly from that country. This is what polite people would call a racket.

Further crises ensued with the Mexican peso crisis in 1995, Brazil in 1998, the Asian financial crisis in 1997–98, and, famously, the utter collapse of the Argentinian economy in 2001.[6] The Argentinian peso was pegged to the US dollar and when the Asian financial crisis hit in 1997, it resulted in high interest rates and additional pressure on the peso. Argentina's debt doubled between 1995 and 2001; by 2000, the interest payment alone on the debt was $9.5 billion. The IMF responded with its biggest ever bailout loan of $6 billion. The fallout, however, continued. The economy went into free fall, followed by riots, and Argentina defaulted on its $88 billion debt. Argentina, arguably more than any other country, had followed the neoliberal economic prescriptions as per Friedman's rulebook. It also had the biggest crash.[7]

Bolivia had also had its own neoliberal programme established under a military junta, although less brutal and violent than those of its neighbours. Debt taken out under dictatorship had expanded considerably when US interest rates rose under Volcker. With Bolivia's return to democracy in 1986 and elections about to be held, inflation and debt ravaged the economy. The newly elected government came up with a radical plan that included the elimination of food subsidies, removing almost all price controls, and allowing the cost of oil to increase to 300 per cent. The US pledged substantial aid if the plan was enacted into legislation. Bolivians never saw the plan, never voted for the plan, and it was not presented to them in the election. Klein writes how the economic programme was initiated all at once, and created a kind of economic shock so overwhelming there was no way for civil society to properly respond. In 1986, the price of tin, Bolivia's main commodity export, dropped 55 per cent.[8]

Similarly, Iraqis never saw or agreed to Bremer's economic orders. Iraqis, much more so than the Bolivians, were also coming out of a period of great disorientation and crisis.

The neoliberal juggernaut continued to obtain control or solidify existing hegemony over economy after economy in the 1990s. As highlighted in the above brief examination of Latin America, it also triggered crisis after crisis. In *Globalisation and Its Discontents*, former World Bank chief economist and Nobel Prize winner Joseph Stiglitz examines how IMF policies directly contributed to the 1997–98 Asian financial crises. Stiglitz says the total $95 billion in bailout funds – including money from the-then G7 countries (Russia was subsequently added, making it now the G8) as well as the IMF, was 'in part, a bailout to the international banks as much as it was a bailout to the country' in question: 'There were billions and billions for corporate welfare, but not the more modest millions for welfare of ordinary citizens.'[9]

The decade offered brand new opportunities, such as tying the new post-apartheid South African government of Nelson Mandela to a devastating IMF and World Bank structural adjustment programme in return for avoiding catastrophic economic collapse. And Russia's transition from communism to democracy was from a closed, state-protected economy to perhaps the most severe neoliberal conditions yet imposed. That it was done under a military state of siege, with the support of the United States and the West, and at the direct expense of the democracy the Russian people had fought for and been promised, is an instructive story for interpreting American actions in Iraq just over a decade later. The resulting poverty and endemic corruption throughout Russia at the hands of the oligarchs is a sad indictment of both neoliberalism and the promise of western democracy. Even communist, supposedly anti-capitalist, China embraced neoliberal free market reforms.[10]

As of 2009, the total debt owed by so-called developing countries was an astounding $3.7 trillion. In 2008, they paid over $602 billion servicing these debts to rich countries, primarily the United States.[11] These figures do not include the additional billions, if not trillions, that American and other western corporations have reaped in these countries by buying up their privatised public assets, replacing government services with foreign corporate ones, and the profit free-for-all as an outcome of the forced deregulation of foreign corporate restrictions, prying open of market access, and the resulting readily available supply of cheap sweatshop labour. As we shall see, expanding this supply of sweatshop labour is one of the clear outcomes of a number of the free trade agreements the US has signed with Arab countries since the invasion of Iraq.

Many of these countries have paid back their initial loans many times over, but are kept in a state of indebtedness due to interest rises, as highlighted by Volker's 21 per cent interest rate rise in the early 1980s. Between 1970 and 2002, sub-Saharan Africa, the poorest region in the world, paid $550 billion on loans totalling $540 billion. Yet it still owed an incredible $295 billion due to interest.[12] In an unfortunately typical example, in 2005 and 2006, Kenya paid as much in debt repayments as it did for providing to its people critical services such as health care, roads, public transportation, and provision of clean drinking water *combined*.[13]

Major fault-lines, however, have appeared in recent years in the edifice of the World Bank and IMF as neoliberal lender and American surrogate. In September 2009, Argentina, Brazil, Paraguay, Uruguay, Ecuador, Bolivia and Venezuela formed their own development bank alternative, the Banco Sur (Bank of the South).[14] This followed a general Latin American-wide move away from World Bank and IMF dependence. The region went from comprising 80 per cent of the IMF's lending portfolio in 2005 to 1 per cent in 2007. Brazil, Argentina and Venezuela openly stated they would never borrow from the IMF again.[15]

It is certainly understandable why these countries would want to be free of the World Bank and IMF. Nearly half (47 per cent) of Ecuador's budget in 2008 went to payments on its debt; education received 12 per cent and health care 7 per cent.[16] In late 2008, Ecuador defaulted on part of its foreign debt, not because it was unable to make payments but because, in the words of President Rafael Correa, the debt was 'immoral' and had been initiated by previously corrupt governments. With the support of a massive public campaign, Ecuador renegotiated to pay back 30–35 cents for every $1 of what it identified as illegitimate debt.[17]

Correa joins Evo Morales of Bolivia, Luiz Inácio Lula da Silva of Brazil, and Hugo Chavez of oil-rich Venezuela as left-leaning South American leaders elected in the last ten years. Since his election in 1999, Chavez has been a vehement critic of US neoliberal imperialism, and in 2007, Venezuela managed to pay off its outstanding IMF and World Bank debt five years ahead of schedule.[18]

The Bush administration's response to Chavez's socialist Bolivarian Revolution, which has seen industry nationalisation and social programme spending, was the same as Nixon's response to Allende in early 1970s Chile: it helped initiate a coup. In this case though, the 2002 coup did not succeed, and only entrenched Chavez's popularity in standing up to decades of US economic and CIA intervention in Venezuela and the rest of Latin America.

As detailed with the examples of Chile and Argentina, often these debts were accrued under dictatorships, with little if any of the loan money ever actually benefiting the people it was supposedly intended for; instead it was used to pay for their repression to keep the dictators in power. We could cite countless other examples: Ferdinand Marcos of the Philippines, Suharto of Indonesia, and Mobutu of Zaire are among the best known who racked up enormous debts, were staunchly supported by the US, ruled with ruthless repression, and left their countries with huge debts and legacies of corruption and fraud for their people to have to pay back. And while there has been so-called debt cancellation for the poorest of the poor countries, this debt cancellation has with almost no exceptions come with further requirements to apply Friedman's disastrous neoliberal formula.

The April 2009 G-20 Summit in London, which was called to address how the world's top 20 economies should respond to the global financial crisis, massively extended the role of one of its chief neoliberal pillars, the International Monetary Fund. The IMF was pledged an additional $500 billion, tripling its budget to $750 billion.[19] Its response to the neoliberal-created global crisis has, unfortunately and not particularly surprisingly, not been to alleviate the human hardship caused by the crisis, but to initiate more loans with the neoliberal structural adjustment conditions that helped create the crisis in the first place.

In an analysis of IMF loans, the Center for Economic and Policy Research (CEPR) found that the IMF's focus was on spending cuts rather than the fiscal stimulus it had promised. In return for a $7.6 billion IMF loan in November 2008, Pakistan had to agree to cut government spending, raise interest rates, and reduce its deficit from 7.4 per cent of GDP to 4.2 per cent within a year. In October of the same year, the IMF and European Union presented a huge bailout package of $25 billion to Hungary, when it came close to defaulting on its foreign debt. Hungary had to agree to the standard neoliberal structural adjustment package – in particular to cut public spending and reduce its deficit.[20] A 2009 report from the UK group Christian Aid detailed how the IMF has continued to force the very poorest countries in the world in sub-Saharan Africa to drastically cut social services and taxes, directly reducing their capacity to address chronic poverty.[21]

In an April 2009 *New York Times* guest editorial, CEPR economist Mark Weisbrot summarised: 'These and other examples indicate that in spite of the depth of the world recession, the Fund is too willing to sacrifice employment, and increase poverty, in pursuit of other goals.'[22]

Those 'other goals' are to retain American-led global power, and to ensure the neoliberal transfer of wealth from poor to rich continues unabated. The response to a crisis the United States was responsible for creating is the same neoliberal debt-control mechanisms of the past 30 years. The bailouts are loans, and will simply result in more debt. US hegemony is dependent on keeping these countries in an ever-deepening spiral of debt; the global financial crisis, alas, appears to be just another opportunity to do so. As we shall see, the US and World Bank/IMF response to the 2011 uprisings throughout the Middle East has been the same: more neoliberal conditional loans to service the debt created by dictators it had long supported.

It is preservation of the system that is the focus, and to ensure that regardless of whether a country is a representative democracy or a dictatorship, decision making is taken out of the hands of government and instead government is beholden to the World Bank, IMF, WTO and free trade agreements.

America has created a global empire where countries are given two choices: acquiesce, or be destroyed. For countries that are already rich, reaping the rewards is allowed with this acquiescence, as in the case of Europe, Japan, Australia, Canada, the Arab oil-producing dictatorships of the Middle East, and now China. Resist and you will be potentially destroyed, like Iraq and Chile and countless others. For most of the planet, there are no rewards, only hardship. The US does not have the world's largest and most powerful military for show. It exists to keep the system in place, to make the rich richer by making the poor poorer, and to be available when a country not only resists, but could potentially impede the very foundations upon which the system depends. This is why Iraq not only had to be militarily invaded, but thoroughly destroyed.

America is responsible for the world's poorest countries being trapped in an endless cycle of poverty, with little money to invest in education, health care, provision of safe drinking water and basic food, and protection of crucial national and environmental resources. Public services must now be subject to the neoliberal law of profit, not need. If the service can't be provided by a corporation for profit, it therefore is not really a necessity. Equally sad, it is forcing a mono-cultural model of free market capitalism onto a wildly culturally diverse global landscape. Forcing traditional people off their land so it can be commodified to pay off national debt and leaving them no recourse but to seek work in urban sweatshops is Neoliberal Capitalism 101. That the world's last remaining wild places, along with the biosphere on which all life depends, are also being destroyed will have future generations asking, over and over, 'why?'

How the US has been able to sustain this system while simultaneously running up its own national debt to unheard-of levels, and how Iraq directly threatened the key element underpinning this American neoliberal power, is the subject of Chapter 9.

8
Containing Iraq: The Gulf War and Sanctions

IRAQ: AN ALTERNATIVE DEVELOPMENT MODEL FOR THE ARAB WORLD

In direct contrast to the World Bank/IMF neoliberal model stood Iraq. As a major oil producing country, it benefited from the US manipulation of the 1973 OPEC crisis and subsequent quadrupling of oil prices. But unlike Saudi Arabia, it steadfastly refused to send its oil profits to the US in return for US protection and client-state status. Instead, it invested its oil revenues back into its own development, and crucially, advocated other oil-producing Arab states do the same.

The development issue and Arab nationalism were crucial. Beginning with Iraq's 1958 revolution and overthrow of its British-installed puppet monarchy, and continuing through the Baathists, Iraqi society had seen dramatic improvements in literacy and the establishment of free education for all. Land reform was introduced to reduce the influence of the large landholding elites created under British rule. It established control over, and reduced the costs of, rent and food prices, began a large-scale new housing programme, and formally recognised unions and peasant organisations.[1] It had also established a free national health care system. By the end of the 1970s, Iraq was widely acknowledged to be the best-educated country in the Arab world. The Baathists also established the right of women to pursue careers and to participate in public life, and on the eve of Iraq's invasion of Iran in 1980, women formed a large percentage of many professions.[2]

When Iraq invaded Kuwait in 1990, these elements were in stark contrast. Kuwait, like Saudi Arabia, was a monarchy with very limited civil liberties, and where dissent was crushed. Dissent was also crushed under the authoritarian regime of Saddam Hussein, but at least the Iraqi people accrued discernible benefits from its oil revenues under Iraq's state-sponsored internal development model.

A delegation from the American University in Washington, DC, who toured the Middle East after the invasion of Kuwait reported that

> Iraq raised the class question, the 'haves' and 'have nots'... on a pan Arab level as it never has been raised before ... [Saddam] managed to tap into tremendous resentment, and this has immense medium and long-term implications. The national question remains to the fore, but the connection with the class question has been made ... even the press financed and controlled by the oil states in the region and in Europe [covered] the fabulous oil wealth of individuals: tales of corruption, gambling and squandering. The corresponding impression is that even if corruption does occur on some scale in Iraq, the surplus has largely been plowed into the country for its own development.[3]

John Perkins, the economic hit-man who had been directly involved in the US plan to guarantee the flow of Saudi petrodollars back to the United States as detailed in Chapter 5, says that in regards to Saddam Hussein and Iraq:

> We would be happy to offer him US government securities in exchange for petrodollars, for the promise of continued oil supplies, and for a deal whereby the interest on those securities was used to hire US companies to improve infrastructure systems throughout Iraq, to create new cities, and to turn the deserts into oases. We would be willing to sell him tanks and fighter planes and to build him chemical and nuclear power plants, as we had done in many other countries, even if those technologies could conceivably be used to produce advanced weaponry ... However, by the late 1980s it was apparent that Saddam was not buying into the ECM [Economic Hit Man] scenario.[4]

America was resolute that Iraq could not remain a strong regional player capable of directly influencing and or challenging Saudi Arabia, with a huge military and oil revenues to support it. In *The Global Gamble*, Peter Gowan provides an in-depth analysis of post-Kuwait invasion politics in the Gulf. Gowan believes that these development issues, and the threat of subversive elements responding to them in Saudi Arabia and other US client states, was a driving motivation for the US invasion: 'a crushing US military victory over Iraq, with no concession to negotiation, was intended to demonstrate unequivocally to all groups in the region who ultimately controlled their destiny and who did not.'[5]

CONTAINING IRAQ: THE 1991 GULF WAR

And so the focused attempt by the US government to create a pliable, US client state did not begin with the 2003 invasion, or with the military planning for the invasion that began in earnest in 2002, or with the election of Bush-Cheney in 2000. It began, at least in this phase, when Iraq under Saddam Hussein invaded Kuwait in 1990 and the UN Security Council (under US leadership) passed UN Resolution 661 and began nearly 13 years of sanctions. The sanctions officially were described as a means to persuade Iraq to surrender its weapons of mass destruction.

But whether the first Bush administration (1989–92), or the Clinton presidency (1993–2000), or the Bush-Cheney administration (2001–08), the sanctions were intended to remove Saddam Hussein from power, because a resurgent post-sanctions Iraq threatened the very viability of US hegemony and its crucial relationship with Saudi Arabia, and hence US capacity to exert influence over other Arab states in the region. By 2002, the sanctions had failed in their purpose of removing Saddam Hussein. They were also nearing the end of their usefulness as an ongoing strategy to contain Iraq, due to the increasing international outcry regarding their devastating effect on the Iraqi people, particularly children. This failure compelled the United States to move to the next level: a military invasion and regime change.

In 1990, Iraq's army and military remained relatively intact after eight years of war with Iran. Iraq had long believed it had territorial rights to Kuwait, which, like Iraq itself, had been granted to the British as part of the post-First World War carve-up of the Ottoman Empire. It was Kuwait's long coastline on the Persian Gulf which was particularly attractive, as Iraq had only one port, Umm Qasar, which was not directly in the Gulf.[6]

Iraq also claimed Kuwait was drilling into Iraq's Rumaila oilfield, and that Kuwait was working directly with Saudi Arabia to reduce the price OPEC charged for oil. Iraq believed Kuwait's activities was costing it $14 billion a year, at a time when it was in debt for at least $80 billion from the war with Iran. At least half that debt had been borrowed primarily from Kuwait and Saudi Arabia and other Arab states.[7]

It is Saudi Arabia's spare capacity for oil production that has made it such a formidable ally and client state of the United States. It has been the only country in the world with the capacity to, if needed, increase or decrease daily production by two to three million barrels. This gives it a tremendous ability to dictate global oil prices; if the rest of OPEC threatens to raise prices, Saudi Arabia can simply counter the rise by releasing its spare capacity into the market, and force prices down. It was Saudi Arabia's willingness to use its enormous oil-producing capacity to manipulate OPEC prices that made it indispensable to America. Kuwait too was a long-time American ally, and similar to Saudi Arabia, was ruled by a royal family supported by the United States.

Iraq invaded Kuwait in August 1990. The takeover of Kuwait meant Iraq had direct control of 20 per cent of the world's oil production. It also had an army of 1 million, with geographical access to influence politically, as well as the potential to outright invade, Saudi Arabia, threatening its additional 20 per cent of the world's oil production.

Condemnation of Iraq's invasion of Kuwait was swift, led by the US and Britain. In August 1990, the UN Security Council passed Resolution 661, which embargoed all UN member states from financial transactions and trade with Iraq, as commercial, industrial, or public utility undertaking.[8] These economic sanctions would stay in place for 13 long years, until the Coalition Provisional Authority was recognised by the United Nations as the new government of Iraq in 2003.

America had historically responded swiftly and with force to any country that chose its own development over allowing unimpeded capital flows to the US and the developed world. American resolve was also strengthened in the absence of the other world superpower, the Soviet Union, which was teetering on the edge of collapse.

There were other considerations as well. George Bush Sr was a former head of the CIA. He, along with most of his administration, wanted to break the US out of the 'Vietnam Syndrome' and display the ultimate military prowess of the United States, particularly in the wake of the near-dissolution of the Soviet Union.[9]

Dick Cheney, US defence secretary and future vice-president under Bush Jr, flew to Saudi Arabia and was able to acquire Saudi permission to station US troops there in order to launch an invasion of Kuwait and repel Iraq.[10] It was this controversial stationing of foreign troops in Islam's most sacred land that was one of the principal grievances of Al Qaeda and Osama Bin Laden.

After rejecting a number of offers to negotiate peace, the United States began bombing Iraq in January 1991, including extensive bombing of civilian infrastructure targets such as power generators, sewage plants, water purification facilities and hospitals.[11] Declassified Pentagon documents show that the US studied Iraq's drinking-water system, assessed its weaknesses, intentionally bombed it during the war, and then shaped the post-war sanctions to prevent its repair.[12] Before the Gulf War, 96 per cent of all Iraqis had access to safe drinking water; three years later, less than half had access. It was then not possible to treat sewage before it went into the Tigris and Euphrates rivers, which were the main source of potable water. There was also wide-scale bombing of the irrigation systems on which Iraqi agriculture depended. The Geneva Conventions state clearly that deliberate attacks on civilian populations and life-support systems are war crimes.[13] UN Deputy Secretary General Martti Ahtisaari described the bombing as a 'near apocalyptic catastrophe for the people of Iraq', leading to starvation and epidemics of deadly diseases.[14] Crippling Iraq's civilian capacity for water purification and electricity distribution, and preventing their repair by prohibiting the necessary foreign parts and assistance under the sanctions meant that the United States had long-term leverage long after the Gulf War itself ended.

Similar to the 2003 invasion, propaganda was an equally important part of the invasion. The Bush administration claimed the war was to 'liberate' Kuwait, despite the fact that Kuwait, like Saudi Arabia, was ruled by a monarchy that governed largely by repression. The vilification of Saddam Hussein began in earnest, with Bush openly comparing him to Hitler and the Nazis.

Media coverage in the first Gulf War was directly controlled by Dick Cheney's Pentagon. The US Department of Defense ran daily media briefings and provided images of 'smart bomb' images hitting their military targets. Later analysis revealed that the smart bombs were not nearly as smart, or as accurate, as portrayed by the Pentagon, and they were only a small proportion of the overall bombardment. There was no release of Iraq casualties statistics, and unlike Vietnam, America's last major war, media coverage in the Gulf War did not allow Americans to identify with the suffering and hardship inflicted by the US military on civilians.[15]

In the wake of the withering bombing, and with the United States and its allies clearly intending to launch a large-scale invasion from Saudi Arabia to repel Iraqi forces from Kuwait, Saddam Hussein agreed to a full and unconditional withdrawal. He asked for time to start the withdrawal of Iraqi troops and to avert an American ground war. Bush's reply was that it was 'too late for that'. On 25 February 1991, Iraq announced it would withdraw fully from Kuwait, agreed to UN Resolution 660, and asked for a Soviet-brokered ceasefire, all of which was rejected by Bush.[16]

On 26 February 1991 Iraq began a full military withdrawal from Kuwait, as had been repeatedly demanded. The Iraqis withdrew in a long convoy of vehicles via the six-lane highway to Basra. After the US bombed and strafed the convoy for over 48 hours, killing thousands of largely defenceless Iraqi troops as well as non-combatants, Iraq's military was largely destroyed. Later it was revealed that large numbers of Iraqi soldiers had been intentionally buried alive by Abrams tanks, which simply ploughed over and buried Iraqis in their trenches.[17]

The United States military had dropped millions of leaflets encouraging Iraqis to rebel against Saddam, along with continuous Voice of America radio broadcasts into Iraq suggesting the same. In response, many Iraqi soldiers deserted, and along with large number of Shia civilians, controlled large areas of southern Iraq. The Kurds in the north also rebelled. But rather than supporting the rebellion it had so openly encouraged, the US military allowed Hussein to order attack helicopters to suppress the rebellion, which he did massively.

A further horror for ordinary Iraqis was a substantial increase in cancers attributed to the US use of depleted uranium rounds. Depleted uranium is also believed to be responsible for Gulf War Syndrome, which is estimated to affect at least 175,000 of the 700,000 US troops who served in Iraq.[18]

CONTAINING IRAQ: THE SANCTIONS 1991–2003

Iraq and the US-led coalition agreed to a ceasefire on 3 March 1991. UN Resolution 687 was passed on April 6, which stipulated that Iraq was to destroy all its chemical, nuclear, and biological weapons and ballistic missiles capable of a range of more than 150 kilometres. The sanctions would remain in place until proof was provided that Iraq had complied with the terms of the resolution, and had withdrawn from Kuwait.[19]

The initial UN Resolution 661 of August 1990 had embargoed all UN member states from financial transactions and trade with Iraq as commercial, industrial, or public utility undertaking. These continued under Resolution 687, despite Iraq meeting the terms of

661 by withdrawing from Kuwait. It was this same UN Resolution 687 that the US would claim that Iraq had violated, and that the US, Britain, and Australia, among others, used to justify the 2003 invasion and 'regime change'.

Similar to Nixon's directing the CIA in Chile to 'make the economy scream' in order to create the conditions to remove Allende and allow neoliberalism to be established, the Iraq sanctions were to make the economy, and the populace, scream to the point of creating the conditions for the removal of Saddam Hussein and allow a neoliberal pliable client state to replace him.

Despite the US successfully making the economy scream in Chile, Chilean support for Allende increased, and it became clear that the Chilean people would not remove him via the democratic process. And after nearly 13 years of sanctions, Saddam Hussein's hold on power continued in 2003, and it was the United States that was widely blamed for Iraqi suffering, both within Iraq and internationally, not the Hussein government. In both countries, only violent military action could remove the obstacles – in Chile, the obstacle to establishing the neoliberal agenda; in Iraq, ensuring that it could and would continue unhindered.

The US government made it clear that the sanctions would remain in place regardless of whether Iraq complied or not. Bush said, 'My view is that we don't want to lift these sanctions as long as Saddam Hussein is in power.'[20] In 1991, Bush ordered the CIA to 'create the conditions for the removal of Saddam Hussein from power'. The CIA organised and funded the Iraqi National Congress,[21] the core of which would form the Coalition Provisional Authority's appointed Iraqi Governing Council 12 years later. And between 1991 and 2001, the United States and British air forces flew 280,000 combat sorties over Iraq, sometimes bombing, and killed hundreds of civilians. Air Force Brigadier General William Looney said in 1999, 'They [Iraqis] know we own their airspace ... We dictate the way they live and talk. And that's what's great about America right now. It's a good thing, especially when there is a lot of oil there we need.'[22]

The sanctions eliminated Iraq's ability to sell oil on the international market, which devastated its economy. Oil was 90 per cent of Iraq's foreign exchange income. The sanctions also devastated Iraq's ability to feed itself. In the 1980s, when it was an American ally and encouraged with US agricultural aid, Iraq had started moving from collective farming to private farming, and to shift from staples to growth-oriented export crops as per the neoliberal development model. Because of the sanctions, Iraq could not import spare parts or fertilisers. Iraq's 1990–91 agricultural output was 80 per cent less than pre-sanctions 1989. By 1999, UNICEF found that 23 per cent of Iraqi babies were born underweight, and one in four children aged 1–4 suffered from chronic malnutrition.[23]

From its election in 1992, the Clinton administration followed the same hard line as the preceding Bush Sr administration regarding Iraq. The sanctions would remain in place as long as Saddam Hussein was in power, regardless of whether Iraq complied with Security Council Resolution 687. In 1998, regime change in Iraq became official congressional and Clinton administration policy.[24]

After considerable international pressure to alleviate the devastating effects of the sanctions, the Oil for Food programme was established in 1995. It allowed UN-approved Iraq oil sales to be used to purchase food and aid. All food contracts had to be approved by the UN, and the money was administered via a UN-monitored account. Purchasing anything other than aid was strictly prohibited. Iraq's $15.9 billion reparations to Kuwait for the invasion came out of the Oil for Food programme. Also, western oil companies were awarded hundreds of millions in compensation for disruption of their operations during the Gulf War, including Halliburton, which was then being run by none other than the ubiquitous Dick Cheney.[25]

Clinton claimed that Saddam Hussein skimmed millions off the Oil for Food programme for his palaces while his people starved, but even if every penny went to the Iraqi people it still was only $170 per person annually, or 50 cents a day.[26]

Corruption on a large scale certainly did occur, as evidenced by the Australian Wheat Board (AWB) scandal. The Australian government's 2006 Cole Inquiry found that AWB had paid over $A290 million in direct bribes to Saddam Hussein's government in return for guaranteed wheat contracts under the Oil for Food programme, almost certainly with Australian government knowledge. AWB officials were later placed in the CPA occupation by the Australian government, where they worked to secure further contracts for Australian wheat.[27]

The United States and Britain sat on the UN Committee responsible for approving contracts under the Oil for Food programme. The stated purpose of the committee, as per the sanctions themselves, was to block Iraq's ability to rebuild chemical or biological weapons. But UNICEF found that $500 million in water and sanitation supply contracts had also been blocked. The US and Britain also blocked chemotherapy drugs, analgesics and radiotherapy equipment. They also prohibited oil infrastructure and telecommunications contracts, which prevented Iraq from increasing its oil capacity and thus its potential to purchase more food or humanitarian supplies. Ninety per cent of all contracts, worth a total $3–5 billion, were blocked by the United States and Britain.[28]

The US and Britain essentially ensured that no economic development could occur in Iraq. The suffering was immense. By 1999, nearly 5,000 Iraqi children were dying each month because of lack of medical care and food, due to the sanctions; UNICEF estimated that 500,000 Iraqi children had died because of the sanctions.[29] UN Humanitarian Coordinator Hans van Sponeck, who ran the Oil for Food programme from October 1998 to March 2000, and his predecessor Denis Halliday both resigned in protest to the humanitarian suffering caused by the sanctions. Halliday described the sanctions as 'a program that they know is killing and targeting children and people. Then it's a program of some sort, and I think it's a program of genocide. I just don't have a better word.'[30]

The Clinton administration remained unmoved. US Secretary of State Madeline Albright, when asked on the investigative journalism programme '60 Minutes' in May 1996 whether the sanctions were worth the deaths of 500,000 children, replied, 'I think this is a very hard choice, but the price – we think the price is worth it.'[31]

In 2002, the United States allowed the UN Security Council to revise the sanctions programme as so-called 'smart sanctions', in order to, according to an editorial in the *Wall Street Journal*, 'deprive Iraq of the propaganda advantage of being the victim of cruel western sanctions'.[32]

There was evidence that Iraq had tried to build a nuclear weapon when it became obvious that the US was intent on military action before the Gulf War, but it did not succeed. It then verified that its destruction of its weapons of mass destruction (WMD) programmes had begun within six months after the Gulf War.[33] The UN's weapons inspections programme verified that Iraq's WMDs had been destroyed, and that its nuclear weapons programme had been abandoned.[34] This was also more famously verified by the US Iraq Survey Group, headed by David Kay, which found no WMDs post the invasion of 2003.

The UN programme for determining Iraqi compliance with destroying its weapons of mass destruction was the United Nations Special Commission, or UNSCOM. In 1998, UNSCOM was found to have been infiltrated by CIA agents. The Iraqis caught them planting bugging and satellite devices to track Saddam Hussein. After the spies were exposed, the US pulled them out and the UN disbanded the disgraced UNSCOM.[35] Iraq did not let inspectors back in until late 2002.

On 15 December, the US initiated Operation Desert Fox, launching 415 cruise missiles and 600 laser-guided bombs, all intended to kill Saddam Hussein. According to the *New York Times*, the targets for Desert Fox were based on intelligence gained in part from the CIA agents' UNSCOM espionage. There was no UN Security Council authorisation for the attack, and they occurred just two days before Clinton's impeachment proceedings concerning his relationship with White House aid Monica Lewinsky were set to begin on 17 December.[36]

Part III

Dollar Dominance:
Controlling the Dollar, Controlling Iraq

9
Threat to the Dollar: Iraq, the Euro and Dollar Dominance

There were only two credible reasons for invading Iraq: control over oil and preservation of the dollar as the world's reserve currency.

John Chapman, former British assistant secretary in the civil service[1]

In the real world ... the one factor underpinning American prosperity is keeping the dollar the World Reserve Currency. This can only be done if the oil producing states keep oil priced in dollars, and all their currency reserves in dollar assets. If anything put the final nail in Saddam Hussein's coffin, it was his move to start selling oil for Euros.

Richard Benson, former Citibank and Chase Manhattan securities analyst[2]

With the sanctions becoming less viable, radical Islam on the rise post-September 11, and a global reaction against neoliberalism in general, American motivation for military action against Iraq was a strong, if not inevitable, consideration. It moved into the inevitable category in November 2000, when Iraq directly attacked another of the underpinnings of US global hegemony, and stopped accepting dollars for its oil and instead insisted on payment in euros.

An absolute key underpinning of the global economy and American hegemony has been that the world's largest and most important commodity, oil, has been sold exclusively in dollars. The world economy in general is also traded in US dollars, making the dollar the *de facto* world currency. In February 2003, on the eve of the US-led invasion, two-thirds of all world trade was denominated in dollars, and more than two-thirds of foreign-held reserves worldwide were also in dollars.[3]

When Iraq switched from selling its oil in dollars to euros in 2000 and encouraged the rest of OPEC to do the same, it presented a much more direct threat to American hegemony than any weapon of mass destruction ever could. This meant that any country wishing to purchase Iraqi oil would need to convert its own currency into euros, which Iraq would then accept as payment. Up to that point, the US dollar had been the only accepted currency for the world's most heavily traded and most valuable commodity. Any country wishing to purchase oil could only do so by converting its own currency into dollars, which would then be accepted by the oil-producing country. These US dollars are held in reserve, in readily accessible investments like US Treasury bills and other interest-bearing government securities. Because the money is in dollars, the investments also must be in dollars, and hence are recycled back into the US economy. This is what in large part allows the US to be in debt for $14,804,647,844,797 ($14.8 trillion) as of October 2011,[4] because so much of the world economy is invested back into the US economy.

If every oil-producing nation followed Iraq's lead and accepted euros instead of dollars, it would mean the end of the American empire. Oil-importing countries – that is, most of the world – would have to convert their dollar reserves into euro reserves, and thus remove the trillions invested in the US economy. A resurgent and regionally strong post-sanctions Iraq, supported politically and economically by European rival oil powers involved in rebuilding its oil-producing infrastructure, would be in a position to encourage vocal US critics Iran and Venezuela to also switch from the dollar to the euro.

In *Petrodollar Warfare: Oil, Iraq, and the Future of the Dollar*,[5] analyst William Clark puts forward his theory that Iraq's switch to the euro, and the threat that other oil-producing countries might follow, was the primary motivation for the US-led invasion. Similar to how the Nixon administration manipulated the 1973 OPEC oil crisis to gain petrodollar ascendancy over the rest of the world, Clark posits that invading Iraq was not only to stop it selling oil in euros, but also to ensure that the euro and Europe could not contest the tremendous economic hegemony the US receives by having oil sales denominated exclusively in dollars. Clark also examines how ongoing US efforts to contain Iran's nuclear programme are actually American attempts to contain Iran's attempts to create a euro-based international oil trading market.

Writing in 1998, before the euro had even been introduced as a currency, Peter Gowan said:

> Directly threatening to US interests in such a scenario would be the impact on the dollar; for Saddam Hussein might have preferred to denominate his capital in marks or yen. As the world's biggest debtor, with its debt denominated in dollars, the US economy would clearly be vulnerable if a significant proportion of Middle East oil revenues were switched to another

currency. For the United States to concede such political power to Saddam was unthinkable.[6]

Former 'economic hitman' John Perkins also recognises the immense power that seigniorage holds for the United States:

> In the final analysis, the global empire depends to a large extent on the fact that the dollar acts as the standard world currency, and that the United States Mint has the right to print those dollars ... It means, among other things, that we can continue to make loans that will never be repaid – and that we ourselves can accumulate huge debts ... A decision by OPEC to substitute the euro for the dollar as its standard currency would shake the empire to its very foundations. If that were to happen, and if one or two creditors were to demand that we repay our debts in euros, the impact would be enormous.[7]

THE EURO THREAT

By the time the Bush administration, along with British support, began in earnest to clamour for the need to invade Iraq and rid the world once and for all of the scourge of Saddam Hussein, much of that world was strongly considering moving to the euro to pay for oil instead of dollars. Emboldened by Iraq's example, this was led by Europe itself. In June 2001, the European Parliament passed a resolution calling on 'the European Union, in dialogue with the OPEC and non OPEC countries, to prepare the way for payment of oil in euros'.[8] A month earlier, there were media reports that 'EU leaders [have] made an audacious bid to lure Russia away from its reliance on the greenback, calling on Moscow to start accepting euros instead of dollars for its exports, dangling the attractive carrot of a boom in investment and trade.'[9]

Russia, like Iraq, is one of the world's largest oil exporters. So is Bush's other famous 'Axis of Evil' member, Iran. In 2002, in an OPEC speech Iranian diplomat Javad Yarjani openly stated that

> It is quite possible that as bilateral trade increases between the Middle East and the European Union, it could be feasible to price oil in euros. This would foster further ties between these trading blocs by increasing commercial exchange, and by helping attract much-needed European investment in the Middle East.[10]

There were also high-level discussion between Russia and Iran regarding the euro for denominating their considerable oil sales.[11] Venezuela's vehemently outspoken critic of US neoliberal imperialism, Hugo Chavez, was also interested. Venezuela is a major oil producer.

It also must have been utterly exacerbating for oilmen like Bush and Cheney to have a fast one pulled on them by Saddam Hussein, despite the sanctions. Under the Oil for Food programme, it had been US companies that were buying up over two-thirds of Iraq's oil production. When Iraq switched to the euro, these same companies then had to take their dollars and exchange them for euros to pay for it. Embarrassingly, if not outright humiliating to companies used to calling the shots, nearly 2.5 billion barrels of Iraq's total 3.3 billion barrels were purchased this way from late 2000 to the start of the invasion.[12]

And so, on the eve of the Iraq invasion, a veritable international coup was forming, with the aim of replacing the dollar with the euro as the global currency for purchasing oil. Iraq had led the way and shown at least to that point that it was possible to defy the United States. If Iran, Venezuela and Russia followed suit, it would mean a great canyon running through the fabric that allowed the United States its global dominance, and would put Europe in position to supersede the US. While it was in no one's interest for this to happen overnight and cause an immediate global economic crisis – and there would probably have been an initial sharing or basket of currencies where the dollar would still be a factor – there was no way the US was going to let this happen at all, sharing or no sharing.

As military analyst Stan Goff puts it, 'Oil is not a normal commodity. No other commodity has five US navy battle groups patrolling the sea lanes to secure it.'[13] And the 725 military installations in 120 countries that the US operated at the time[14] were most definitely not for show, nor to protect any 'freedom' other than the freedom of the United States to dictate its power whenever, however and wherever it wanted. America would soon show that it would be a monumental mistake to, as Bush might put it, 'misunderestimate' US resolve.

Former German Chancellor Helmut Schmidt understood this. In 1997, when the euro was still in its inception stage, he stated that 'Americans do not yet understand the significance of the euro, but when they do it could set up a monumental conflict, it will change the whole world situation so that the United States can no longer call all the shots'.[15]

Iraq's move to the euro, and the very real possibility of the euro replacing the dollar more broadly for oil sales, helps explain why Germany, France and Russia were so very unreceptive to American and British assertions that Iraq had to be dealt with militarily. And as we shall see in Chapter 14, European and Russian companies had signed contracts to develop Iraq's oil post-sanctions which were potentially worth $1.1 trillion,[16] at the direct exclusion of those same US companies now humiliatingly having to pay for Iraq's oil in euros. And it was Britain's adherence to the dollar as the *de facto* global currency – and reaping many of the benefits as a result – that influenced its ongoing decision to stick with the pound and not join the rest of Europe in the euro. Its dogged support of the US in the sanctions meant that it too was shut out of the post-sanctions Iraq oil contracts. And lest we forget, it was the only country to support the invasion with actual ground troops.

As usual, it was Saudi Arabia who ensured American interests were upheld. Youssef Ibrahim, a member of the US Council on Foreign Relations, told CNN in February 2003 that 'The Saudis are holding the line on oil prices in Opec and should they, for example, go along with the rest of the Opec people in demanding that oil be priced in euros, that would deal a very heavy blow to the American economy.'[17]

But with radical Islam on the rise, and with elements within Saudi Arabia clearly funding Al Qaeda (see Chapter 14), reliance on Saudi Arabia was looking more and more like a short-term gamble. In one of the (very) few mainstream media articles in the American or British press examining the issue in any sort of depth, business writer Faisal Islam of the UK *Observer* revealed the following 2002 Congressional testimony by a former US ambassador to Saudi Arabia:

One of the major things the Saudis have historically done, in part out of friendship with the United States, is to insist that oil continues to be priced in dollars. Therefore, the US Treasury can print money and buy oil, which is an advantage no other country has. With the emergence of other currencies and with strains in the relationship, I wonder whether there will not again be, as there have been in the past, people in Saudi Arabia who raise the question of why they should be so kind to the United States.[18]

The answer, of course, was given when the United States invaded Iraq not long after, answering for the Saudis and the rest of the world 'why they should be so kind to the United States.'

A NEW AMERICAN WORLD ORDER: NIXON, THE GOLD STANDARD AND THE SAUDIS

And so, it all comes back to Saudi Arabia. America was utterly reliant on Saudi Arabia and its ability to dictate, among other crucial oil-related terms, that oil be priced in dollars. As Faisal Islam summarised a month before the Iraq invasion, this is what allowed the US to

> ... carry on printing money – effectively IOUs – to fund tax cuts, increase military spending, and consumer spending on imports without fear of inflation or that these loans will be called in. As keeper of the global currency there is always the last-ditch resort to devaluation, which forces other countries' exporters to pay for US economic distress. It's probably the nearest thing to a 'free lunch' in global economics.[19]

That 'free lunch' was also established as result of the Nixon administration's manipulation of the OPEC oil embargo in 1973. As we have seen, at the same time they were 'making the economy scream' in Chile and instituting the world's first neoliberal regime, Nixon and his Secretary of State Henry Kissinger were also ensuring the OPEC embargo would ultimately benefit the United States. That their actions would also cause distress and hardship for the majority of the American public, who would have to deal with the hyper-inflation and substantial increases in gasoline prices, was apparently not taken into consideration.

This was on top of the already turbulent economic consequences that occurred when Nixon abandoned the Bretton Woods gold standard in October 1971. The free-floating dollar resulted in significant inflation – so severe that the administration went to the extraordinary measure of instituting wage and price freezes by the end of the same year. Rampant inflation continued throughout the 1970s.[20]

A crucial aspect of that manipulation was to ensure that the dollar remained as the *de facto* world currency, even after the US pulled out of the Bretton Woods requirement that all dollars be backed by gold. Once the US pulled out, there was nothing to stop countries from buying oil in whatever currency they chose. Pricing oil in a variety of currencies, however, was volatile for those countries selling oil, and OPEC was in negotiation with Europe and other industrialised countries to devise a basket of currencies, including the dollar itself, to replace the US dollar as an exclusive monopoly for oil trade.

While assuring the rest of the world that it would not impede moves to a basket of currencies to replace the dollar, Nixon was secretly and successfully negotiating with Saudi Arabia to guarantee that international oil sales would continue to be priced exclusively in dollars. In return for ongoing American support for the ruling stability of the Saudi royal family, the Saudis agreed to ensure OPEC would continue to price oil in dollars, and also to deposit their surplus oil revenues in American and British private banks – banks which had just been freed from the capital constraints of the Bretton Woods agreements, which Nixon had also recently ditched. Petrodollar recycling was thus born, and the first billions of what would become trillions began flowing into the US.[21]

As David Spiro writes in *The Hidden Hand of American Hegemony: Petrodollar Recycling and International Markets*, which examines this history in detail, 'clearly something more than the laws of supply and demand ... resulted in 70 percent of all Saudi assets in the United States being held in a New York Fed account.'[22]

Nixon and Kissinger's manoeuvring was part of a long-standing American relationship with the Saud royal family. In 1945, US President Franklin Roosevelt ensured that Saudi Arabian oil would be under US domain when he entered into an agreement with Saudi Arabia's King Saud. The US would protect and guarantee the Saudi regime, in return for exclusive access to Saudi oil.[23]

Rather than trying to prevent the oil embargo and its subsequent price shock – which Nixon probably could have done with a phone call – or reining in Israel in the Yom Kippur War – which also almost certainly could have been accomplished with a phone call – Nixon and Kissinger instead manipulated the crisis to solidify American dominance. It was Kissinger who negotiated the secret arrangements to ensure the resulting increase in Saudi oil revenues would go to American and British banks.

As well as the banks, that other mainstay of the American free enterprise system – weapons manufacturers – also benefited. Saudi Arabia accounted for nearly a quarter of all US weapons exports from 1950 to 2000. In 2002, the year before the Iraq invasion, they purchased $5.2 billion worth.[24]

In January 2001, former Saudi Arabian Minister of Oil Sheikh Yaki Yamani said in an interview that '... the Americans were behind the increase in the price of oil.' Yamani had been oil minister for 24 years (1962–86), and had been opposed to the American plan. He elaborated that 'King Faisal sent me to the Shah of Iran, who said: "Why are you against the increase in the price of oil? That is that they want? Ask Henry Kissinger – he is the one who wants a higher price."'[25]

And so what had seemed at the time like a weak acquiescence to the power of the Arab sheikdoms to arbitrarily force an economic crisis on the US from the rapid rise in gasoline prices, was in fact a massive swindling of the United States to smash the agreed-upon rules of the global economy for its own benefit. Or, to be more precise, the benefit of its banks and other corporations.

The resulting hyper-inflation and long queues for gasoline which so defined the 1970s in America were then the ultimate justification that Keynesianism did not work, and that only through the neoliberal disembowelling of government spending on social programmes, consumer protection and environmental preservation could America return to prosperity. In a few short years, Ronald Reagan would be elected as a result, and American – and world – history would take a very different turn. Market forces and corporate profit would now be the ultimate measures of American success, not the social well-being of its people. The result was the neoliberalised, free market, globalised world that we live in today, with the US exerting control over much of the global economy.

10
Dollar Challenge Redux:
The Global Financial Crisis and Iraqi Oil

In June 2003, the US military occupation moved back to accepting only dollars for Iraq's oil, and eliminated the acceptance of euros. It did so despite the fact that the euro was valued 13 per cent higher than the dollar, and thus directly reduced the revenue value of Iraq's oil sales.[1]

While the invasion of Iraq might have staved off the euro's challenges to American dollar dominance, it was at best a stop-gap solution. In the wake of the global financial crisis that exploded in 2008, faith in the dollar as the world's *de facto* currency – and America's ability to keep it stable – has been greatly diminished. Initiated by its neoliberal mania for deregulation, the US faces a renewed challenge to its dollar hegemony, although this time it was clearly of its own making.

It was, after all, America that was responsible for creating the crisis in the first place. American banks and investment firms had been allowed by the federal government to flood the US housing market with cheap credit and subprime adjustable rate mortgages that were almost certainly never going to be repaid. These extremely risky, if not outright worthless, mortgages were then chopped up and fraudulently sold as AAA-rated investments to unsuspecting investors all over the world. When the US housing market peaked in 2006 and prices steadily declined, combined with millions of these adjustable rate mortgages resetting at higher interest rates that people had no hope of paying, the related investments went bust, as did the global market for buying them. Millions have lost their homes in the ongoing wave of foreclosures.

Legislation to prevent this exact type of scenario had been enacted during the Great Depression. The Glass-Steagall Act prohibited the merger of commercial banks and investment firms to ensure mortgages would not be subject to the type of casino speculation that had brought on the Great Depression. It was repealed in 1999 during the heyday of neoliberal mania under the Clinton administration as part of US requirements for joining the World Trade Organization.[2]

The American government's response to the crisis was to spend $16 trillion to bail out the very banks and financial institutions that were responsible for the crisis. This astonishing figure was revealed in the first ever federal audit of the Federal Reserve in July 2011.[3] Combined with the profligate military spending on the invasions of Iraq and Afghanistan and the global (and domestic) 'War on Terror' now estimated to cost $4 trillion,[4] US debt had increased by $10 trillion in just ten years.

The Federal Reserve's subsequent policy response has been to keep interest rates at near-zero levels to encourage borrowing and to promote economic growth. This in turn has meant much lower returns for US Treasury bills and other American interest-bearing instruments, and subsequently lower returns for the rest of the world's countries which have their vast dollar reserves that are needed to pay for oil and other commodities invested in these Treasury bills.

As a result, calls for a new global currency regime away from the dollar have become a chorus, with many now suggesting that what was unthinkable a few years ago is now inevitable. Former US Federal Reserve chairperson Alan Greenspan has suggested the euro could eventually replace the dollar. UN Under- Secretary-General for Economic and Social Affairs Sha Zukang also called for a shift away from a single currency.[5] A 2011 World Bank report predicted that the dollar will be abandoned as the world's single currency before 2025.[6]

French President Nicolas Sarkozy has been particularly vocal. In 2009, he said

> A new international monetary system is required. Following World War II, there was a single superpower in the United States, and it was normal that there was a single great currency. Today, we have a multipolar world, and the system must be multimonetary. In the world as it is now, there can't be submission to what a single currency dictates.[7]

In October 2009, long-term Middle East correspondent Robert Fisk of Britain's *Independent* newspaper broke the story that Gulf oil-producing countries, along with China, Russia, Japan and France, were planning a new system to replace the dollar as the *de facto* currency for global oil sales by 2018.[8] The dollar would be replaced by a basket of different currencies including a new currency for the Gulf Co-operation Council countries of Saudi Arabia, Kuwait, the United Arab Emirates, Oman, Qatar and Bahrain. Other currencies would include the euro, the Chinese yuan and Japanese yen. Gold would also be included in the mix.

China was cited as one of the most enthusiastic participants in the secret meetings. According to the US Treasury, as of 2011, China has over $1.15 trillion in US Treasury bills.[9] It has developed a somewhat mutually dependent relationship with the US. China buys American debt in the form of US government securities, which helps keep the US government and economy stable. In return, America consumes an enormous amount of Chinese products, so very cheaply made in the sweatshops resulting from China's wholehearted embrace of US-driven free market neoliberalism. Many of these sweatshops are producing goods for American corporations – goods which had previously been manufactured by blue-collar workers in the US – so there is an added benefit to shareholders of those companies. This arrangement has been relatively stable as long as the American economy continues to buy Chinese goods, and as long as US government securities provided a decent rate of return. But with recent events, neither the US economy nor US global leadership are looking like particularly good bets. The US, after all, was responsible for creating the financial crisis in the first place.

Saudi Arabia, Kuwait, the United Arab Emirates and Qatar have an estimated $2.1 trillion in dollar reserves.[10] With the Middle East importing a vast amount of goods from China, as does the rest of the world, these dollars are then exchanged for Chinese yuan in order to buy Chinese goods. If China could buy oil in yuan, the Middle East countries could then buy Chinese goods with the yuan they would be holding in reserve from oil sales. It would certainly make more sense.

If successful, it would easily be one of the most significant events in financial – and because of its potential for repercussions – quite possibly world history. It was immediately denied by the countries in question, and any such moves will obviously be fought by the US, judging by its actions in Iraq. But as the Chinese economy, along with India and Brazil's, continue to grow, the US will have less leverage to continue the status quo. That long-term allies like Saudi Arabia and the other Arab Gulf states, along with Japan, are involved is a profound message that US leadership is openly being questioned if not outright challenged.

There is also the crucial issue of China now competing with the US for dwindling oil reserves as we enter the era of peak oil. Fisk's story in the *Independent* quoted Sun Bigan, China's former special envoy to the Middle East, that 'Bilateral quarrels and clashes are unavoidable. We cannot lower vigilance against hostility in the Middle East over energy interests and security.'[11] China has successfully competed with US companies for oil concessions recently in Iraq, and unlike the US, is willing to do business with Iran. There has also been speculation that US support for rebelling forces in Libya has been about blocking Chinese access to that country's resources, Libya being one of many African nations, like Sudan, where China has been particularly active.[12]

These moves to create a new global currency programme were all highly predictable. In December 2004, a full year-and-a-half after the US invaded Iraq to eliminate these threats to its dollar dominance, the *Economist* predicted:

> If America keeps on spending and borrowing at the present pace, the dollar will eventually lose its mighty status in international finance. And that would hurt; the privilege of being able to print the world reserve currency, a privilege which is now at risk, allows America to borrow cheaply, and thus spend much more than it earns, on far better terms than are available to others.[13]

The vast hollowing-out of the US economy – as a result of 30 years of relentless neoliberal cutbacks on government education and health care spending, deregulation of financial markets which led to the global financial crisis, and privatisation of remaining government services – has seen a massive transfer of wealth from the working and middle class to the wealthiest percentage of American society. Real wages have barely risen since before the onslaught of neoliberal reforms under Reagan, and income inequality is now worse than Egypt's. In 1973, the average hourly wage was $14.73; in 2009, adjusting for inflation, it was $15.96, an increase of a dollar and some change, over 36 years. Top-income earners meanwhile saw their hourly wage increase by 30 per cent. An October 2011 report by the Congressional Budget Office revealed that income exploded by 275 per cent for the wealthiest 1 per cent, but only 18 per cent for the bottom 20 per cent between 1979 and 2007.[14]

The US has crippled itself and its economic ability to be the ultimate consumer of China's, let alone the world's, products. Invading Iraq only postponed what is becoming increasingly obvious: that neoliberalism is destroying the domestic foundations of American economic dominance.

AMERICAN PETRODOLLAR HEGEMONY POST-INVASION

But in the short term at least, the Iraq invasion has guaranteed the continued petrodollar recycling so crucial to America's superpower status. These petrodollar flows to the US economy, just prior to the Iraq War and the initial years after the invasion, have been significant. The global price of oil more than doubled from 2002 to 2005, and would hit record highs in 2008. Oil export revenue in 2002 for oil-exporting countries was $262 billion; in 2005 these revenues had risen to $614 billion.[15] IMF Europe Director Saleh Nsouli said:

> The majority of oil exporters' central bank reserves remain invested in the dollar. And oil sales are still priced, invoiced, and settled in dollars. It is thus likely that purchases of US reserves will continue to take place, even though not necessarily in the traditional channels. Oil exporters' preference is for investing their petrodollars in the United States ... .[16]

Writing for global financial analyst *RGE Monitor* in April 2008, Rachel Ziemba estimated in her report 'Petrodollar Recycling: Focus on the Banks' that

> ... Central banks and sovereign funds of oil exporters had an estimated $2.5 trillion in foreign exchange holdings at the end of 2007. Most of those assets have found their way into [dollar] bonds, equities, and other assets classes but a share are still in [bank] deposits, especially dollar deposits.[17]

In an in-depth analysis of petrodollar recycling from 2002 to 2006, the New York Federal Reserve Bank also concluded that 'Although it is difficult to determine where the funds are initially invested, the evidence suggests that the bulk are ultimately ending up in the United States.'[18] The authors emphasise the difficulty in tracking petrodollar revenues, but conclude that about half of the petrodollar revenues have been spent on imports, while the other half of remaining revenues has gone towards purchasing foreign investment assets. Countries like Japan and China who have seen their exports increase as a result, have largely invested these petrodollars back into the US financial markets, or into purchasing US Treasury notes, bonds and other forms of debt. The report concludes, 'Our analysis indicates that most petrodollar investments are finding their way to the United States, indirectly if not directly.'[19]

As we've seen earlier, this has continued, with Saudi Arabia, Kuwait, United Arab Emirates and Qatar holding an estimated $2.1 trillion in dollar reserves as of 2011. As a result of the invasion, this book is still talking about petrodollars, not petro-euros.

IRAQ: THE NEW SAUDI ARABIA

Since the invasion, Iraq has not been in a position to recycle any excess oil revenues. As of mid-2011, it was still only producing 2.7 million barrels, nowhere near its 1979 peak of 3.7 million barrels per day.[20] Its oil production has been stymied by ongoing security issues, and as examined in Chapter 21, civil society opposition to American backed legislation that would have semi-privatised its oil industry. However, despite the lack of legislation, and therefore of questionable legality, the Iraqi Oil Ministry has signed contracts with a number of foreign firms since 2008. These contracts were the biggest in the history of the industry, and if fulfilled, Iraq is now in position to produce an astonishing 12 million barrels a day by 2017, dependent on increased security and significant improvements in infrastructure.[21]

In comparison, Saudi Arabian production averaged 8.4 million barrels a day in 2010.[22] It is certainly capable of pumping well beyond that, and it utilised its estimated spare production capacity of 2.5–3 million barrels a day to increase production in 2011 when a number of Arab producers had their production challenged in the midst of the Arab Spring.[23] But as revealed in the Wikileaks release of US diplomatic cables in 2010, there are real concerns within senior circles of the American government that its oil reserves have been seriously overstated.[24]

If Iraq produced anywhere near the 12 million barrel mark it would cause serious problems for the rest of OPEC. If Iraq chose to release all 12 million barrels, the world market would be flooded, driving the price down significantly. It would certainly be in position to rival, if not outright replace, the Saudis' exclusive ability to maintain their role as *de facto* US surrogate. Iraq at present still has observer status in OPEC, meaning it cannot vote, and has been exempt from OPEC's quota system since its invasion of Kuwait in 1990. While it is expected to be eventually reinstated, it could choose not to.

The advantage for the US is obvious. Whether in OPEC or not, the US's *de facto* control of the Iraqi government means *de facto* control over Iraq's oil. With peak oil becoming more of a political reality over the coming years, what oil remains will obtain even further geopolitical significance, as detailed in Chapter 14. And even though all US combat troops had technically left Iraq by the end of 2011, as agreed, US military bases, thousands of contractors, and the world's largest embassy remains. The Iraqi government can always ask US troops to return. And there is always the option of re-escalating military engagement with an Iraqi government suddenly found to be 'supporting terrorists'.

Thanks to the fine work of investigative journalist Greg Palast, we now know that there were high-level discussions within the Bush administration strongly advocating that once the US got control of Iraqi oil, that production be hugely increased so that the US would no longer have to rely on the good-will of the Saudi royal family to do American bidding within OPEC.[25] This reliance, as we shall see, was becoming increasingly tenuous post-9/11.

The potential to simply replace its reliance on Saudi Arabia with an Iraq under a military occupation, and the immense benefits to the United States of this arrangement as long as oil continues to be priced in dollars, means that American hegemony can potentially extend well into the future. And just as the US invaded Iraq when it switched to the euro, any moves to create a new global trading currency will be met with similar force, whether political, economic, military, or, most likely, a combination of all three. The question is whether after pushing its economic hegemony to its outer limits from wars and Wall Street bailouts, and eviscerating its middle class to the point it can no longer be the engine of global consumption, whether a US system entrenched in neoliberalism can still rise to the challenge.

11
Containing Iraq: Oil, Imperialism and the Rise of Corporate Rule

The Gulf War, the subsequent sanctions, and the 2003 invasion are, unfortunately, directly consistent with nearly a century of British, French and American intervention in the Middle East. The ferocious resistance that the US has encountered to its rule in Iraq has defined the Iraqi people ever since its artificial creation as a nation by the British just after the First World War.

IRAQ: A CREATION OF BRITISH IMPERIALISM

Prior to the First World War, the nation state that is now Iraq did not exist. The area that is now Iraq consisted of three districts of the Ottoman Empire which had been administered by Turkey since the 1600s: Basra in the south, Baghdad in the centre, and Mosul in the north. The Mandate of Mesopotamia was entrusted to Britain by the League of Nations when the Ottoman Empire was divided up in April 1920 at the San Remo conference following the First World War; France was granted the mandates of Lebanon and Syria. Britain, France and Russia had already met and divided up the post-First World War world amongst themselves in the 1916 Sykes-Picot Agreement; the subsequent Balfour Declaration committed Britain to establishing a Jewish homeland in the Arab Middle East. In May 1920, the League of Nations upheld Sykes-Picot and Balfour.[1]

The British had promised Arab states independence after the war if they fought with them against Turkey and the Ottoman Empire. When the British entered Baghdad in 1917, Lieutenant General Stanley Maude said, 'We do not come into your cities and lands as conquerors or enemies, but as liberators ... The Arab race may rise once again to greatness.'[2] Independence, however, was not forthcoming. Just as in 2003 and similar broken promises of Iraqi sovereignty post-invasion, the Iraqis rebelled. In June 1920, in *Ath Thawra al Iraqiyya al Kubra*, or the Great Iraqi Revolution of 1920, Iraqis revolted against the British all along the Euphrates River valley, and an Iraqi provisional government was declared in August.[3]

The British response was brutal, particularly regarding the modern airfare advantage they held. One Royal Air Force officer proudly noted that 'Within forty five minutes a full size village can be practically wiped out and a third of its inhabitants killed or injured.'[4] The insurgency was soon crushed, with an estimated 6,000–9,000 Iraqis killed, versus 500–2,000 British. The British also used chemical weapons, despite their use having been internationally condemned in the First World War. Winston Churchill commented, 'I do not understand this squeamishness about the use of gas. I am strongly in favour of using poison gas against uncivilised tribes.'[5]

In *Oil, Power and Empire*, Lawrence Everest outlines the British founding of the modern state of Iraq.[6] In 1921, with resistance largely eliminated, Iraq was created in Cairo, Egypt at a secret meeting of British officials. Iraq means 'cliff' in Arabic, and replaced the area's better-known name of Mesopotamia. Self-determination was not considered an option.

The modern state of Iraq and its religious and cultural mix of Sunnis, Shias and Kurds is a British invention. As mentioned previously, the long-standing border issues and grievances regarding Kuwait that led to the first Gulf War were also established by the British. More specifically, Kuwait had been a British protectorate since 1899. Much smaller in size and population, it was given 310 miles of coastline, whereas Iraq was given only 36 miles and had no direct port on the Gulf. Kuwait had been part of the Ottoman Empire's district of Basra, and therefore Iraqis believed it should have been part of Iraq and not a separate country. The British clearly intended to keep Iraq weak, and to ensure it would not become powerful enough to ever be a threat to British domination of the area.

The British also established the long-standing Sunni minority dominance of Iraqi governance by establishing and selecting a Sunni monarch for the colonial government, Faisal ibn Husayn. The British also created a strong and loyal base of support by granting large landholdings to a small number of tribal leaders, thus concentrating wealth and political power in a small base. Britain, however, retained the real power and had a full veto over Iraq's military and finances, controlled its foreign policy, and, crucially, had direct control of Iraq's oil. Overall, the British relied on the Sunnis to control the country via the monarchy and their place in the military hierarchy. In other words, they created the political situation of Sunni minority rule that Saddam Hussein and the Baathists replicated. The Anglo-Iraqi Treaty of 1922 also dictated that British officials would be appointed to specified posts in 18 departments to act as advisers and inspectors. Similarly, the CPA ensured that Iraq's post-sovereignty government in June 2004 would have pro-free market, neoliberal advisers in its government.

IMPERIALIST HISTORY OF IRAQ: OIL

In March 1925, Iraq's British-installed King Faisal signed a 75-year-concession granting the British-controlled Turkish Petroleum Company all rights to Iraq's oil, with modest royalties.[7] By 1928, pressure from the United States to be included in Middle East oil production forced the Red Line Agreement, which divided up the Middle East into areas controlled by US, British, French and Dutch oil companies. Under the renamed 'Iraqi Petroleum Company' (IPC), Shell of the Netherlands, British Petroleum, Total of France, and the entities that would become American companies Exxon and Mobil, carved up the substantial reserves discovered in Iraq's north in 1927.

The IPC quickly gained a total monopoly of Iraqi oil production, and it deliberately restricted Iraqi oil output in order to keep prices and profits artificially high. The Red Line Agreement stipulated that no single power would develop oil without the participation of the other companies. The IPC cartel became the model for all future oil ventures and control.[8] The Red Line Agreement is an excellent example of the American government pursuing a vigorous foreign policy on behalf of its corporations.

In 1932, the British League of Nations mandate ended and Iraq became an independent nation. Nothing really changed, however, as the British still controlled the monarchy, British troops were stationed in the country, and there were British officials throughout the government. Granting sovereignty while retaining actual control was also practised in June 2004 in Iraq, by the United States, the UK and Australia, as examined in Chapter 20.

The post-Second World War political landscape of the Middle East was determined in 1944, when US President Franklin Delano Roosevelt told British Ambassador Halifax that 'Persian [Iranian] oil is yours. We share the oil of Iraq and Kuwait. As for Saudi Arabian oil, it's ours.'[9] The subsequent deal that Roosevelt struck with Saudi Arabia's King Saud meant that in return for American protection of the Saudi regime, the United States would have exclusive access to Saudi oil. This alliance has proven to be one of the absolute crucial underpinnings of American hegemony.

In the post-Second World War world, oil was an even more vital commodity. The Allies had triumphed at least in part because they had better oil supplies and access, largely due to their control of the Middle East. Middle East oil took on a more direct geopolitical importance in the oil-dependent post-war global economy. It also provided consistent and huge profits. Middle East oil cost 5–15 cents a barrel to produce in the mid-1950s, while selling for around $2.25 a barrel. From 1948 to 1960, western oil companies earned $12.8 billion in Middle East oil profits from a $1.3 billion investment. By 1960, the US and its oil corporations controlled 60 per cent of Middle East oil, and Great Britain 30 per cent.[10]

THE US POST-SECOND WORLD WAR: CORPORATE IMPERIALISM

After the Second World War, the United States was by far the dominant western power. Secretary of State John Foster Dulles, and his brother, Allen Dulles, head of the newly created CIA, represented the more conservative, pro-corporate and free enterprise foreign policy of the Eisenhower administration (1952–60). Both Dulles brothers had previously worked as lawyers representing major US corporations with significant foreign interests. It was these corporations who had the most to lose from the developmentalism occurring in the Southern Cone countries and elsewhere, and the placing of limitations on US capital via tariffs and state protection of industries. Such activities were viewed as definitive first steps to full-blown communism by the Dulles brothers.

In *Overthrow*, author Steven Kinzer writes that 'As the twentieth century progressed, titans of industry and their advocates went a step beyond influencing policy makers; they became the policy makers.'[11] The Dulles's are a clear example of this, as was Philander Knox, secretary of state under the Taft administration, and like the Dulles's a former corporate lawyer. Knox orchestrated the removal of Nicaraguan President Zelaya in 1909 on behalf of his former corporate clients, the Philadelphia-based La Luz mining company.[12] The examples become even more stark when we examine the corporate connections regarding the awarding of Iraq reconstruction contracts in Chapters 18 and 19.

John Foster Dulles was famously anti-communist and a devout Christian. 'For us, there are two sorts of people in the world', he said in 1953, summarising his foreign policy vision. 'There are those who are Christians and support free enterprise, and there are the others.'[13]

As part of its post-Second World War role, the United States had taken over the British and French colonial roles of enforcing borders and maintaining the previous colonial power arrangements in the Middle East. It displayed how seriously it took this new responsibility in 1953, when, in response to the democratically elected government of Mohammed Mosaddegh nationalising the Iranian oil industry, the CIA engineered a bloody coup that removed Mosaddegh and installed the Shah in his place. Mosaddegh's progressive reforms had been so influential that in 1952, *Time* magazine had named him 'Man of the Year'.[14]

The Dulles's former legal firm, Sullivan and Cromwell, was hired to work out the legal conditions for Iranian oil. Under the newly formed National Iranian Oil Company, 40 per cent of Iran's oil went to US companies, and 10 per cent each to French and Dutch companies. British Petroleum lost its pre-nationalisation monopoly, but secured a new share of 40 per cent. Profits were split with the new government of the Shah on a 50-50 basis.[15] Iran under the Shah would prove to be one of the most loyal, and brutal, of all American client states over the next 25 years. In 1948, the state of Israel was established, and became another key US client state in the region.

In 1954, in response to the democratically elected Arbenz government in Guatemala expropriating land belonging to the United Fruit Company, with full compensation, the CIA initiated another coup and deposed Arbenz. United Fruit had been one of the Dulles brothers' former clients.[16] Under John Foster Dulles' foreign policy leadership, the US aligned itself with dictatorships, especially in Latin America, and with anti-popular, anti-democratic movements. It was a pattern of US economic and foreign policy that continued unabated through the Kennedy and Johnson administrations of the 1960s, leading up to its more dramatic escalation in Vietnam, and then in Chile under Nixon.

Since the early 1980s, American intervention in other countries' governments has taken place to ensure their adherence to the neoliberal debt-dependency agenda set by the World Bank and the IMF, and since 1996, the more specific market liberalisation dictates of the World Trade Organization. The US directly initiating regime changes, either by coups or more direct military intervention in support of US corporate capital access, hardly began then.

In *Overthrow*, Kinzer identifies 14 countries in which the US directly and intentionally overthrew governments to protect or create economic interests, beginning in Hawaii in 1893 and concluding with Iraq in 2003. He focuses on only those countries where the US played the primary role in deposing the government in power.

Kinzer is blunt that in nearly every instance intervention was done on behalf or at the behest of US multinational corporations when their interests – that is, their share of the particular market – was threatened: '[American] corporations came to expect government to act on their behalf abroad, even to the extreme of overthrowing uncooperative foreign leaders. Successive presidents have agreed that this is a good way to promote American interests.'[17]

From 1893 through to the Second World War, the US sent military forces to overturn governments in Hawaii, Cuba, the Philippines and Puerto Rico (the latter three included in the Spanish–American War), and Nicaragua. Its 1903 intervention in Colombia to secure the building of the Panama Canal saw the creation of an entirely new country: Panama. As well as Iraq, Kinzer also identifies Vietnam, Granada (1983), Panama (1989), Afghanistan (2002), Chile and Guatemala (1954), and Iran (1953) although the latter three were coups and not direct invasions. The US also invaded Mexico, Haiti and the Dominican Republic, but their leaders were not overthrown. Kinzer states that 'No nation in modern history has done this so often, in so many places so far from its own shores.'[18]

Kinzer's list is barely the tip of the iceberg, however, in terms of countries the US has intervened in. In addition to Chile, the US supported the establishment of right-wing neoliberal regimes in Argentina and other countries pursuing developmental-ism throughout South America in the 1970s, and the Reagan administration supported right-wing reactionary forces in Nicaragua and El Salvador in the 1980s. Nor does his list include the US role in the horrific bloodbath in Indonesia in the 1960s in the name of eradicating communism, or the Arab dictatorships like Saudi Arabia, Kuwait and Egypt, that would not be able to exist without US support, or the US role in the 1975 dismissal of the highly progressive Gough Whitlam government in Australia, or America's eradication of its own native Indian population. The list, unfortunately, is long.

That Kinzer begins his examination of US direct interventions with that of Hawaii in 1893 is significant. US corporate interests were able to muster American government support to overthrow the Hawaiian monarchy to establish a sugar industry. Kinzer describes as a 'quirk of history' that the multinational corporation rose to prominence simultaneously as the US became a world power.

SANTA CLARA BLUES: THE RISE OF CORPORATE DOMINATION

However, this simultaneity was not a coincidence. The rise of the modern multinational corporation as we know it today, and its ability to significantly influence American foreign policy, can be traced directly to the 1886 US Supreme Court decision in *Santa Clara* vs. *Pacific Railway* that recognised corporations as having the same legal rights as flesh-and-blood citizens, and were therefore protected under the Constitution's Bill of Rights.

The *Santa Clara* decision recognised the corporation as a 'person' under the US Constitution's 14th Amendment, which was passed in 1868. The 14th Amendment granted constitutional rights to newly freed slaves and their descendants after the American Civil War. The amendment forbids any state to 'deprive any person of life, liberty, or property, without due process of law; nor deny to any person within its jurisdiction the equal protection of the laws'.[19] It is this specific use of the word 'person' that corporation lawyers claimed protected the corporation, because corporations were corporate 'persons'. It is ironic that corporations succeeded at this time in being recognised as legal persons, whereas flesh-and-blood female persons and native Indians would have to wait many years before they were afforded the same recognition and protection under the Bill of Rights.

Being recognised and protected as a legal individual – a 'person' – allows corporations to give donations to political parties, and to lobby on behalf of legislation just as natural persons, that is, citizens, are allowed to. Similarly, just as there are no limits on how much wealth or property a natural person can possess, there are no limits on corporations in terms of their size or the amount of property they are able to hold: for example, buying out other corporations in order to increase their market share and hence their size, wealth, and power. The only constraint is related to monopoly issues, which in last 30 years of neoliberal mega-mergers, is barely that.

Examining the *Santa Clara* decision and the recognition of corporations as legal persons allows a better understanding of not only how corporations are able to influence public debate, but also provides an understanding of why a corporation, an artificial entity constructed exclusively for commercial purposes, is allowed to have such access to the political process in a democracy. It also provides an explanation for the sheer size, wealth and power of large multinational corporations, their dominant role in society, and why neoliberalism's emphasis on 'individual' freedom to be free from government interference has overwhelmingly benefited corporate 'individuals' more than any other element in society.

The corporate-dominated American society and culture that is now so very entrenched was not always so. In part due to their mistrust of British monopoly crown corporations, for approximately the first hundred years of US history, the corporate form was extremely restrained and was primarily limited to providing a public service or good, such as building a canal or road. Their charters were limited in time, there were limits to the number of shareholders, and the corporation would cease to exist when the road or canal was finished. They were prohibited from being able to purchase or merge with other corporations, and were strictly prohibited from accessing the political process. They could be taxed, buy property, and pursue litigation, but they were specifically and intentionally denied the rights that natural 'persons', or citizens, had under the US Constitution's Bill of Rights.[20]

The American Civil War (1861–65) saw a weakening of corporate restraints to facilitate production of war-related materials for the North. After the war, the railroads emerged as the most powerful corporations in the United States, and they lobbied to be recognised as corporate persons and be entitled to the same rights as flesh-and-blood citizens under the Constitution's Bill of Rights.

Even before the war had ended, in 1864, US President Abraham Lincoln foresaw the inevitable rise of corporations and the influence they would have over the democratic process:

> I see in the near future a crisis approaching that unnerves me and causes me to tremble for the safety of my country. As a result of the war, corporations have been enthroned and an era of corruption in high places will follow, and the money power of the country will endeavour to prolong its reign by working upon the prejudices of the people until all wealth is aggregated in a few hands and the Republic is destroyed. I feel at this moment more anxiety for the safety of my country than ever before, even in the midst of war.[21]

Finally, in 1886, in the landmark Supreme Court decision of *Santa Clara* vs. *Pacific Railway*, the Supreme Court gave *de facto* recognition to the fact that corporations were persons under the Constitution. Efforts to eliminate child labour, unsafe working conditions, the legal recognition of unions, and other efforts were struck down because the corporation was protected by the 14th

Amendment. Previous state restrictions on the size or activities of corporations were also eliminated, allowing them to merge and acquire further corporations, resulting in mega-monopolies like John D. Rockefeller's Standard Oil. Eliminating previous state restrictions on the size of corporations, while simultaneously granting them the 'right' to lobby and eventually to donate to political parties, facilitated their rapid rise to become a dominant aspect of US foreign policy.[22]

Writing in 1934, regarding the political realities at the end of the nineteenth century, social historian Charles Beard said, 'Here, then, is the new realpolitik. A free opportunity for expansion in foreign markets is indispensable to the prosperity of American business. Modern diplomacy is commercial. Its chief concern is with the promotion of economic interests abroad.'[23]

These protections and 'rights' under the legal guise of 'corporate personhood' have given the corporation as an 'individual' the ultimate power and benefits under neoliberalism. It is this issue of 'rights' that is at the heart of the neoliberal conundrum. On the one hand, it promotes the individual's right to be free of government-imposed coercion, and that it is the individual's unrestricted participation in the market that best expresses their aspirations and freedom. In doing so, it assumes equality between all participants in that market. But by allowing all legally recognised individuals to participate, it ensures that the biggest, most powerful of those individuals – almost without exception, corporations – will be the largest beneficiaries.

Not only is it ludicrous that an individual worker could possibly send the same price signals, as advocated by Hayek and Friedman, as a multinational corporation. But neoliberal ideology also does not address the inherent protections that a corporation enjoys that individual human market participants do not, such as limited liability, and the ability to financially influence and have access to the political system. Campaign donations (via political action committees – PACs), lobbying, and running advocacy campaigns – these are areas where multinational corporations have the ability to significantly distort market and price signals in ways that human individuals cannot.

In 1976, Orlando Letelier addressed the issue of the different capacities of individuals, relative to Friedman's application of neoliberalism, to Chile:

Friedman's theories are especially objectionable – from an economic as well as a moral point of view – because they propose a total free market policy in a framework of extreme inequality among the economic agents involved: inequality between monopolistic and small and medium entrepreneurs; inequality between the owners of capital and those who own only their capacity to work, etc. Similar situations would exist if the model were applied to any other underdeveloped, dependent economy.[24]

It has been corporate individuals, not human ones, who have purchased the privatised assets of governments, who have provided the outsourcing when governments cut back on social spending like health care and education, and whose profits have rapidly increased via deregulation, and who, as entities legally dedicated to profit, have spectacularly benefited from neoliberalism's emphasis on economic growth.

As a result, 95 of the world's 150 largest economic entities were corporations at the time of the Iraq invasion, as measured by gross domestic product and revenue outputs.[25] The Iraq invasion, among unfortunately countless other examples, has displayed for all to see that the United States is at best a feeble democracy in which corporations are utterly dominant over human citizens. Not until a citizens' movement successfully rescinds these corporate rights and protections, and restores the Bill of Rights for the exclusive benefit of the flesh-and-blood people who over several generations have shed blood for the rights enshrined in them, can the United States ever hope to have any level of meaningful democracy. Removing artificial entities exclusively dedicated to profit (that would be corporations) from the political process is addressed in the Conclusion.

12
Iraq: Resistance and Revolution

Iraq in the 1950s was still under the control of its British-imposed monarch. Poverty and inequality were deeply entrenched, despite the country's copious oil resources. In 1952, 55 per cent of all privately held land belonged to 1 per cent of all landowners, or 2,480 families.[1] Eighty per cent of Iraqis were illiterate, and there was only one doctor for every 6,000 people.[2]

There was consistent resistance. Resistance to British colonial rule was eerily similar to later resistance to the American military occupation decades later. In *Al-Wathbga* ('the leap'), tens of thousands of Iraqis took to the streets to protest the 1948 Portsmouth Agreement, which ratified the ongoing presence of British troops in Iraq. On 27 January 1948, an anti-government protest became a street battle in which 300–400 people were killed by the police and military. Another uprising took place in November and December 1952, when anti-British and anti-monarchy protests became nation-wide, known as *Al-Intifada*, 'the uprising'. This too was brutally suppressed.[3]

On 14 July 1958, General Abdul Karim Qasim and the Free Officers Group seized power in what is known in Iraq as the '14 July Revolution'; they shot the king and crown prince and declared Iraq a republic. This was a time of rising Arab nationalism throughout the Middle East. In 1956, Egypt under Gamel Nasser seized control of the Suez Canal from Britain and France, and a nationalist government took power in Syria. Syria and Egypt joined together to become the United Arab Republic (which dissolved in 1961). Nasser called for Arabs to stand up against American and British imperialism. In 1957–58, there was a substantial uprising against the US-backed regime in Lebanon. The US sent a battalion of 14,000 Marines and the Navy Sixth Fleet to Lebanon to support the Lebanese government in the face of protests and unrest. There was concern that the new Iraq government under Qasim might attempt to resolve Iraq's long-standing issues with Kuwait with military action, or nationalise its oil industry. In April 1959, CIA Director Allen Dulles told the US Congress that the situation in

Iraq was 'the most dangerous in the world'. The 14,000 marines still deployed in Lebanon remained as a deterrent.[4]

The US, however, did not take military action against the new Iraq government. Qasim was viewed as less radical than Egypt's Nasser, and Iraq did not nationalise its oil or make any military moves against Kuwait. There was also the risk of a Soviet response regarding any US military action, and the United Arab Republic (Egypt and Syria) had announced that it would fight any American intervention in Iraq. The *New York Times* (1958) reported that 'intervention will not be extended to Iraq as long as the revolutionary government in Iraq respects Western oil interests.'[5]

The new Iraqi government pursued a number of progressive domestic and foreign policy reforms. Iraq demanded the full withdrawal of British troops; established diplomatic relations with the Soviet Union and communist China, and in general pursued a neutral foreign policy. It also brought in land reform to reduce the power of the elites created by the British. It established control over, and reduced the costs of, rent and food prices; began a large-scale new housing programme, formally recognised unions and peasant organisations, and lifted the ban on Iraq's Communist Party.[6]

Qasim also started focused negotiations with the American, British, French and Dutch-controlled Iraqi Petroleum Company for increased royalties and partial government ownership. The IPC refused to make any concessions. In response, Iraq formed the Organization of Petroleum Exporting Companies (OPEC) with other oil-producing nations, most notably Iran, Kuwait and Venezuela, in Baghdad in 1960. In 1961, Iraq passed Law Number 80, which withdrew the IPC's concession rights in the areas that it was not actually producing, and allocated the rights to these undeveloped fields to its soon-to-be-formed Iraq National Oil Company.[7] When American efforts for new Iraqi oil legislation failed in 2007, Law Number 80 remained the law of the land.

The American government's reaction to Qasim was, unfortunately, predictable. With US State Department support, the IPC started to intentionally slow oil production with the aim of bankrupting the Qasim government. The US and Iran under the Shah both funded Kurdish rebels against Qasim. The Kurds had not benefited from the new republic, and were agitating for further autonomy and greater share of oil post-revolution.

On 8 February 1963, in a Baathist coup, Qasim was assassinated. The new government was given formal recognition by the Kennedy administration within hours of Qasim's death. The Baathists recognised Kuwait, and promised to honour existing IPC arrangements. The US responded by supplying the new regime with weapons to fight the Kurds, who two years earlier had been supplied with weapons by the US to fight Qasim.[8]

Like Indonesia two years later, the CIA provided the Baathists with a list of suspected communists, intellectuals and leftists. The Baathists unleashed a wave of terror and an estimated 3,000–5,000 communists were summarily killed in house-to-house witch hunts. Up to 35,000 people in total were killed; anyone who was viewed as belonging to the leftist opposition was targeted.[9]

The Baathists were removed nine months later in another coup, but by 1968 and after a few other coups in the interim, they were back in power. In 1972, Iraq nationalised the Iraqi Petroleum Company's oilfields after signing a friendship treaty with the Soviet Union, its trading and security partner. With Soviet help and protection, Iraq significantly boosted its oil production over the previous low levels of the IPC.[10]

As examined earlier, Iraq invested its considerable oil money internally and advocated other Arab states to do the same. This was in direct contrast to the Saudis, who invested their petrodollars back into the US economy via US investment banks, which drove the global hegemony of US neoliberal power. It was this internal investment in its own development, and its advocacy that other Arab countries do the same, that would later prove such a threat to American control of the region.

As detailed in Kanan Makiya's *Republic of Fear* (originally published under the pseudonym Samir al-Khalil), the Baath Party was a ruthless regime that relied on terror and repression to maintain power, particularly under Saddam Hussein. But Khalil also outlines how the Baathists dramatically modernised Iraqi society and advocated state-sponsored, oil-funded, industrial development. They attacked illiteracy, and established free education for all. Iraq by the end of the 1970s was widely acknowledged to be the best-educated country in the Arab world. The Baathists also established the right of women to have careers and to participate in public life. On the eve of Iraq's invasion of Iran in 1980, women formed 46 per cent of all teachers, 29 per cent of all doctors, 46 per cent of all dentists and 70 per cent of all pharmacists.[11]

AMERICAN ALLY: SADDAM HUSSEIN AND THE IRAN–IRAQ WAR

For American-Iraqi relations, 1979 was a pivotal year. First, Saddam Hussein became president of Iraq. In February, the Shah was deposed in the Iranian Islamic Revolution. In November of the same year, the US Embassy was taken over, and 52 American embassy personnel were held hostage for 444 days in response to demands that the Shah be returned to Iran to face trial. And in December 1979, the Soviet Union invaded Afghanistan.

It was at this time that the US Carter administration announced the Carter Doctrine, which said that the Gulf region and its oil were directly US strategic interests, and that any attempt to control them would be met by force if necessary. The Carter Doctrine was ultimately about ensuring and protecting American market access to oil. Carter's National Security Adviser Zbigniew Brzezinski outlined the doctrine's three main points: first, guardianship of the oil industry 'with all its political, economic, and military ramifications'; second, containing the Soviet Union and its influence, and third, protecting 'the moderate states in the region, which could be toppled by local upheavals, as happened with Khomeini's ascendancy in Iran'.[12] By 'moderate states', Brzezinski was referring to Arab states like Saudi Arabia and the recently deposed Shah who ruled with ruthless, US-supported repression.

The new Iranian regime presented numerous problems to Iraq as well as to the United States. The Shia-dominated Iranian Islamic Republic and its leader, Ayatollah Khomeini, called on Iraqi Shias to overthrow the Sunni-dominated Baathist regime. Iraq also wanted to repossess the Shatt al Arab waterway, which it had conceded to Iran in the 1975 Algiers Agreement, after the CIA and Iran had supported a Kurdish insurgency.[13]

On 22 September 1980, Iraq invaded Iran and thus began eight long years of hellish war between the two countries, as well as eight years of the United States supporting one side and then the other, sometimes in secret, sometimes openly, at times simultaneously. Iraq believed Iran would be militarily incapable of defending itself after the upheaval of the revolution, and that Iran's army was in disarray because the military upper command had been purged. Iraq also believed Iran would not be able to obtain spare parts for its US weapons that had been purchased under the Shah, and which were now frozen by the US. With the Soviet Union bogged down in Afghanistan, Iran would not be able to rely on any overt military assistance from Russia.[14]

The Carter administration used Iraq's invasion of Iran as a means of negotiating for the release of the Americans held hostage in Iran. It promised weapons to Iran, and told Iraq to withdraw its forces from Iran.[15] This occurred in 1980, a presidential election year in the United States. Gary Sick, National Security Council staff member under Carter from August 1976 to early 1981, claims that Republican presidential nominee Ronald Reagan was in secret negotiations with the Iranians to ensure the hostages would not be released before the US election. In *October Surprise: America's Hostages in Iran and the Election of Ronald Reagan* (1991), Sick outlines how Reagan promised the Iranians that once elected, his administration would lift US economic sanctions and allow Israel to ship weapons to Iran. Iran sent the embassy hostages home the day Reagan was inaugurated, 21 January 1981.

The Reagan administration played both sides against each other. When Iran began to win and threatened to take Iraq, Reagan started supporting Iraq rather than see the balance of power in the region threatened. Reagan removed Iraq from the US official list of state sponsors of terrorism, and then in 1983, put Iran back on the list. Reagan also approved $5 billion in aid to Iraq, and facilitated the flow of British and French weapons.[16]

Crucially, the Reagan administration also supplied Iraq with the building-blocks for chemical and other weapons of mass destruction during this time. Referring to a 25 May 1994 Senate Banking Committee report, journalist William Blum summarises these efforts as follows: 'From 1985, if not earlier, through 1989, a veritable witch's brew of biological materials were exported to Iraq by private American suppliers pursuant to application and licensing by the US Department of Commerce.'[17]

These biological materials were used as chemical weapons against Iranian forces. They were also used, famously, against Kurdish insurgents who were rebelling against Saddam Hussein while Iraq was at war with Iran. The infamous poison gas attack at Halabja, Kurdistan, occurred on 16 March 1988 in a military operation to capture Halabja from Iranian and Kurdish forces. Five thousand Kurds were killed.[18]

This attack is particularly famous because it became the consistent refrain of three American presidents – Bush Sr, Clinton, and Bush Jr – as proof of the utter evil of Saddam Hussein and the dire necessity for regime change. It would reach a veritable crescendo in the lead up to the 2003 invasion.

The direct complicity, and hypocrisy, of Reagan administration officials such as Secretary of State George Schultz and future Bush Jr Department of Defense Secretary Donald Rumsfeld, and their direct ties to supplying Iraq with chemical weapons, is shameful.

Despite what is about to disclosed, Bechtel was one of the biggest winners of reconstruction contracts in 2003 post-invasion Iraq.

In 1983 and 1984, Rumsfeld met at least twice with Saddam Hussein in Baghdad. Reagan had appointed Rumsfeld as a special 'peace envoy to the Middle East'. Officially, Rumsfeld was there to express American concern over Iraq's repeated use of chemical weapons against Iranian troops. But declassified State Department papers show that Rumsfeld was actually there to negotiate the building of the Aqaba oil pipeline, to be constructed by the Bechtel Corporation. The pipeline would allow Iraqi oil to go to the Jordan port of Aqaba on the Red Sea, avoiding the Persian Gulf. Iraq was at war with Iran at the time, and Iranian warships were attacking its oil shipments. In 2002, Rumsfeld told CNN that he cautioned Hussein about chemical weapon use when he went to Baghdad in December 1983 and March 1984. Official State Department transcripts show Rumsfeld never brought it up with Hussein, and that it was never discussed.[19]

Rumsfeld was under the direct supervision of Reagan's Secretary of State George Schultz; Schultz had been CEO of Bechtel before becoming secretary of state. Schultz and the Reagan administration continued to covertly attempt to secure the pipeline deal even after the State Department publicly condemned Iraq's use of chemical weapons against Iran in March 1984. This included attempts to circumvent congressional approval to guarantee loans and risk insurance through the federal government's Export Import Bank and the Overseas Private Investment Corporation, and guarantees from Israel to the Iraqi government that it would not attack the pipeline. The Iraqi government rejected the pipeline project in December 1985.[20]

Bechtel's involvement with the Hussein regime went far beyond merely trying to build a pipeline. Bechtel sold Iraq chemical infrastructure, with US government approval, that they knew Hussein would almost certainly use to build weapons of mass destruction. Jim Vallette, research director of the Sustainable Energy and Economy Network, made the following findings:

[In 1988] Bechtel signed a contract to consult in the construction of a petrochemical complex (PC-2) south of Baghdad, just four months after the Hussein government infamously 'gassed the Kurds' with mustard gas. The Bechtel design involved 'dual-use' technology. According to the Middle East Defense News, 'a key feature of the PC-2 project was the plan to manufacture ethylene oxide, a precursor chemical that is easily converted to thyodiglycol, which is used in one step to make mustard gas.' When U.N. weapons inspectors arrived in 1991, they declared the industrial complex that PC-2 was a major part of the 'smoking gun' that proved that Iraq was pursuing a 'Weapons of Mass Destruction' (WMD) program.

The US Department of Agriculture's Commodity Credit Corporation funded Bechtel's construction of the PC-2 ... After the imposition of sanctions, Iraq defaulted on the loan. In other words, in 1990, U.S. taxpayers paid for Bechtel's construction of an Iraqi chemical weapons factory, and now in 2003, they are paying Bechtel $680 million to rebuild Iraq after the U.S. destroyed and invaded the country under the pretext of preventing Iraq from developing weapons of mass destruction.[21]

In Iraq's December 2002 Declaration to the United Nations regarding its compliance with the terms of UN Resolution 687 and verification that it had destroyed its weapons of mass destruction (WMDs), it listed 24 specific American companies that had helped initially to build them. Also cited were the specific aid and credits supplied by the US Departments of Energy, Defense, Commerce, and Agriculture, and that Iraq had received nuclear expertise from US weapons labs.[22] The original report was 11,800 pages. The US was able to obtain it before it was released to the UN, and promptly cut 8,000 pages before resubmitting it. A Berlin newspaper was able to obtain, and release, a full copy.[23]

A 1987 *New York Times* headline perhaps put the US position best: 'Keeping Either Side from Winning the Persian Gulf War'. The US wanted both sides to lose and be decimated so that the US could step into the vacuum.[24]

Despite its anti-American rhetoric, the United States found that Iran under Ayatollah Khomeini had some redeeming features. Khomeini attacked and violently suppressed Iranian leftists, many of whom had supported action against the Shah. Iran also did not align itself exclusively with the Soviet Union, and it kept oil flowing to the US and the West.[25]

In 1985, the Reagan administration secretly began supplying arms to Iran via Israel, and then used the proceeds to secretly finance the Nicaraguan Contras, after Congress had officially prohibited the Reagan administration from funding the Contras. When the Iran-Contra scandal broke in the waning days of the Reagan presidency, the US had to reassure all other countries in the region that it wasn't seeking to destabilise them. The US also moved quickly to end the Iran–Iraq war. On 2 July 1988, the USS *Vincennes* warship shot down an Iranian passenger plane, killing all 290 passengers. The United States claimed it was an accident; regardless, Iran accepted a UN ceasefire with Iraq 16 days later.[26] The war had been horrible for both sides, with hundreds of thousands dead.

Two years later, Iraq would invade Kuwait and precipitate nearly 13 years of American foreign policy designed to contain Saddam Hussein and the Baathist regime, leading to a full military invasion in March 2003.

Part IV

Losing Out: The US Eliminated from Oil and Other Iraqi Markets Post Sanctions

13
State of Play: Neoliberalism Wounded, US Hegemony Challenged

On the eve of the 2003 Iraq invasion, the international neoliberal agenda as detailed thus far was not only being questioned, it was arguably in jeopardy. By mid-2002, the easy speculative profits that had been identified by Letelier as a key plank of the neoliberal agenda in Chile was over. The 1997 Asian crisis was followed by the complete economic collapse of Argentina in 2001. Clearly, the neoliberal structural adjustment policies of the World Bank and the IMF were not actually benefiting the countries involved.

Former IMF economist Davison Budhoo summarised the effectiveness of the IMF's policies: 'The majority of those nations that have followed the IMF's advice have experienced profound economic crises: low or even declining growth, much larger foreign debts and the stagnation that perpetuates systemic poverty.'[1]

A global resistance movement to free market neoliberalism had emerged, also known as the anti-globalisation movement, led by social movements in the global South and then joined by unions and grass-roots activists in the developed countries. Meetings of the WTO, World Bank, IMF, G8 and other international economic meetings were met with mass protests and direct action. The 1999 Seattle WTO meeting was shut down by protesters. The Multilateral Agreement on Investment (MAI) had been beaten back. The inherent problems of the North American Free Trade Agreement (NAFTA) had come to the fore in both Mexico and the United States. The Free Trade Area of the Americas (FTAA), which proposed establishing a NAFTA free trade zone for the entire North and South American continents, was vigorously opposed throughout the region and would soon face ultimate defeat. Political change was brewing throughout Latin America, based on and openly expressed as direct opposition to neoliberalism and the US agenda. Hugo Chavez and Luiz Inácio Lula da Silva had been elected presidents of Venezuela and Brazil respectively, the first of a wave of anti-neoliberal candidates who would soon take power throughout Latin America.

Joseph Stiglitz summarised, in 2002, when American planning to invade Iraq began in earnest:

> International bureaucrats – the faceless symbols of the world economic order – are under attack everywhere. Formerly uneventful meetings of obscure technocrats discussing mundane subjects such as concessional loans and trade quotas have now become the scene of raging street battles and huge demonstrations. The protests at the Seattle meeting of the World Trade Organization in 1999 were a shock. Since then, the movement has grown stronger and the fury has spread. Virtually every major meeting of the International Monetary Fund, the World Bank, and the World Trade Organization is now the scene of conflict and turmoil.[2]

MULTILATERAL AGREEMENT ON INVESTMENT AND THE WORLD TRADE ORGANIZATION

Thus far we have examined a number of substantial tools that the United States has utilised in order to impose a capital-dependent, free market, neoliberalism upon other countries. These are military coups (and in the case of Iraq, outright military invasion), the dollar's dominance as the global currency for oil, and the structural adjustment programmes of the World Bank and the IMF. In the mid-1990s, they were joined by two new tools: the market liberalisation pressures of the World Trade Organization, and free trade agreements (FTAs). Both would play a major role in the subjugation of Iraq.

We begin with an exploration of what was arguably the peak attempt at imposing an international neoliberal regime that would have elevated the rights of capital far above any social, environmental, or health concerns: the Multilateral Agreement on Investment (MAI). The MAI was put forward, unsuccessfully, at approximately the same time as the WTO. Its ultimate defeat, combined with the international blowback to the World Bank/IMF agenda, motivated the United States to invade Iraq to both protect and expand its free market neoliberal hegemony.

Prominent neoliberal and corporate globalisation critic David Korten described the MAI as potentially 'the most anti-democratic, anti-people, anti-community international agreement ever conceived by supposedly democratic governments'.[3]

THE MULTILATERAL AGREEMENT ON INVESTMENT

The Multilateral Agreement on Investment was initiated in 1991 by the US Council for International Business. The core element of the MAI was 'to ensure the ability of speculators and multinational corporations to move capital in and out of countries without governmental involvement or public interest rules'.[4] It would do so by eliminating restrictions on purchasing private property, businesses, and natural resources. Any foreign business would be able to compete with local firms with no impediments. Traditional government-provided services such as education, health care, and any other services would be subject to competition; any government-provided service was considered a monopoly. Referring to these provisions as 'investor rights', corporations would have the right to sue governments for lost profits if these 'rights' were restricted.

Had it been successful, the MAI would have guaranteed the following rights for investors and corporations:

1. The right to compete against domestic companies in all economic sectors;
2. The right to acquire any business or property in any sector of a country's economy, including natural resources and strategic industries such as communications and defence;
3. The right to convert currency and move money across borders without constraints, fostering the sorts of currency crises that resulted in the Mexican peso collapse and the 1997 Asian financial meltdown;
4. The right to move production facilities without limit or penalty, regardless of the impacts on workers or the host community;
5. Freedom from conditions (called performance requirements). These conditions were often placed on investment by governments to protect against the worst aspect of speculation and to ensure that corporations met basic rules of conduct.
6. The right of investors, that is, corporations, to sue governments for cash damages, to be paid for from public funds, for restitution if an investor claims its rights have been violated. Such disputes would be settled by third party international courts, which would be limited to considering only the commercial aspects of the dispute.[5]

This last point is the crucial investor-state dispute resolution, in which international commercial tribunals and the corporate right to profit would have *de facto* sovereignty over national governments and their laws.

The MAI was the ultimate global Bill of Rights for unrestrained corporate profit. Any protection of local businesses, labour, minority populations, land reform for indigenous peoples, or environmental regulations that in any way imposed additional costs would not be allowed if they interfered with these investor rights. Even protests, public boycotts and union strikes were cited in the MAI as possible areas of compensation if they resulted in lost profits. Government-imposed sanctions – for example, local councils prohibiting purchase of products from a country or company because of their environmental or human rights abuses – would also have been eliminated.

Implementation of the MAI was led by the Organisation for Economic Co-operation and Development (OECD), representing the world's top 30 or so economies – the so-called 'developed' world. When the MAI text was leaked during OECD negotiations, it was met with a significant global campaign by environmental and social justice activists and NGOs to defeat it. When the OECD announced termination of the MAI in 1998, its defeat was viewed as a major victory for global civil society, and combined with the mass non-violent shut-down of the 1999 Seattle WTO Meeting, was a significant rollback of what had appeared to be an unstoppable neoliberal juggernaut.[6]

The MAI attempted to place the corporate right to profit for investors above all others, and to take neoliberal ideology to a level where government interference in the market would have been virtually illegal. Ordinary human individuals would have no democratic recourse to challenge these 'rights'.

The US would doggedly try to insert the MAI, or as many provisions of it as possible, especially the investor-state conditions, into its subsequent focus on signing individual or regional free trade agreements. Much of what the US imposed in Iraq under the Bremer economic orders was rooted in the MAI wish list, as are many of the individual free trade agreements the US has negotiated, as examined below and in more detail in Part V of this book (chapters 22–25), which deals with the US Middle East Free Trade Area.

THE WORLD TRADE ORGANIZATION

The World Trade Organization came into being almost simultaneously as the MAI negotiations, and was established in early 1995 to administer the Uruguay Round of the General Agreement on Tariffs and Trades (GATT). GATT had begun in 1947 when 18 countries met, with the aim of reducing tariffs on trade. A number of subsequent meetings, or rounds, concluded with the 1986 Uruguay round, which involved 108 countries.[7]

Similar to the MAI's attempt to prevent any impediments to investment, the WTO attempts to eliminate barriers to free trade. It does so by setting internationally agreed standards. If a country has set higher standards that prohibit trade relative to protecting human health or the environment, that country must prove the necessity of those standards, and must do so on scientific grounds. These types of disputes are settled in the WTO's dispute-settlement system, where a country presents its case to a panel of WTO-selected experts; these sessions are closed to the public and media. If a panel finds a country guilty because its standards or legislation were not warranted, the panel has the power to impose economic sanctions or fines.

One example is the United States and Canada's challenge to a European Union (EU) ban on hormone-fed imported beef. The EU claimed that such beef contained carcinogens; the EU had to prove to the WTO panel that eating this beef actually posed a health risk. Despite a lengthy report by independent scientists showing that some hormones added to US meat are 'complete carcinogens' – capable of causing cancer by themselves – the WTO's three-lawyer tribunal ruled in 1998 that the EU did not have a 'valid' scientific case for refusing to allow the import of US beef. The losing EU countries were required to pay the US $150 million each year as compensation for lost profits.[8]

In 2006, the US, along with Canada and Argentina, challenged the EU's ban on crops grown with genetically modified organisms (GMOs), and received a similar ruling that such restrictions in the name of protecting citizens' health and protecting food security are 'an unfair restraint of trade'.[9] If the world's second most powerful political entity, the EU, is unable to successfully protect its own citizens, it is doubtful if Arab countries that have joined the WTO as part of the US Middle East Free Trade Area process will be able to successfully resist similar efforts by Monsanto and other corporate agricultural giants to manipulate their agriculture.

The WTO is ultimately undemocratic, and erodes national sovereignty; it highlights neoliberalism's preference for unelected, and in the case of the WTO, secret courts rather than legislation or direct democratic participation. Although voting in the WTO is by consensus, and each country has one vote regardless of its size, the United States and Europe can still dominate proceedings because they have control over the World Bank and the IMF, and can threaten or directly cancel loans and other crucial investment credit investment if countries drop out of the voting or fight a ruling.[10]

The Uruguay Round also included the General Agreement on Trade in Services (GATS). GATS addresses what are usually government-provided services such as electricity, water, health, education, and equally controversially, financial services. Similar to the MAI, it limits a government's ability to support local businesses, or provide subsidies for efficiency, or for renewable sources of energy. These are viewed as an unfair advantage versus other sources of energy like coal or gas, regardless of their environmental impacts. Foreign-ownership limits were also eroded.[11]

One of the most contentious issues with neoliberalism in general is the privatisation of services that have traditionally been provided by publicly owned utilities, and handing them over to corporations dedicated to profit. As Friedman and Hayek state, there should be no government provisions of services that the private sector cannot do more efficiently: motivated as they are by accruing profit, they are therefore naturally more efficient.

As part of a World Bank structural adjustment programme, in 1999, Bechtel and UK-based United Utilities won the contract to privatise the Bolivian city of Cochabamba's water supply. In a few years, Bechtel would be one of the biggest contract winners for Iraqi reconstruction, despite, or perhaps because of, the following. The Cochabamba contract prohibited people from using private wells without paying the water-supply companies, and also stipulated that people could not even collect rainfall. Bechtel and United Utilities then raised the price by over 300 per cent, equivalent to one-quarter of the average income in the city, population 850,000. Many people could not pay and faced losing their access to water. Mass protests ensued, and two people were killed and over 30 wounded when troops opened fire. The Bolivian government broke the contract with Bechtel, and took back direct public control of Cochabamba's water service. Bechtel and United then sued the deeply impoverished Bolivia in a World Bank trade court for $25 million in lost profits.[12] Bechtel and United finally withdrew the lawsuit in 2006.

As examined earlier, it was the need to adhere to WTO-required deregulation that led to the repeal of the US Glass-Steagall Act that had separated the activities of banks and investment firms, and which in turn led to the global financial crisis. Domestic US efforts to try and ensure government stimulus money would go towards creating and sustaining American jobs have also been weakened because they violated WTO rules on banning policies that favour local jobs and provision of services. Further WTO deregulation requirements, enthusiastically pursued by the Clinton and Bush Jr administrations, facilitated the creation of banks that were then 'too big to fail'.[13]

In Chapter 27, we'll examine the WTO's Trade Related Aspects of Intellectual Property Rights Agreement (TRIPS), which defines genetic materials and seed plasmas as private property protected by patents and intellectual property rights, and how this in turn has facilitated US agribusiness giants' attempts to establish genetically modified seeds and crops worldwide, including in Iraq and the Middle East.

The 1999 WTO meeting in Seattle proposed to substantially expand the powers of the WTO and was met with huge protests, and the talks broke down. In 2003, the EU and the US, along with extensive lobbying by the International Chamber of Commerce, tried to include the MAI's investor-state dispute resolution process into the expanded Doha Round of WTO negotiations. This would have allowed corporations to sue governments directly in the WTO, rather than having to ask the corporation's own government to sue on their behalf. Steadfast refusal by the global South, combined with the huge 2003 protest in Cancun, Mexico that greeted the 2003 WTO ministerial meeting, forced the US and the EU to back down, and it was removed from the 2005 Hong Kong WTO ministerial agenda.[14]

A further contentious point has been Europe and the United States' continued subsidising of their agricultural industries. Reducing agricultural tariffs while simultaneously allowing its food exports to be subject to the type of casino speculation that brought on the global financial crisis is a hallmark of US intentions with Iraqi agriculture and the US Middle East Free Trade Area. As Joseph Stiglitz wrote just before the Iraq invasion:

> The critics of globalization [neoliberalism] accuse Western countries of hypocrisy, and the critics are right. The Western countries have pushed poor countries to eliminate trade barriers, but kept up their own barriers, preventing developing countries from exporting their agricultural products and so depriving them of desperately needed export income.[15]

While the full intent of WTO expansion has not been realised due to developing countries' and social movements successful resistance, the accession programme to initially join the WTO means that member countries have had to liberalise their economies and implement many pro-neoliberal policies. The accession programme is covered in more detail in the examination of the US Middle East Free Trade Area (chapters 22–25), which stipulates WTO membership as a prerequisite for membership.

The neoliberal debt-restructuring and market-liberalisation programmes outlined thus far resulted in a tremendous amount of money flowing from the Third World to the First: an estimated $4.6 trillion from 1980 to 2004, with $340 billion in 2002, the year before the Iraq invasion.[16] This economic and political control was a crucial pillar of American global power. The United States was not going to allow any potential threat to this crucial arrangement to go unaddressed, and as we saw earlier, this money has kept on flowing post-invasion.

The MAI and the WTO were arguably the peak of unrestrained neoliberalism, and their respective defeat and setback signalled the end of the easy speculation and profits that had come with the World Bank and the IMF structural adjustment programmes. The momentum of neoliberalism had been slowed. The insatiable American need for further capital expansion, however, had not been slowed, leading inevitably to the invasion and occupation of Iraq.

NAFTA, THE FTAA AND FREE TRADE HEGEMONY

In January 1994, when the North American Free Trade Agreement (NAFTA) came into effect between the United States, Canada and Mexico, the US initiated yet another tool to impose its free market neoliberal hegemony. NAFTA had been initiated by the Bush Sr administration, and came into effect in January 1994, during Clinton's first term. It eliminated tariffs and other trade impediments between the three countries. Among other problems, NAFTA has meant that Mexican peasants have had no protection against highly subsidised US agricultural products, in particular, corn.

The 1.3 million farmers who lost their livelihoods as a result of NAFTA then had little recourse but to seek work in the *maquiladoras* (sweatshop factories) that proliferated seemingly overnight along Mexico's border with the United States. These factories, of course, had replaced much of the manufacturing that had, previous to NAFTA, been done in the United States.[17] Those who couldn't find work formed the nucleus of the 60-per cent increase in the number of illegal immigrants entering the United States during NAFTA's first eight years. And, in the endless 'race to the bottom', Mexican workers willing to work for $5 a day were very soon beaten out by workers in China who, under an authoritarian government, would work for a dollar a day.[18]

This displacement of rural agricultural populations has been the hallmark of free market neoliberalism in all its guises. NAFTA, combined with the relentless World Bank and IMF structural adjustment of the Mexican economy, as detailed earlier, has significantly contributed to the drug cartel violence that has engulfed the country in recent years. Similarly, US neoliberal policies imposed upon Iraq have contributed to the massive diaspora of the Iraqi population and the endemic internal violence that has plagued the country since the invasion.

In forming NAFTA, the US was also able for the first time to include the crucial investor–state dispute resolution. Corporations could now directly sue a government if it felt its right to free trade and investment was being impinged, and there was not a damn thing the democratically elected governments of Canada, Mexico, or the United States could do if they didn't like or agree with the secret court's decision. One of the best-known cases was when Metalclad, an American company, was refused permission by a Mexican city government to build a hazardous waste dump due to human health and environmental concerns. Metalclad sued and won under NAFTA, and Mexico had to pay compensation to Metalclad. In another equally famous case, the Canadian government banned the gasoline additive MMT due to health concerns. MMT was legal and available in the United States. After the US exporter sued, Canada repealed the ban on MMT and had to compensate the company.

By 2002, when the propaganda began in earnest regarding the need to invade Iraq, it was obvious to many Americans that NAFTA had been a disaster for their country. The United States was also meeting a great deal of resistance to its efforts to form the Free Trade Area of the Americas (FTAA), a NAFTA-style Free Trade Agreement for all the countries of the North and South America, and which ultimately failed. The much smaller Central American Free Trade Agreement (CAFTA) was also in trouble, and a watered-down version was eventually passed by the US Congress, by only one vote.

14
Losing Out: The Geopolitical Significance of Iraq's Oil

The problem is that the good Lord didn't see fit to put oil and gas reserves where there are democratically elected regimes friendly to the interests of the United States.

US Vice President Dick Cheney, 1998[1]

By 2002, the decade-long period of economic sanctions against Iraq was not serving the purpose of removing Saddam Hussein from power and installing a compliant client state. International pressure and condemnation was growing regarding the humanitarian toll the sanctions were taking on ordinary Iraqis, in particular, children. The sanctions also strengthened sympathy for Iraq from other Arab states, who viewed the sanctions to be punitive, and helped sustain smouldering anger about the US invading an Arab state in the first Gulf War. The ongoing presence of US troops on the sacred soil of Islam in Saudi Arabia was a key issue for Osama Bin Laden and others.

A potentially oil-rich, post-sanctions resurgent Iraq directly threatened the funding of the neoliberal project via Saudi petrodollars, as well as the potential stability of Saudi Arabia as the rock of US support in the Arab Middle East and its ability to manipulate OPEC and oil prices. While the sanctions had successfully contained Iraq's ability to regain its potential status as a regional power, it was also clear that the sanctions could not be held in place forever.

US ELIMINATED FROM POST-SANCTIONS OIL AND OTHER MARKETS

Iraq under Saddam Hussein posed a number of other challenges to America. Saddam Hussein had signed a number of contracts with European and Russian companies to help significantly increase Iraq's oil production once the sanctions were lifted. American companies were thus excluded from a ready-made market expansion of the world's most precious market commodity.

The Wall Street Journal highlighted the serious geopolitical situation:

... the European companies will have grabbed the best deals ... International politics is creating an uneven playing field for U.S. companies and could lead to a major power shift away from the U.S. oil industry ... Indeed, the companies that win the rights to develop Iraqi oil fields could be on the road to becoming the most powerful multinationals of the next century.[2]

France and Russia had signed deals in the 1990s with Iraq for its post-sanctions oil. If honoured, Total/Fina/Elf would have had exclusive rights to develop the Majnoon and Bin Umar regions, worth $7 billion.[3] A Russian consortium led by LukOil had exclusive rights to develop the massive West Qurna oilfields in southern Iraq, estimated at 70 billion barrels, approximately half of Iraq's reserves.[4] Australia's BHP had also been negotiating with Saddam Hussein's government to develop the Halfayeh oilfield post-sanctions. The total of these contracts were estimated to be worth up to $1.1 trillion in the long term.[5]

The United States was thus eliminated from any future access to developing the world's second largest oil reserves. This explains why the United States kept the sanctions in place, no matter what Iraq did in terms of actual compliance. Ending them would mean the US would lose access to Iraqi oil, so in the meantime it ensured no one else had access either. This was one of the central diplomatic bargaining chips in the lead-up to the invasion as the US pressured (unsuccessfully) UN Security Council members Russia and France to support military action on Iraq. In addition, there were other market considerations besides oil. Before the first Gulf War, Iraq had proved to be a lucrative export market for other US products, particularly agricultural products. For example, in the 1980s, the United States was exporting 20 per cent of its rice crop to Iraq.[6]

Iraq also posed issues because of its socialised command-and-control economy. Iraq, despite the sanctions, existed as a staunch anti-neoliberal, anti-US client state, which had eliminated corporate investors, American or otherwise, from participating in any of its markets post-sanctions: agriculture, health, education, manufacturing, etc. This precluded US or western capital from directly owning or investing in Iraqi industries. Based on past experience, restricting, let alone eliminating US corporations from its markets would be reason enough for the US to take very decisive action.

THE GEOPOLITICAL SIGNIFICANCE OF IRAQ'S OIL

Direct control of Iraqi oil would guarantee no new rival could emerge to challenge the superpower status of the United States. This was implicit in the Bush administration's pre-invasion identification of long-term US energy needs, and its focus on Iraq.

In May 2001, the US Energy Task Force released its National Energy Plan, better known as the (Dick) Cheney Report, which provided the blueprint for America's long-term energy needs. This public policy document recommended that the US 'conduct an immediate policy review toward Iraq that includes military ... assessments'. The report is a mandate to 'make energy security a priority of our trade and foreign policy', and that 'U.S. national energy security depends on sufficient energy supplies to support U.S. and global economic growth.'[7]

Cheney projected that US oil consumption would jump from 19.5 million barrels per day (mbd) to 25.5 mbd by 2020, and that the US will have to import two-thirds of that figure. This would mean an increase from the then 10.4 million barrels imported per day to 16.7 million. As of 2001 and the release of the Cheney Report, the US consumed 25 per cent of oil produced worldwide, and imported just over half that figure.[8]

The Cheney Report's clear focus was on securing additional sources of foreign oil for the United States. Cheney dismissed any possibility that these energy needs could be met in any meaningful way through conservation or renewable technologies. It placed a high priority on increasing access to Persian Gulf supplies and on an expanded military build-up to ensure that this happened. It made clear that most of this future oil supply would have to come from Persian Gulf countries, which accounted for 65 per cent of known world reserves. No other single region accounted for more than 9 per cent.[9]

Cheney was at the centre of an ongoing legal battle to release the contents of his highly controversial Energy Task Force meetings, which he adamantly refused to do. Cheney was sued by environmental groups to release information that, when finally disclosed, revealed that he had met widely with oil, gas and nuclear industry representatives at the exclusion of environmental, renewable and efficiency representatives.

The US has been diversifying to protect itself against the political instability of any and all Persian Gulf countries, and now relies on substantial imports from Nigeria, Colombia and Venezuela, among others. As of 2003, the area of the world thought to be a great bastion of undeveloped oil reserves – the Caspian Sea Region – posed substantial logistical, military, and political impediments compared to the more certain and established supplies in the Middle East.[10]

THE KEYS TO THE KINGDOM: IRAQI OIL

On the eve of the invasion, Iraq was estimated to have the world's largest proven oil reserves outside of Saudi Arabia: over 112 billion barrels, or 11 per cent of the world's total. In addition, the US Energy Department estimated that Iraq had up to 220 billion barrels in undiscovered reserves, bringing the Iraqi potential total to the equivalent of 98 years of US annual imports. The combined figure would make it equivalent to Saudi Arabia's 260 billion barrels of total reserves, and also put it in a similar position as the Saudis regarding having enough supply to substantially influence world oil prices.[11] Iraq's oil is also the cheapest in the world to access: $1 per barrel to get out of the ground, compared to $4 in the North Sea and Russia, or $3 in the rest of the Middle East.[12]

At the time of the invasion, the world supply of oil was already decreasing, while world demand was increasing. China was projected to match US consumption by 2020, and will be competing directly with the US (and the world) for an increasingly smaller supply. New oil discoveries dropped from an average of 47 billion new barrels discovered per year to only 14 billion in the 1990s. Meanwhile, oil consumption was increasing in the United States. Between 1991 and 2001, US demand for refined oil products increased by 17 per cent, compared to 7 per cent worldwide and 7 per cent for Europe.[13]

Iraq's copious oil reserves would allow the US to end its dependence on Saudi Arabia, which has the world's largest supply of oil. As previously examined, because of their dominant supply, the Saudis have been able to control world oil prices and provide stability of supply to the US advantage in return for American military protection, as established by Roosevelt in 1945. While the US actually imported only 18 per cent of its oil from the Persian Gulf at the time of the Iraq invasion,[14] it is price stability at as low a price as possible and guaranteed supply that the Saudis have provided since the Nixon initiated OPEC oil crisis of the 1970s.

That asset changed dramatically with the 9/11 attacks when it was revealed that 15 of the 9/11 hijackers were Saudi nationals, and that Al Qaeda allegedly received widespread financial and other support from within Saudi Arabia. The Saudi government was viewed as reluctant to crack down on these sources of support. With radical Islam on the rise, there was concern both in the US Congress and the Bush administration that the Saudi ruling family could be overthrown by a popular – and very likely by US definitions, extremist – uprising.[15] Extremist or not, the Middle East is a volatile area. Having direct military control of a major oil-producing client state in the region would provide a bulwark against upheaval of whatever kind, for example, the eruption of the Arab Spring protests that began in early 2011.

In *The Hidden Hand of American Hegemony*, David Spiro revealed a CIA memo marked 'Secret, Not Releasable to Foreign Nationals' that clearly showed this to be a US security concern long before 9/11. The memo's title was 'Saudi Arabian Foreign Investment' and said that 'Temporary dislocation of international financial markets would ensue, if the Saudi Arabian government ever chose to use its accumulated wealth as a political weapon.' The memo had been reviewed for declassification in May 1985.[16]

And, as previously examined, control of Iraq's oil would also potentially provide the US with the opportunity to have more direct control over, or even eliminate, OPEC. It is in OPEC's interest to keep prices as high as possible to maximise profits. But when other countries within OPEC have advocated raising the price per barrel, the Saudis have been able to counter with the threat of releasing more oil of their own, driving the price down. Saudi Arabia has traditionally been the only country in the world with enough oil to utilise this threat – a threat which as long as it remained a strong and steadfast ally, was a major asset to the United States. Just as the Saudis could influence and determine global oil price and supply availability, so, potentially, could a post-sanctions Iraq under Saddam Hussein. The US could not, and would not, allow this to happen.

Inherent in Bush's 2002 National Security Strategy was that no rival to the US be allowed to rise in the post-Cold War geopolitical world. Russia, one of the few nations with the potential to rival American power, is heavily dependent on its oil-producing revenue. The control of Iraq's oil production would mean control over the global oil market; a cut in the oil price via Iraq in combination with Saudi Arabia would mean a cut in Russia's own hegemony, and more importantly, a direct impediment to its ability to economically rival the US. The US already did this when, on its behalf, the Saudis helped sabotage the Soviet Union economy to help speed its downfall, as highlighted earlier.

Alternatively, China and Europe are both dependent on oil imports. Raising the price of oil would have similar deleterious impacts on their economies, which the US did not hesitate to do when Nixon manipulated the OPEC oil crisis. Control of world oil prices means in large part control over the economies of Europe, China, Russia and any other present or future rivals to US hegemony.

With Iraq now having the potential to flood the world oil market with up to 12 million barrels per day as soon as 2017, continued US control over Iraq means immense potential economic control over the rest of the world, and an ultimate geopolitical weapon to remain unchallenged as the world's sole superpower.

The 2002 Baker Report was commissioned by James A. Baker, former Bush Senior secretary of state, Reagan's secretary of the treasury, and chief architect of the first structural adjustment programmes; it stated:

> Tight markets have increased US and global vulnerability to disruption and provided adversaries undue potential influence over the price of oil. Iraq has become a key 'swing' producer, posing a difficult position for the US government ... Iraq remains a de-stabilising influence to ... the flow of oil to international markets from the Middle East. Saddam Hussein has also demonstrated a willingness to threaten to use the oil weapon and to use his own export program to manipulate oil markets.[17]

The Baker Report provides a succinct explanation of why the US would not lift the sanctions regardless of proof that Iraq had complied with UN Resolution 687, or regardless of the humanitarian suffering. It also explains why the US invaded: to eliminate Iraq's future capacity to manipulate global oil supply, demand, and/or cost, and to influence other Arab producers to reinvest their sizeable oil revenues back into their own economies.

The past century of US foreign policy had been dedicated primarily to ensuring American corporations had access to foreign markets. The US has regularly initiated coups or direct military intervention in countries throughout the world that had closed off, or threatened to close off, their markets in support of internal development. In 1953, it initiated a coup in Iran when the Mossadegh government nationalised its oil industry. And the start of the neoliberal experiment had been its brutal installation in Chile, and another US-supported and initiated coup in direct response to wholesale nationalisation under Allende. The history of the modern corporation is the history of US imperialism to ensure access to, and control over, markets. And there is no larger or more important global market than oil. Given the significance of Iraq, it is reasonable to assume the pattern of US intervention would continue in order to guarantee its economic interests.

15
The Push for War

As well as removing significant threats to US hegemony and the neoliberal agenda, installing a new, pro-market, neoliberal US client state in Iraq would also provide immense opportunities. Direct control of Iraq would ensure the continuation of the neoliberal agenda in the face of global opposition. Control of the only nation that could potentially match Saudi Arabian production meant the potential elimination – via wholesale replacement – of the need to rely on Saudi Arabia for petrodollar reinvestment, or to rely on the Saudis to control oil politics via OPEC. It would provide additional control over the Saudis themselves, and further motivation for it and other Arab client states to continue their support of American policy in the Middle East, as well as strengthening Israel as the US regional anchor.

The military seizure of Iraq, with its well-educated, professional population of 28 million, would also provide a brand new market for American products. It had a nationalised industrial infrastructure that could be privatised, at least in theory, for instant and spectacular speculative profit. And, crucially, Iraq would provide a base for creating a neoliberal mass market in an area of the world that had not been fully accessed: the Middle East. Bush announced the US Middle East Free Trade Area almost simultaneously with the declaration that major combat operations were over in Iraq in May 2003.

It was in this geopolitical context that the September 11 terrorist attacks occurred in 2001, and that the Bush administration's National Security Strategy (NSS) was launched in 2002. The NSS received international notoriety for stipulating the US right to pre-emptively attack any and all countries or entities which it deemed to be a *potential* threat to its security. Crucially, it linked free markets and free people as one and the same, by pledging 'a new era of global economic growth through free markets and free trade', and for America to ensure an 'efficient allocation of resources, and regional integration'.[1] The NSS suggested that what it had previously achieved via coups and structural adjustment programmes, the WTO, and free trade agreements, it was now willing to seize with overwhelming force.

The NSS clearly stated that the US had the right to pre-emptively strike terrorists or 'rogue states', and, crucially, that 'free markets and free trade were key priorities' for American national security. As well as being identified as rogue states in Bush's 'Axis of Evil' speech, Iraq, Iran and North Korea were also impediments to any expansion of US capital and free trade. Because post-sanctions Iraq posed a direct threat to the United States' ability to maintain the policy prescriptions of international neoliberalism, it was thus a 'rogue state'.

The case of Iraq is unique and alarming because it is an enforced neoliberalism imposed under an American military invasion and occupation. Iraq therefore represents a new, distinct and substantial development in US neoliberal policy and hegemony. Rather than control being exerted through debt restructuring, Iraq was the object of a direct military invasion which then sought to establish a neoliberal, capital-dependent, free market state. This strategy was determined *before* the invasion. A distinction must therefore be made regarding Iraq and the previous 25 years or so of US neoliberal imperialism.

Identifying the US government's actions in the context of the state's responsibility to actively create markets, and to prevent any loss of position relative to existing markets, provides a clearer understanding of the motivations, both economic and ideological, of the decision to invade Iraq despite considerable public opposition and lack of credibility of other arguments.

NEOCONSERVATIVES, THE PNAC, AND THE BUSH NATIONAL SECURITY STRATEGY

The Bush administration did not need the motivating political factors associated with September 11 and the National Security Strategy which flowed from it, nor Iraq's switching to the euro, to begin planning a military invasion and regime change. Regime change was already US congressional policy as of 1998, and had been the policy of the previous Clinton administration.

The Bush administration was renowned for its collection of neoconservatives, or 'neocons'. David Harvey states that neoconservatives believe in and are committed to neoliberalism and its manifestation via corporate power, private enterprise and marketisation, but neocons distinguish themselves from neoliberals by their commitment to establishing order via use of the state's monopoly of violence, and their attention and focus on issues of morality. For example, the woman's right to choose and the debate regarding abortion cannot be resolved through the market.[2] While these are relevant distinctions, Bush administration policies were clearly neoliberal in practise and intent.

The leading officials of the Bush administration had openly advocated for war on Iraq years before they took office. The Project for the New American Century (PNAC) is a Washington-based think tank created in 1997 by, among others, former Bush Jr administration officials Defense Secretary Donald Rumsfeld, Dick Cheney, Deputy Defense Secretary Paul Wolfowitz, Cheney's former Chief of Staff Lewis Libby, Bush's National Security Council Middle East expert Elliott Abrams, and Zalmay Khalizad, who would serve as US ambassador to Iraq from 2005 to 2007. In September 2000, the PNAC produced a white paper titled 'Rebuilding America's Defenses: Strategy, Forces and Resources for a New Century', in which the PNAC outlined what was required of America to expand and maintain its global empire.

In addition to substantially increasing the size of the military, the report also called for the US to 'fight and decisively win multiple, simultaneous major theater wars', and to 'perform the constabulary duties associated with shaping the security environment in critical regions'. It also emphasised securing interests vital to American security, like oil. Chillingly, it states: 'The process of transformation, even if it brings revolutionary change, is likely to be a long one, absent some catastrophic and catalyzing event – like a new Pearl Harbor.'[3] Or, as we shall see, September 11.

The PNAC also formed the Committee for the Liberation of Iraq, which met with then National Security Adviser Condoleezza Rice in order to formulate a plan to 'educate' the American public about the need for war in Iraq. George Schultz, secretary of state during the Reagan administration, was the advisory board chair; a long-term advocate of military intervention in Iraq,[4] he had direct connections to the Bechtel Corporation, which reaped substantial profits from the Iraq invasion.

The PNAC's vision of US global domination, beginning with the seizing of Iraq, was the culmination of a plan at least ten years in the making. In 1992, following the collapse of the Soviet Union, the Department of Defense drafted a document that 'envisioned the United States as a colossus astride the world, imposing its will and keeping world peace through military and economic power'.

It also stated that 'no rival superpower [be] allowed to emerge in Western Europe, Asia, or the territory of the former Soviet Union'.[5] When leaked in its final form, however, the proposal drew so much criticism that it was withdrawn and repudiated by President Bush Sr.

Dick Cheney, Bush Jr's vice-president, was defence secretary in 1992. The document was written by Paul Wolfowitz, who at that time was defence undersecretary for policy. He was, famously, the deputy defence secretary in the Bush Jr administration and, like his then employer, Donald Rumsfeld, was an outspoken advocate regarding the need to wage a brand new war on Iraq.

On 20 September 2002, Bush Jr released the US National Security Strategy. It is an ideological match to the PNAC's 'Rebuilding America's Defenses' report issued a year earlier. In many places, it uses exactly the same language to describe America's new place in the world. The US launched two major theatre wars, in Afghanistan and Iraq, under the Bush Jr administration, as per the PNAC's vision.

International law and the UN Charter provide for only two legitimate reasons for war: individual or collective self-defence in response to an attack, or if an action is authorised by the UN Security Council. The National Security Strategy declared the United States had the right to strike pre-emptively, in clear violation of the UN Charter. The NSS also distinctly identified market freedom with political freedom. While not stated directly, the NSS essentially said that a threat to market freedom, such as Iraq, was a major threat to freedom itself. The NSS is a *de facto* declaration that the US would move militarily to create a free market, neoliberal state if and when it believed its freedom – freedom in the context of the neoliberal corporate individual's ability to participate freely in the global market – was threatened. The US made a number of moves during this time to ensure that its ability to act unilaterally was not impeded, withdrawing from ratification of the International Criminal Court, the Chemical Weapons Convention, and the Kyoto Protocol on Climate Change.

THE OIL INDUSTRY AND THE THINK TANKS PUSH FOR WAR

Exercising their freedom as individuals to operate unfettered in the marketplace, and utilising the Supreme Court's decision recognising cash and corporate contributions as protected free speech, the corporate sector donated record amounts of money to the 2000 Bush-Cheney election campaign. The oil and gas industry contributed over $26 million to Bush's Republican Party in 2000, and another $18 million in 2002. ExxonMobil alone gave over $2 million for the two election cycles. ExxonMobil also spent over $54 million on lobbying in Washington, DC, from 1997 to 2004.[6]

The Bush administration is particularly renowned for its direct links with the oil and gas industry, and for having a very pro-active policy agenda that directly favoured fossil fuel industries. Bush himself is an ex-oil executive, and his administration had, as of 2002, 41 former oil and gas industry executives. As well as his connections to Halliburton, Cheney is a past director of the American Petroleum Institute. Secretary of State and former Bush National Security Advisor Condoleezza Rice is a former director of Chevron, and has the dubious distinction of having an oil tanker named after her. As of 2004, she held $225,000 worth of Chevron stock in a blind trust. During 2002, when the planning to invade Iraq began in earnest, the top hundred officials in the Bush administration had the majority of their personal investments, almost $150 million, in the energy and natural resource sectors.[7]

THE CORPORATION AS INDIVIDUAL: THINK TANKS PUSH FOR WAR

America's oil and gas industry also directly funded some of the most outspoken invasion advocates: the neoliberal policy think tanks examined earlier. These think tanks then supplied a seemingly endless stream of press releases and research to conservative talkback radio programmes and to Fox News, as well as demanding that more mainstream media include their research in order to be balanced and unbiased.

ExxonMobil is the merged entity of the two original American companies of the Iraq Petroleum Company, which dominated Iraqi oil for 45 years before being banished when Iraq nationalised its oil industry in 1972. ExxonMobil was particularly generous in funding these right-wing think tanks: it gave $405,000 to the Competitive Enterprise Institute (CEI) in 2002.[8] CEI advocated the US invasion and pressed for the privatisation of the Iraqi economy, particularly its oil industry.[9]

The American Enterprise Institute, of which ExxonMobil's CEO Lee Raymond was vice-chair, received $255,000. Its vice-president for foreign and defence policy studies, Danielle Pletka, said, 'For as long as Saddam is in power, he will threaten the U.S. and the rest of the world. There is no benefit in waiting; the danger must be met head on.'[10] One of the AEI's senior fellows was pro-war hawk, Richard Perle, who served on the National Defense Policy Board as an adviser to Donald Rumsfeld. ChevronTexaco, the second largest US oil company after ExxonMobil, gave $45,000 to the AEI.[11]

The Heritage Foundation advocated that the war should be about protecting 'Iraq's energy infrastructure against internal sabotage or foreign attack, to return Iraq to global energy markets, and ensure that U.S. and world energy markets have access to its resources.'[12] It received $75,000 from ExxonMobil and $15,000 from ChevronTexaco in 2002.

Anthony Cordesman of the Center for Strategic and International Studies, which received $145,000 from ExxonMobil, argued: 'We need a formal Bush Doctrine that ... says quite clearly that Gulf security and the continued flow of oil is a vital U.S. national security interest, and that we will remain committed to military confinement ... .'[13] ChevronTexaco, in one of its highest levels of so-called philanthropic support, gave $110,000. The Project for the New American Century and the Heritage Foundation were also explicit in their calling for the wholesale privatisation of the Iraqi economy as part of an American invasion.

The Washington, DC-based think tanks outlined above were instrumental in advocating neoliberalism as both ideology and government policy beginning in the 1970s. They played a crucial role in corporate America's large-scale political and cultural response to the Powell memo, as outlined previously. Similar to the campaign donations and other financial connections to the Bush-Cheney administration, the corporate funding of think tanks is protected by the 1886 *Santa Clara* vs. *Pacific Railway* US Supreme Court decision that recognises corporations as 'persons', establishing that they had the same 'rights' as flesh-and-blood persons under the US Constitution and Bill of Rights.

16
Invading Iraq:
Bush's Agenda from Day One

It is now well documented that Bush and Cheney intended to invade Iraq and seize its oil from the very first days of taking office. In the February 2004 issue of *The New Yorker*, journalist Jane Mayer revealed documentation that Cheney had begun urging that the US militarily seize Iraq's oil within the first two weeks of taking office, several months before the 9/11 terrorist attacks. A previously undisclosed National Security Council (NSC) document, dated 3 February 2001, concerns Cheney's newly formed Energy Task Force which, as examined in the previous chapter, was set up to develop long-term US energy policy. Cheney had only been in office two weeks; Bush's presidential inauguration was 20 January. Cheney directed the NSC staff to cooperate fully with the Energy Task Force as it considered the melding of two seemingly unrelated areas of policy: 'the review of operational policies towards rogue states', such as Iraq, and 'actions regarding the capture of new and existing oil and gas fields'.[1]

Former Treasury Secretary Paul O'Neill also confirmed that invading Iraq was at the top of the administration's agenda from day one. 'Go find me a way of doing this', Bush said at the very first National Security Council meeting in January 2001.[2] Based on interviews with O'Neill and several other officials, former *Wall Street Journal* writer Ron Suskind revealed in *The Price of Loyalty* that the early planning was very much focused on Iraq's oil wealth. A Pentagon document, 'Foreign Suitors for Iraqi Oilfield Contracts', dated 5 March 2001, features a detailed map of oilfield locations and potential areas of exploration.[3]

On 17 September 2001, six days after the 9/11 attacks, Bush signed orders to invade Afghanistan and also to prepare full war plans for Iraq. He sent former CIA chief James Woolsey to London to gather evidence linking Saddam Hussein to 9/11. These included allegations that Iraqi agents met with Mohammed Atta, ringleader of the 9/11 attacks; that Al Qaeda had travelled to Iraq to celebrate Saddam Hussein's birthday; that Iraq had trained

Al Qaeda operatives, and that Iraq was linked to anthrax that had been mailed to US senators in October 2001.[4] These allegations were widely reported in mainstream media, and they were all fully disproved before the invasion.

In January 2002, Bush gave his famous State of the Union address identifying Iraq, Iran and North Korea as an 'axis of evil'. Bush then directed the CIA to step up its financial and military support for anti-Hussein agents in Iraq, and to increase intelligence gathering. Yet, the *New York Times* reported a few weeks later that the CIA had found 'no evidence that Iraq has engaged in terrorist operations against the United States in nearly a decade, and the agency is also convinced that President Saddam Hussein has not provided chemical or biological weapons to Al Qaeda or related terrorist groups.'[5] A Congressional committee also came to the same conclusion.[6]

And, in September 2002, the Pentagon's Defense Intelligence Agency concluded that there was 'no definitive, reliable information' that Iraq either possessed or was manufacturing chemical or biological weapons.[7] In 1998, the International Atomic Energy Agency had certified via inspections that Iraq no longer had a nuclear weapons programme.[8]

But on 12 September 2002, one day after the one-year anniversary of 9/11, Bush said in his address to the United Nations General Assembly that Iraq was one of the 'outlaw groups and regimes that accept no law of morality and have no limit to their violent ambitions'.[9] In his January 2003 State of the Union speech, Bush warned Americans that Saddam Hussein had or could have

> ... biological weapons materials sufficient to produce over 25,000 litres of anthrax; enough doses to kill several million people ... materials sufficient to produce more than 38,000 litres of botulinum toxin; enough to subject millions of people to death by respiratory failure ... materials to produce as much as 500 tons of sarin, mustard, and VX nerve agent ... upwards of 30,000 munitions capable of delivering chemical agents.

Bush also stated that, during the 1990s, the Hussein regime had 'an advanced nuclear weapons development program', and that 'The British government has learned that Saddam Hussein recently sought significant quantities of uranium from Africa.'[10]

The world now knows that none of this was true, and, crucially, that Bush at the time knew that it wasn't true. Former Ambassador Joseph Wilson had been sent to Niger by the CIA a year earlier to investigate links to Saddam Hussein purchasing uranium; Wilson publicly stated there was no truth in Bush's uranium claims.[11] And Iraq did let UN inspectors back into the country in late 2002, and no evidence of WMDs were found.

More to the point, the Bush administration itself had openly admitted that Iraq had been successfully contained. On 24 February 2001 Secretary of State Colin Powell said, regarding Saddam Hussein, that 'frankly, they [UN sanctions] have worked. He has not developed any significant capability with respect to weapons of mass destruction. He is unable to project conventional power against his neighbors.'[12]

A short two years later, on 5 February 2003, Powell would embarrass himself before the United Nations Assembly and a global television audience when he claimed that minimally Iraq had enough chemical weapons capacity to 'enable Saddam Hussein to cause mass casualties across more than 100 square miles of territory, an area nearly five times that size of Manhattan'. And despite Wilson's having openly declared there was no merit to the story, Powell also stated that 'Since 1998, his efforts to reconstitute his nuclear program have been focused on acquiring the third and last component, sufficient fissile material to produce a nuclear explosion.'[13]

Much of Powell's detailed description on Iraq's non-existent weapons programmes was false information gained under torture from terrorist suspect Ibn al-Shaykh al-Libi, who the US had sent to Egypt for torture. The veracity of his confession had not been verified, and like much of the information gained from the administration's enthusiastic embrace of torture, it was subsequently proven to be worthless. Egypt was a common destination for the torture of detainees sent there by the US.[14]

Powell also already knew what Mohammed ElBaradei of the International Atomic Energy Agency (IAEI) would tell the UN a few weeks later on March 7: 'After three months of intrusive inspections, we have to date found no evidence or plausible indication of the revival of a nuclear weapon program in Iraq.'[15]

Bush also knew that any weapons of mass destruction that Iraq had ever possessed were supplied in large part by his father's and Ronald Reagan's governments. The *Washington Post* reported in 2002 that 'The administrations of Ronald Reagan and George H.W. Bush authorized the sale to Iraq of numerous items that had both military and civilian applications, including poisonous chemicals and deadly biological viruses, such as anthrax and bubonic plague.'[16] As examined in Chapter 12, the Reagan administration publicly condemned Iraq's use of chemical weapons but continued to assist Iraq and supply materials.

Iraq's December 2002 Arms Declaration to the UN stated that it had imported over 17,000 tons of chemicals, as well as equipment for making chemical weapons, from the US and its allies between 1983 and the start of the first Gulf War. American companies directly supplied chemical components, including for nerve gas, and $782 million in dual-use technology.[17] These components were all subsequently destroyed as per its compliance with the sanctions.

The public propaganda war, however, had been largely won. A *Washington Post* poll of September 2003 found that 69 per cent of Americans believed Saddam Hussein was probably involved in 9/11.[18] Bush finally publicly admitted two weeks after the poll that there was no evidence of Iraq's involvement.[19]

We know this was propaganda due to the Downing Street Memo of 23 July 2002, which were the leaked minutes of a meeting of senior UK government, defence and intelligence figures. It featured a discussion regarding how best to make the case for invading Iraq, and the best strategy to ensure it would happen, despite the considerable lack of evidence to support its justification. Foreign Secretary Jack Straw was quoted as saying that it was clear that Bush had 'made up his mind' to take military action but that 'the case was thin' regarding Iraq's weapons of mass destruction and ties to Al Qaeda. The discussion then focused on the need to manipulate the UN weapons inspection process to provide the legal pretext for invading, and that pre-war air strikes would need to be significantly increased in order to soften Iraqi infrastructure in preparation. The memo was leaked to the UK press in May 2005.[20]

The decision to invade Iraq had been made much earlier than that. In evidence presented to the 2006 Australian government's Cole Inquiry into the Australian Wheat Board's alleged bribes to Saddam Hussein during the sanctions, it was revealed that John Dauth, then Australia's ambassador to the United Nations, told AWB Chairman Trevor Flugge in early 2002 that Australia would participate in military action to invade Iraq and overthrow Saddam Hussein. Flugge, who a year later would be appointed to oversee Australia's role in the Coalition Provisional Authority's Ministry of Agriculture, then reported the conversation to the AWB Board of Directors meeting on 27 February 2002. Minutes from the meeting state Dauth 'believed that US military action to depose Saddam Hussein was inevitable and that at this time the Australian government would support and participate in such action'.[21] The

Australian Wheat Board was thus given advance notice of the Australian Howard government's intention to participate in the US invasion of Iraq, a full 13 months before the Australian, American, or British public were informed.

The evidence, or at least supporting evidence, for the administration's true plans for Iraq were not difficult to ascertain, even in the face of the official Bush administration propaganda and outright lies stating otherwise. The *Wall Street Journal* reported in 2002 that Bush's real goal in Iraq was to make the Middle East safer for American interests. It then reported in January, 2003 that

> Executives of US oil companies are conferring with officials from the White House, the Department of Defense and the State Department to figure out how best to jump-start Iraq's oil industry following a war, officials say ... The Bush Administration is eager to secure Iraq's oil fields and rehabilitate them, industry officials say. They say Mr. Cheney's staff hosted an informal meeting with industry executives in October, with ExxonMobil Corp, ChevronTexaco Corp, ConocoPhillips and Halliburton among the companies represented.[22]

The article also said the Bush administration hoped that Iraq's oil would be able to pay the actual costs of an American occupying army. Both Cheney and the oil companies denied that any such meeting took place. Between 31 January and 4 March 2003, before any declaration of actual war took place, the Bush administration issued nine tenders for post-invasion reconstruction contracts.[23]

In April 2011, it was revealed that BP and Shell had had extensive discussions with British Trade Minister Elizabeth Symons, who agreed to lobby the Bush administration on their behalf to ensure they would not miss out on the post-invasion Iraqi oil bonanza. The revelations were part of a number of documents uncovered by oil researcher and activist Greg Muttitt showing that oil was definitely a consideration in the Blair government's decision to support the invasion,[24] and are detailed in his book *Fuel on the Fire*. Blair, of course, had famously claimed that Saddam Hussein was able to launch weapons of mass destruction within 45 minutes of ordering their use.

Consistent public criticism that the Bush administration's interest in Iraq was more about accessing its oil than about its ties to Islamic terrorism were not helped by a series of leaked quotes strongly suggesting otherwise. Lawrence Lindsey, at the time US chief economic adviser, was quoted in the *Wall Street Journal* on 16 September, 2002: 'When there is a regime change in Iraq, you could add three to five million barrels of production to world supply each day. The successful prosecution of the war would be good for the economy.' Grant Aldonas, US Under Secretary for Commerce, said to a business forum in October 2002 that '[War] would open up this spigot on Iraq's oil, which certainly would have a profound effect in terms of the performance of the world economy for those countries that are manufacturers and oil consumers.'[25]

Former UN Weapons Inspector Scott Ritter's *Endgame: Solving the Iraq Crisis* (2002) provides compelling evidence Iraq had complied with UN weapons inspections requirements and possessed no weapons of mass destruction, nor did it possess an effective armed forces capable of defending itself. The overwhelming conclusion is that the US invaded Iraq not because Iraq had weapons of mass destruction, but because it didn't. Much to its shame, America would attack with the full brunt of its 'Shock and Awe' devastation, knowing full well that Iraq had followed the dictates of the sanctions, had destroyed its weapons of mass destruction and was therefore largely defenceless.

Part V

Regime Change:
Opportunity to Create a Brand New,
Neoliberal, Free Market State

17
Regime Change:
The Bremer Economic Orders

When the Occupation troops stood back and allowed Basra's hospitals, universities and public services to be burned and looted, while they defended only the oil ministry and oilfields, we knew we were dealing with a brutal force prepared to impose its will without regard for human suffering. From the beginning, we were left in no doubt that the US and its allies had come to take control of our oil resources ... We reject and will oppose all moves to privatise our oil industry and natural resources. We regard this privatisation as a form of neo-colonialism, an attempt to impose a permanent economic occupation to follow the military occupation.

Iraqi Federation of Oil Unions (IFOU) President Hassan Juma'a Awad, 2005[1]

On 20 March 2003, the Bush administration directly applied its National Security Strategy's 'efficient allocation of resources, and regional integration' when, along with Britain and Australia, it invaded Iraq. The US-dominated 'Coalition of the Willing' wasted little time in radically transforming Iraq's economy and political institutions into a neoliberal, free market-oriented state, with deliberate and systematic planning to ensure that Iraqis had no say in determining their own national interest, other than the model of self-determination upon which the United States had already decided. The brutal nature of the occupation has not been an exercise in counter-terrorism, as the US has consistently claimed, but a systematic and intentional means of mass repression to ensure its neoliberal agenda is fully implemented and unchallenged. The result has been an utterly devastated country. That the US has been stymied in much of what it wanted to accomplish in Iraq is a testament to the tremendous resistance, both peaceful and militant, of the Iraqi people.

The Coalition Provisional Authority was established in May 2003 by the United States, the UK and Australia, and was the official governing body of the military occupation until the so-called handover of sovereignty to an appointed Iraqi government on 28 June 2004. The CPA had full executive, legislative and judicial authority over Iraq during this time.

Bush appointed Paul Bremer, a long-time diplomat with a number of ambassadorial postings over a 30-year career, to head the CPA. Bremer's official title was 'administrator', and he was given vast powers to initiate and implement CPA policies. He had previously served as the State Department's counter-terrorism head. He left government service in the 1980s to work as a senior executive for Henry Kissinger and his private consulting firm, Kissinger Associates, which provided advice to dictators like Suharto in Indonesia.[2] Kissinger, of course, had figured prominently in Nixon's manipulation of the OPEC embargo crisis, and in initiating the violent coup that would usher in the first national experiment in neoliberalism in Chile.

With UN Security Council Resolution 1438, the United Nations formally acknowledged the occupation of Iraq by the Coalition and recognised the CPA as the occupation government. The resolution included the requirement that the CPA promote the welfare of the Iraqi people through the effective administrative of the country, restore security and stability so that the Iraqi people could 'freely determine their own political future', and comply fully with international law governing occupying powers.[3] The Bush administration delegated its authority from Resolution 1438 directly to Bremer, who could create laws by his signature alone, without any consultation or approval from the rest of the CPA.

Iraq's crippling sanctions were thus lifted by the UN Security Council. In their place, the Security Council established the Development Fund for Iraq, to be controlled by the CPA and overseen by a board of representatives from the World Bank, IMF and the UN, which would control Iraqi oil revenues. The UN thus granted control of Iraq's economy and reconstruction to the US and the Coalition, to be overseen by the pillars of neoliberalism and the Washington Consensus.

If there had been any doubt regarding American intentions to allow Iraq's future to be determined by Iraqis, they were quickly dispelled, and the specifics of a pro-free market, neoliberal US client state were already being articulated. Defense Secretary Donald Rumsfeld announced in May 2003 the 'Core Principles for a Free Iraq': 'Decisions will favour market systems ... The Coalition will encourage moves to privatise state owned enterprises.'[4] That Iraq was under a military occupation and not free was a matter of semantics.

Washington Post journalist Rajiv Chandrasekaran was based in Baghdad's Green Zone during the CPA's tenure. In *Imperial Life in the Emerald City: Inside Iraq's Green Zone* (2006), he interviewed Bremer soon after his arrival to run the CPA:

> 'What's your top priority?' I asked. 'Economic reform', he said. He had a three step plan. The first was to restore electricity, water, and other basic services. The second was to put 'liquidity in the hands of the people' – reopening banks, offering loans, paying salaries. The third was to 'corporatize and privatize state-owned enterprises,' and to 'wean people from the idea that the state supports everything.' Saddam's government owned hundreds of factories. It subsidized the cost of gasoline, electricity, and fertilizer. Every family received monthly food rations. Bremer regarded all of that as unsustainable, as too socialist. 'It's going to be a very wrenching, painful process, as it was in Eastern Europe after the fall of the Berlin Wall,' he said.

'But won't that be very complicated and controversial?' Chandrasekaran asked. 'Why not leave it up to the Iraqi's?' 'If we don't get the economy right, no matter how fancy our political transformation, it won't work,' he said.[5]

A month later, in June 2003, Bremer said, 'Economic growth will depend on the birth of a vibrant private sector. And this will require the wholesale relocation of resources and people from state control to private enterprise, the promotion of foreign trade, and the mobilisation of domestic and foreign capital.'[6]

A 'free' Iraq, according to the dictates of the US occupation, would be unfettered by government interference with market signals, and would be a country in which individuals, human and corporate, would not be restricted by a semi-socialised economy, as Iraq had been under Saddam Hussein and the Baath Party. The irony, of course, is that this could only occur with massive government interference and intervention: military invasion and occupation.

And just in case there was any confusion, Bremer said the following regarding any Iraqis opposing this new and 'free' Iraq: 'We are going to fight them and impose our will on them and we will capture or … kill them until we have imposed law and order on this country. We dominate the scene and we will continue to impose our will on this country.'[7]

The CPA was actually the second American occupation authority in Iraq. The CPA and Bremer replaced the Office of Reconstruction and Humanitarian Assistance, headed by retired Lieutenant General Jay Garner; the ORHA was the US authority on the ground in

Baghdad from 21 April, ten days after US troops secured Baghdad. Garner had been hired on 17 January 2003 to run the post-war occupation of Iraq – more than two full months before the Coalition had 'decided' to invade. In 1991, after the first Gulf War, Garner had overseen the military operation to protect the Kurds in northern Iraq from retaliation by Saddam Hussein.[8]

Before arriving in Baghdad, Garner and the OHRA had drawn up a list of Iraqi cultural sites to be protected once the US entered Baghdad, and which, based on advice from archaeologists, would be subject to looting. The list was ignored. In images televised around the world, in April 2003, Iraq's National Museum, National Library and Archives were ravaged by looting. Artefacts which had been protected for thousands of years simply disappeared, probably lost forever. Eighty-four per cent of Iraq's universities and higher education institutions were looted and many were outright burned and destroyed, as well as thousands of regular schools.[9] Iraq's national seed bank was also looted, a key issue, as we shall see, for Iraqi agriculture. The Red Cross reported that Baghdad's health care facilities, including hospitals, had totally collapsed.[10]

US troops did, however, protect the Ministry of Oil, which documented and housed the administration for Iraq's oil wealth. Rumsfeld famously responded to global outrage at the lack of protection by stating, 'Freedom's untidy.'[11]

There was considerable conflict between the State and Defense Departments once Garner and the OHRA arrived in Baghdad on 21 April. The conflict centred on the role of the Iraqi exiles supported by the Bush administration neocons and the Department of Defense, but who were not trusted and who were viewed as opportunists by US Secretary of State Colin Powell. There was also fundamental disagreement on the timeline for a handover of power to Iraqis, and what form that would take. In the absence of a political plan, and with the mandate that he was in charge, Garner announced that elections would take place within 90 days.[12] But then in early May, Garner and the OHRA were very quickly replaced by Bremer and the formation of the Coalition Provisional Authority.

THE BREMER ECONOMIC ORDERS

While the evidence suggests that there was no political plan, there certainly was an economic one, and Bremer wasted little time in laying the foundations for a neoliberal, free market, US client state. Reducing the size of government and government expenditure is a cornerstone of neoliberal, free market ideology. It is the third element of Friedman's three-part formula for neoliberal government policy: cutting back the size of the state.

On 23 May, five days before the UN recognised the CPA's authority as the occupation government, CPA Order Number Two dissolved Iraq's entire army, air force, navy, Ministry of Defence, and Intelligence Service. Non-officers received a one-time severance payment and no pension. Officers received a monthly stipend, provided they weren't senior Baath Party members. Iraq's army, Bremer decided, would be reduced to 40,000, would focus exclusively on border control, and would not have any tanks or artillery.[13]

The majority of Baath Party members were not supporters of Saddam Hussein or his policies, but belonged to the Baath Party because membership was essential for advancement in any profession. In Bremer's first executive order, CPA Order One, 120,000 government workers were fired throughout the Iraqi ministries, including 10–15,000 teachers. In a country of 28 million people, where unemployment already stood at 50 per cent, Bremer sacked a workforce of over 500,000 people.[14] The CPA also passed a wage law that fixed public-sector workers' salaries – which in Iraq's state-owned economy was more or less the entire country – at US$35 dollars a month, whereas foreign workers were earning up to $1,000 a day.[15]

In July 2003, under increasing international and Iraqi public pressure for the US and the CPA to ensure Iraqi self-determination was being recognised, Bremer announced the formation of the Iraqi Governing Council (IGC). The IGC was chosen largely from the collection of Iraqi exiles of the CIA-created Iraqi National Congress. In doing so, Bremer immediately broke an American promise to hold a larger and more representative assembly of Iraqis that would then choose Iraq's first governing body. Instead, the CPA/ Bremer-controlled IGC would choose a committee to organise a constitutional convention, and then organise a national referendum on a constitution. The IGC, however, had no actual power, which remained with the CPA and in particular with Bremer.[16]

In one of its first actions, the CPA also cancelled scheduled Iraqi local elections. Further anti-democratic suppression occurred when, post-invasion, over a hundred newspapers began operating, a number of them with anti-CPA content. The CPA passed an order prohibiting the local media from inciting attacks on other Iraqis – and on Coalition forces.[17]

Saddam Hussein's Baath Party ran Iraq on semi-socialist principles, with most industries state-owned. Prior to its economy being devastated by UN sanctions and two wars, Iraq was widely recognised as having the Arab world's best and most accessible education and health care systems. Chandrasekaran summarises daily economic life under Saddam's Baathist government:

> Government jobs, either in a factory or a ministry or in the security services, were plentiful and guaranteed you a salary for the rest of your life. Paychecks were low, but the cost of most goods and services was subsidized by the government. Gasoline was sold for less than a nickel a gallon. Nobody paid for electricity, not even the state-owned factories that guzzled hundreds of megawatts. Every family received monthly food rations from the state. Education, even college, was free. So was health care. The price of fertilizer was so heavily subsidized that Iraqi farmers would often sell their annual allotment in Jordan and Syria instead of using it to grow crops.[18]

Iraqis blamed their economic woes on Saddam for launching war with Iran, and then invading Kuwait and bringing on the sanctions after the devastation of the first Gulf War. 'But all along', Chandrasekaran writes:

> ... there was little, if any, recognition among ordinary Iraqis that their economic system was rotten to the core. After all, it was the same system that had given them a good life a generation earlier. The thinking among those Iraqis was that if Saddam and the sanctions were gone, they'd be wealthy again.[19]

The CPA wasted no time in implementing a market-oriented, radical neoliberal economic system, with Friedman's three-part formula of privatisation, deregulation and severe cutbacks in government services as the cornerstones for the new Iraqi economy. Any and all regulations limiting corporate powers were quickly dismantled. Within a few months, the CPA announced that nearly all Iraqi industries were open for sale to foreign investors, the vast bulk of which were state-owned enterprises (SOEs). Kamil Mubdir Gailani, the Iraqi Governing Council's finance minister, announced the Bremer privatisation orders at an IMF/World Bank meeting in Dubai in September 2003.[20]

The CPA thus attempted to move the entirety of Iraq's economy, with the exception of oil, from state-owned enterprises to an almost entirely privatised one to be owned, controlled, and for the benefit of, foreigners. It would be the CPA, not Iraqis, who would determine the selling price, and then write the subsequent budgets of how the revenue would be spent. Not only did the CPA Order 39 authorise and fast-track the wholesale sell-off of Iraqi publicly owned industries, but it specified there could be no preferential treatment for Iraqis. Order 39 also included the crucial investor–state provisions, meaning if any investor feels the Iraqi government is impeding its right to profit, it can directly sue in a third-party international dispute settlement court. Previous protections limiting foreign ownership of Iraqi businesses to 49 per cent had ensured majority Iraqi ownership. Now foreign corporations could buy up 100 per cent of these industries, and also keep 100 per cent of the profits.[21] Their sole requirement was to maximise profits; if the people of Iraq accrued any benefit from it, it would be a matter of luck, not intent.

Money from the sell-off of Iraq's state-owned industries would go into the Development Fund, which the United States would then in turn use to pay for the occupation and to provide insurance and financial guarantees for more American corporations to do business in Iraq. Oil revenues also went into this fund. The outright fraud associated with the CPA's handling of this fund is a stunning indictment of the US occupation, as we are about to see.

Tariffs, duties and other taxes on imports were also rescinded, thus facilitating an influx of cheap foreign products and eliminating any protection for Iraqi industries.[22] Iraqi farmers would have no protection against wheat and other agricultural imports from Australia, the US and other countries.

Foreign banks were now allowed to own up to 100 per cent of domestic Iraqi banks, and were also allowed to establish their own private-sector banks. Foreign branches and domestic subsidiaries of foreign banks were guaranteed equal treatment to that of Iraqi domestic banks. Foreigners were also allowed to lease land for up to 40 years.[23]

CPA Order 49 eliminated the Iraqi graduated income tax and the top rate of 45 per cent, and created a flat tax of 15 per cent on individuals and corporations. An Iraqi earning $100 a month would pay the same percentage of tax as a multinational corporation earning billions.

Although Iraqis were not technically eliminated from buying the state-owned enterprises or becoming shareholders once the industries were sold, few if any could afford to do so. Iraq's economy was in a shambles after the devastation and subsequent looting of the invasion, which had followed nearly 13 years of sanctions and the destruction from the first Gulf War.

Bremer announced that privatisation of the SOEs would begin by October 2003, along with a host of other forced neoliberal reforms.[24] Monthly food rations, on which the majority of the population depended upon, would be eliminated by November, and would be replaced by cash payments. Food subsidies, along with the below-market price subsidies for gasoline and electricity, were to be eliminated after February 2004. These would pave the way for Iraq to join the World Trade Organization. Bremer also announced that a trust fund would be established to provide Iraqis with annual cash rebates from oil sales, to be modelled after the one in the state of Alaska. It was the first and last mention of any trust fund for ordinary Iraqis. 'It's a full scale economic overhaul,' Bremer said. 'We're going to create the first real free market economy in the Arab world.'[25]

Neoliberal theory dictates that the state has a responsibility to create markets where they did not exist before. In a July 2003 address to a World Economic Forum special meeting in Jordan, Bremer claimed that

Markets allocate resources much more efficiently than politicians. So our strategic goal in the months ahead is to set in motion policies which will have the effect of reallocating people and resources from state enterprises to more productive private firms. We have to move quickly with this effort. Getting inefficient state enterprises into private hands is essential for Iraq's economic recovery.[26]

Even mainstream financial journalists were stunned at the audacity of the plans. 'By almost any mainstream economist's standard, the plan ... is extreme – in fact, stunning', wrote *New York Times* economic columnist Jeff Madrick.[27] Neil King of the *Wall Street Journal*, said that the intent was 'to remake Iraq's economy in the US image'.[28] The *Economist* described the plans as ' ... fulfilling the wish list of international investors ... Let's go to the yard sale.'[29] The *Guardian*'s Rory McCarthy described it succinctly: 'Iraq was effectively put up for sale yesterday, when the US backed administration unveiled a sweeping overhaul of the economy, giving foreign companies unprecedented access to Iraqi firms which are to be sold off in a privatisation windfall.'[30]

'An even more radical form of shock therapy than pursued in the former Soviet world,' said Joseph Stiglitz, former World Bank chief economist and Nobel Prize winner.[31] Michael Bleyzer, a former executive of Enron, summed up the goal when he briefed Defense Secretary Donald Rumsfeld and other officials of the Bush administration: 'We want to set up a business environment where global companies like Coca-Cola and McDonalds could come in and create a diversified economy not dependent on oil.'[32]

It was clear that the US viewed Iraq as nothing more than an ultimate neoliberal, free market plaything that they could do with as they pleased. No country had ever been subjected to the radical degree and intensity of wrenching economic change that the US was attempting in Iraq. The ultimate wish list guaranteeing the right of profit above all others was accomplished via a few scribbles of Bremer's pen.

LAYING THE FRAMEWORK FOR NEOLIBERAL INSTITUTIONS

This 'full scale economic overhaul' was not undertaken by an occupying force taking advantage of chaos and lack of scrutiny, shielded by overwhelming military strength. The master plan for this ultimate neoliberal transformation of Iraq had already been spelled out in startling detail in a draft February 2003 contract between the US Agency for International Development (USAID), the official US government aid agency, and the BearingPoint Corporation – a full month before the purported final decision was made to invade.

The confidential, 101-page document, 'Moving the Iraqi Economy from Recovery to Sustainable Growth', reads like a neoliberal manifesto. It clearly stated that any and all decisions regarding Iraq's economy would be determined by the CPA and the military occupying force, and not Iraqis. For example, 'The new [occupation] government will seek to open up its trade and investment linkages and to put into place the institutions promoting democracy, free enterprise and reliance on a market driven private sector as the engine of economic recovery and growth.' It outlined the specifics of a 'broad based mass privatization program', and a 'world class exchange' for trading stocks. The awarding of contracts would be 'blind as to whether the investor is from that country [Iraq] or elsewhere'.[33] BearingPoint also was awarded the contract to implement the plan on the ground in Iraq. The contract, valued at $79 million for the first year, was followed by USAID awarding BearingPoint the follow-on contract worth up to $225 million in September 2004. BearingPoint was to promote 'private sector involvement ... especially in the oil and supporting sectors'.[34]

The Iraqi population was not presented with these plans as a political platform. Indeed, Iraqis were openly prohibited from even seeing, let alone determining, them. Isam al-Khafaji, who worked directly with the CPA in the first months of the occupation, verified that 'Many radically new sweeping changes, for example the law on foreign investment, Iraqis were not allowed to review it. They were not even given the chance to look at it before it was passed.' Iraqi businesses complained they'd been cut out of the bidding process, and that others had been prevented from doing business by the CPA.[35]

Any Iraqis who opposed the mass privatisation plans, or for that matter the military occupation of their country in general, were quickly cut out of the CPA-initiated and controlled political and electoral system. As the occupation repression quickly intensified, there were much worse potential consequences for being seen to oppose US rule, as the horrors of Abu Ghraib and Fallujah would reveal less than a year later. It was clear that the CPA's intention was that Iraqis would have no say or sovereignty over their own economic future.

Although the CPA's neoliberal economic policies were embedded as law, they were not successfully implemented. The CPA had to back down on the fast-tracking of the privatisation plans, due to substantial public resistance and the fact the CPA's actions were illegal under international law. The mass sell-off of the SOEs have been put on hold by successive elected Iraqi governments, despite considerable pressure to approve them. The ongoing legal issues and the critical lack of security, as well as in many cases dilapidated and out-of-date facilities, have meant few buyers. In July 2006, Iraq's Industry Minister Fawzi Hariri declared that privatisation would not happen 'for at least five to 10 years'.[36] In October 2010, the Iraqi government announced plans to privatise, either partially or in full, at least two hundred state-owned industrial enterprises over the next four years.[37] The Iraqi government and its ministries are fond of making announcements, and, like many others, this one was not particularly detailed in how it would actually be accomplished.

18
Reconstruction and Corruption:
The Next Klondike

At a conference in Washington in early 2004 for companies hoping to obtain government contracts, Iraq was promoted as 'the next Klondike' by James Clad, an official with the US Overseas Private Investment Corporation.[1] As delineated in Rumsfeld's 'Core Principles for a Free Iraq', access to contracts for this next Klondike would be limited to companies whose countries 'supported the Iraqi people's liberation', that is, that directly supported the invasion. French, German and Russian firms were cut out from the reconstruction contract bonanza because of 'security concerns', despite the fact that three out of four Iraqi power stations were built by firms from those countries.[2]

More importantly, Iraqis themselves were also cut out of benefiting economically from their own reconstruction. Iraq was only in need of reconstruction due to the intentional destruction of its infrastructure from the first Gulf War, sanctions, and the recent 'Shock and Awe' devastation of the invasion. By awarding contracts almost exclusively to American firms, with a few large crumbs thrown in for its Coalition partners, the US was ensuring Iraqis would be utterly dependent on the occupation for basic functioning and essential service provision. Even worse, American contractors reaping enormous profits would largely be paid out of the Development Fund with Iraq's own money.

At the heart of the CPA was the clear intention of privatising the Iraqi economy and selling off its industries, which would then, along with oil revenue, pay for the occupation itself. It is also clear that the intent was to pursue further radical neoliberal economic prescriptions. The way the CPA went about establishing these, and the manifest corruption, fraud, and cronyism inherent in the CPA, helped ensure that they would not succeed.

In US congressional hearings held early in February 2007, it was revealed that nearly $12 billion of CPA-controlled money could not be properly accounted for, with no clear accountability or record keeping regarding who received it, or why. The money was flown from the US to Baghdad in shrink-wrapped $100 bills. According to Bremer, the use of cash was necessary because of the breakdown in Iraq's banking system.[3] This was Iraqi money which had been handed over by the UN's Oil for Food programme to the CPA for humanitarian and reconstruction purposes.

Fraud and corruption was extensive. Already in 2006, an audit conducted by the US government found that only 49 of the 136 projects that were originally pledged to improve Iraq's water and sanitation would be finished; and about 300 of an initial 426 projects to provide electricity were completed, but most were not fully operational.[4] There are few success stories regarding US reconstruction efforts, and few of the benchmarks of electricity, clean water, adequate health care, and other key areas have been met. The insurgency has certainly made reconstruction efforts challenging. But if the US had provided direct assistance to Iraqis, rather than outsourcing to its own corporations which got rich regardless of their ability to perform the work, the militant resistance would have had much less reason to have ever occurred in the first place.

The real looting in Iraq was done by the US and its contractors, not poor people rioting in Baghdad's slums. In August 2011, a report by the Commission on Wartime Contracting, a body set up by the US Congress, found that at least $30 billion and as much as $60 billion had been lost to fraud and waste in outsourcing military contracts to private corporations in Iraq and Afghanistan, and averaged about $12 million each and every day.[5] With so many contracts containing guaranteed cost plus profit incentives – which means the contractor is guaranteed a profit regardless of what work is actually accomplished – it's a wonder any reconstruction occurred at all.

Despite ongoing investigations by the Special Inspector General for Iraq Reconstruction and other government agencies, relatively few individuals have faced any criminal charges or accountability. And, as we shall see with Halliburton and Bechtel, fraud and waste were hardly impediments to further contracts.

The corruption, intentional fraud, lack of accountability, and outright incompetence in the reconstruction contracts is spectacularly exemplified by Custer Battles,[6] which was a business partnership between 33-year-old ex-Army Ranger Michael Battles, and fellow ex-Ranger Scott Custer. Battles arrived in Baghdad shortly after it fell with $450 in his pocket, looking for reconstruction contracts. Custer Battles was able to secure a $16 million CPA contract to provide security for Baghdad airport, primarily armed guards and baggage screeners, and to do it quickly.

Custer Battles then won the contract to transport thousands of tons of Iraq's new currency from Baghdad airport, where it arrived after being printed overseas. The company created a number of false invoices from sham companies registered in the Cayman Islands and Lebanon, claiming that Custer Battles was leasing trucks and other relevant equipment from these companies. The invoices were highly inflated, which, in the cost-plus contract, the higher the costs, the higher the profits.

The company found a number of abandoned Iraqi Airways forklifts at Baghdad airport, which they simply repainted. They then claimed the forklifts had been leased and flown in from overseas, and charged the CPA thousands of dollars a month. After a meeting with CPA officials, a Custer Battles employee left behind a company spreadsheet. The spreadsheet clearly delineated that Custer Battles had charged the CPA $9,801,550 for work that had only cost $3,738,592. Custer Battles was banned from any further contracts in September 2004; by that time, it had received over $100 million in government contracts.

The CPA itself resembled the executive infrastructure of a US corporation, both in structure and content. The vast majority of Bush administration appointees to the CPA were Republican Party donors, or individuals who had personal connections to Bush and/or Cheney. Many had no expertise in the area that they were appointed, and few could speak Arabic or had any knowledge of the country they were assigned to help rebuild. 'The criterion for sending people over there was that they had to have the right political credentials,' said Fredrick Smith, the deputy director of the CPA's Washington, DC office. Many senior CPA advisers were hired as a result of well-connected Republicans recommending them.[7] The most astounding example was when six recent university graduates with Republican connections ended up being appointed to manage Iraq's $13 billion budget, even though they had no previous financial management experience.[8]

Somewhat typical of the CPA appointees was Peter McPherson, who was appointed head of the CPA's Office of Private Sector Development. McPherson took a leave of absence as head of Michigan State University to go to Baghdad. He had been the director of USAID for seven years under Reagan, and so did have a relevant development background. Before that, he had served as deputy director of personnel in the Gerald Ford administration, and had formed a close personal relationship with Dick Cheney,

Ford's chief of staff. He had also been a senior vice-president of Bank of America.[9]

As one of the few journalists covering the reality of the economic transformation, who also had high-level access, Chandrasekaran's interviews of McPherson and other CPA officials clearly reveal why the US was in Iraq. McPherson told Chandrasekaran that his mission was to pursue Friedman's three-part formula of deregulation, privatisation and cutbacks. He favoured 'a supply side economic strategy: reduce the role of government through privatisation, eliminate subsidies for electricity and fuel, cut tariffs, lower taxes, promote foreign investment, and enact pro business laws'.[10] This would create the environment for new businesses, would create jobs, and boost economic growth.

One of the first things McPherson did was to initiate an analysis of the Ministry of Industry's 150 factories and 48 companies to determine their potential worth for privatisation. Another CPA staff member, Glenn Corliss, was put in charge. In comparison, Germany had a team of 8,000 people working on the privatisation of former East German factories after unification. The CPA had three for all of Iraq. Corliss found that only 13 of the ministry's 48 companies were capable of turning a profit. These included cement, fertiliser, phosphate, and petrochemical firms.[11]

Despite the fact that he was not a doctor and had no actual health background, James K. Haveman was appointed by Bush to run the Iraqi Health Ministry. Haveman had been the community health director for the Republican governor of Michigan, who recommended him for the job. Haveman announced his first priority in the post-invasion, war- and sanctions-ravaged country was to initiate an anti-smoking campaign.[12]

As an initial step towards eliminating Iraq's national health care system and replacing it with a privatised one like the US's, where approximately 50 million people have no health coverage whatsoever, Haveman's other priority was to privatise Kimadia, Iraq's state-owned firm that purchased and then distributed drugs and medical supplies. When he encountered the same problems that Corliss had faced, he focused on reducing costs by slimming down the number and types of medicines that the state would purchase. Haveman envisioned an American, market-based system for Iraq with co-payments and primary care clinics. The Health Ministry was handed over to the Iraqis in March 2004, three months before the official sovereignty handover. The new Iraqi Minister for Health Aladdin Alwan claimed that 40 per cent of the 900 drugs deemed essential by the ministry were not available. Only 6 of the 32 drugs used in public clinics for the management of chronic diseases were in stock.[13]

In the face of the overwhelming evidence, McPherson recognised that it would not be possible to launch the privatisation programme until Iraq was stable. So he focused on eliminating the state subsidies such as free electricity and free petrol or diesel, which ran to hundreds of millions of dollars a year. Without the subsidies, only the truly viable companies would survive. McPherson referred to this as 'shrinkage'. As state-owned firms shrank or went bankrupt, new businesses would take their place. Or, more likely, they would be replaced by imports, thanks to the CPA eliminating tariff protections.

'I thought the privatisation that occurs sort of naturally when somebody took over their state vehicle, or began to drive a truck that the state used to own, was just fine,' McPherson said in response to Baghdad's bus drivers running their state-owned vehicles and collecting and keeping the fares.[14]

McPherson left Baghdad in the summer of 2003, and was replaced by Thomas Foley, an investment banker and major Republican Party donor, and former classmate of Bush's at the Harvard Business School. Foley took his title as the head of the CPA's Office of Private Sector Development literally. A week after arriving, Foley told a contractor from BearingPoint, who later told Chandrasekaran,[15] that he intended to privatise all of Iraq's state-owned enterprises within 30 days.

'Tom, there are a couple of problems with that,' the contractor said. 'The first is an international law that prevents the sale of assets by an occupation government.'

'I don't care about any of that stuff,' Foley told the contractor, according to her recollection of the conversation. 'I don't give a shit about international law. I made a commitment to the president that I'd privatise Iraq's businesses.'

CPA LEGALITY

The international laws that Foley didn't 'give a shit about' were the Hague Resolutions of 1907. Article 43 states that an occupying power 'must re-establish and insure as far as possible, public order and safety, while respecting, unless absolutely prevented, the laws in force in the country'. Article 55 states that an occupying power 'shall be regarded only as an administrator and usufructuary of public buildings, real estate, forests, and agricultural estates belonging to the hostile state' and must 'safeguard the capital of these properties'.[16]

The United States, the UK and Australia have all ratified this treaty and it is binding as law. Furthermore, UN Security Council Resolution 1483 which recognised the CPA as the occupation government, specifically called on the Coalition 'to comply fully with their obligations under international law including in particular the Geneva Conventions of 1949 and the Hague Resolutions of 1907'. It also required that the US and the CPA promote 'economic reconstruction and the conditions for sustainable development'.[17]

Meanwhile, a remarkable political event was taking place in Iraq which was beyond America's control. Iraq's leading Shia cleric, the Grand Ayatollah al Sistani, issued a *fatwa*, or holy order, calling for Iraq's new constitution to be drafted by elected, not appointed, representatives. Bremer's plan had been for the CPA (that is, Bremer), to handpick with the Iraqi Governing Council a preparatory committee to draft the constitution. Sistani's *fatwa* instead insisted that the people drafting the constitution be elected. The Governing Council could not ignore the *fatwa*; nor could Bremer and the CPA without risking considerable political unrest. Sistani's *fatwa* changed the dynamics of the CPA and its timeline for establishing the economic orders. There was also increased civil agitation and protests demanding sovereignty, as well as international pressure. On 15 November 2003, Bremer announced that the CPA would hand over sovereignty to Iraqis by June 2004. The CPA focus then changed to meet the deadline.[18]

In February 2004, Foley proposed to lease Iraq's factories in place of privatisation, but by then the insurgency was under way and there were still legal issues with whether the CPA had the authority to lease, let alone sell, Iraq's factories.[19] Bremer's attempt to substitute food rations with cash payouts also failed, with the US military vetoing it due to fear of food riots and the lack of personnel needed to implement a new system on which the entire population was dependent.

Foley's approach was also directly counter to US claims that it was in Iraq to establish democracy for the Iraqi people. Foley was by no means unique. The intention and passion to privatise Iraq's industries, and to follow Friedman's neoliberal rulebook as quickly as possible, was not met with the requisite skill base and resources to do so. Regardless of intent, the CPA's legacy is one of ineptitude, fraud and scandal. And ultimately failure, as it was not able to successfully transform Iraq into Bremer's 'first real free market economy in the Arab world'.

Based on his time in Iraq, including stretches outside the Green Zone, Chandrasekaran says that what

> ... the CPA's economic team failed to grasp was that the mostly Western educated participants [the former exiles] were by no means representative of Iraqi society. Their desire for a fundamental economic restructuring – abandoning Saddam's centrally planned, socialist welfare state for a globalized, free-market system – had little resonance on Iraqi streets. To most Iraqis, even those who would later become ardent critics of the American occupation, the political side was a no brainer: Saddam was a brutal tyrant who had to go. When it came to economics, however, there was no such consensus.[20]

19
Reconstruction and Corruption: The Halliburton and Bechtel Contracts

A core principle of neoliberal ideology is that freedom is best enhanced by individuals operating unhindered by government in the marketplace, in order to send the appropriate price signals. The awarding of contracts to corporations with close ties to the Bush administration reveals another reality of neoliberalism: that it is the largest, most powerful individuals in the marketplace that are able to substantially influence those signals.

Reducing the role of government, and turning over government services to the private corporate sector is a cardinal principle of neoliberalism, and one of the three cornerstones of Friedman's formula. Outsourcing would prove to be one of the many controversies of the Bush administration's conduct of the war in Iraq, in part because of the immense opportunity it provided for those close to the administration for personal and substantial profit.

The issues of neoliberalism rewarding the largest and most powerful corporate individuals is highlighted by the fact that the 70 or so companies that received Iraq contracts during the CPA donated more money to President Bush than they did to any other candidate during the previous twelve years.[1] The windfall that has come to Cheney and other government officials from US government contracts with firms with which they had direct connections blurs the line between outsourcing as a fundamental neoliberal ideology to reduce the role of government, and war profiteering and criminal culpability. Here we'll briefly examine Halliburton and Bechtel as the two most blatant examples.

HALLIBURTON AND CHENEY

It was the Bush administration's Vice-President Dick Cheney who had the closest ties, and who has received the most direct financial benefits, from the war on Iraq. Widely regarded as the most powerful and influential vice-president in American history, Cheney has had an ongoing and extremely lucrative connection to Halliburton, a major oil services and infrastructure company. Cheney was CEO of Halliburton 1995–2000.

Halliburton has operations in approximately 80 countries. As well as oil-related services, it also provides a range of outsourcing services to the US military, from delivery of petrol to meals. It is based in Houston, Texas, but in March 2007 it opened a second headquarters in Dubai, the United Arab Emirates. In 2007, Halliburton sold its controversial subsidiary, Kellogg, Brown and Root (KBR), which had won many of the Iraq contracts.[2]

Halliburton was awarded a two-year, no-bid contract worth up to $7 billion to fight oil fires in Iraq and to pump and distribute Iraqi oil. The contract was awarded in March 2003, before the war had even started, and before, at least in theory, the Bush administration had made the decision to invade. The highly controversial contract was awarded under a Bush administration waiver that allowed government agencies to handpick companies. The contract, not announced until two weeks after being awarded, was 'cost-plus', which means that the company was guaranteed a profit on top of recovering all costs.[3]

Halliburton stands accused of a series of scandals surrounding its Iraq contracts. The Pentagon found that Halliburton subsidiary KBR overcharged the US military more than $61 million for fuel delivered in Iraq through September 2003.[4] In late January 2004, Halliburton admitted that it took $6 million in kickbacks in return for awarding a Kuwaiti-based company lucrative work supplying US troops in Iraq.[5] KBR was found in February 2004 to have overcharged the military another $27.4 million for meals served.[6] And the company was repeatedly warned that the food it was serving 110,000 troops in Iraq was 'dirty', with a military audit finding 'blood all over the floors of refrigerators, dirty pans, dirty grills, dirty salad bars, rotting meat and vegetables'.[7] KBR also submitted a bid for cafeteria services that the Pentagon said appeared to be inflated by $67 million, which was rejected.[8]

Yet KBR was handed a new $1.2 billion contract in mid-January 2004, the day after the story broke about the kickbacks.[9] Awarded in an open bidding process, the new contract was supposed to address charges of corruption and cronyism surrounding KBR's no-bid contract worth up to $7 billion granted in March 2003, before the start of the war. Both contracts were to repair Iraq's oil infrastructure, with the second contract superseding the first.

Previous to its Iraq contracts, KBR had received a long-term deal to supply US military provisions. The Iraqi portion of that contract was worth 'in excess of $2bn', according to officials of the Defense Contract Management Agency in Baghdad.[10] Reuters reported that as of January 2004, Halliburton had already done nearly $6 billion worth of military business in Iraq.[11]

In a country with an unemployment rate at the time of over 60 per cent, Halliburton imported cheap labour from South Asia to guarantee even higher profits. One of its subcontractors, Tamimi, organised 180,000 meals a day for 60,000 US troops and administrators. The company employed 1,800 Pakistanis, Indians, Bangladeshis and Nepalese in its kitchens and paid them an average salary of $3 a day and granted leave once every two years. It used only a few dozen Iraqis for cleaning.[12]

Halliburton's 2002 annual report described counter-terrorism as offering 'growth opportunities'. Thanks to its no-bid guaranteed profit contract, Halliburton's sales rose 39 per cent to $4.1 billion in its 2003 third quarter.[13] Its stock price rose from $10 before the Iraq War to $41 three years later.[14] This quadrupling was in large part due to the billions in contracts it received for Iraqi reconstruction.

In 2006, the Pentagon cancelled Halliburton's contracts and put them out to open bidding. Between March 2003 and June 2006, the company had already received over $18.5 billion in contracts from the US government for work in Iraq.[15]

VICE-PRESIDENT DICK CHENEY'S TIES WITH HALLIBURTON

'I severed my ties with Halliburton when I became a candidate for Vice President in August 2000,' Cheney stated on 22 January 2004. Far from severing his ties, the *Wall Street Journal* found that Cheney had 189,000 shares in Halliburton and 500,000 unvested stock options when he was running for office.[16] He also has received $211,000 a year in deferred income from the company, and his retirement package is worth $20 million.[17]

As defence secretary under the first President Bush, Cheney had commissioned Halliburton to write a report on how all planning and support for military operations, such as preparing food, laundry, and cleaning toilets, could be done by one company. In August 1992, this outsourcing contract was awarded to Halliburton – three months before Cheney's employer, President Bush Sr, lost the election to Bill Clinton. The then-unemployed Cheney was subsequently hired as CEO of Halliburton in 1995, after abandoning plans to run for president.[18] He resigned from Halliburton to become Bush's running mate in 2000.

Cheney famously summarised the geopolitical reality of oil supply: 'The problem is that the good Lord didn't see fit to put oil and gas reserves where there are democratically elected regimes friendly to the interests of the United States.'[19] Cheney has been adamant that he played no part in the awarding of contracts to Halliburton. But *Time* magazine disclosed that on 5 March 2003, an Army Corps of Engineers official wrote in an email 'We anticipate no issues since action has been coordinated with VP's office.' Three days later, Halliburton was awarded the two-year, no-bid contract worth up to $7 billion to fight oil fires in Iraq and to pump and distribute Iraqi oil.[20]

HALLIBURTON, CHENEY AND THE UN SANCTIONS ON IRAQ

Halliburton received the Iraq contracts despite its atrocious track record up to that point, for example, conducting $73 million worth of business in Iraq in direct violation of the UN sanctions.[21] It also did extensive business with two other nations the United States had prohibited companies dealing with because of their ties to terrorism – Iran and Libya – as well as some of the most repressive regimes of the late twentieth century, such as Burma (Myanmar).[22]

During Cheney's tenure as CEO in 1997, the US General Accounting Office found that the US Army was unable to ensure that KBR adequately controlled costs. KBR was charging $86 for a $14 sheet of plywood. The Army sued KBR for $6 million in overcharges from 1995–97. The company was also under investigation by the SEC for artificially inflating revenue by $234 million over four years while Cheney was CEO.[23] In May 2003, Halliburton admitted that, during Cheney's tenure, KBR had paid $2.4 million in bribes to Nigerian government officials in return for more favourable tax arrangements for building a refinery.[24]

During Cheney's tenure, Halliburton gave $1,212,000 in campaign contributions to both parties, though primarily to Republicans. Also under Cheney's tenure, the number of Halliburton subsidiaries in offshore tax havens increased from 9 to 44. Halliburton went from paying $302 million in taxes in 1998 to getting an $85 million tax refund in 1999.[25]

BECHTEL

Another sizeable contract winner was the Bechtel Corporation, the largest engineering company in the United States. Privately owned and headquartered in San Francisco, Bechtel had projects in 50 countries and over $27 billion in revenue in 2009.[26]

As examined earlier, Bechtel's willingness to do business with Saddam Hussein included directly supplying him with chemical weapons capacity. Yet Bechtel still received a no-bid contract from the US Agency for International Development (USAID) in 2003 for emergency repair or rehabilitation of power-generation facilities, electrical grids, municipal water systems, sewage systems, airport facilities, the dredging, repair and upgrading of the Umm Qasr seaport (before the seaport was even occupied by US forces), and reconstruction of hospitals, schools, ministry buildings, irrigation structures and transportation links. The contract was worth up to $680 million over 18 months. USAID granted an additional $350 million on the contract in September 2003, raising the ceiling to $1.03 billion. Bechtel then received an additional $1.8 billion contract for similar work in early January 2004, this time in an open bidding process and in partnership with the Parsons Corporation.[27] Essentially, the contract was to repair much of the infrastructure intentionally destroyed and then prevented from being repaired during the sanctions.

Bechtel received the contracts despite being renowned for its questionable construction techniques, such as installing the San Onofre nuclear reactor in California 180 degrees backward. It was also found guilty of overcharging the city of San Francisco tens of thousands of dollars for upgrading the city's water systems. Its handling of Boston's 'Big Dig' tunnel project to reroute a major highway under the city went from a 1985 estimated cost of $2.5 billion to $14.6 billion, making it the world's most expensive highway. Bechtel is also listed 730 times for hazardous waste spills on the EPA's Emergency Response Notification System database for 1990–97.[28]

Bechtel has been a major beneficiary of forcing countries to open their water, sewage and other services to bidding by private corporations, as per the General Agreement on Trade in Services (GATS) provisions of the WTO, for example, the water supply privatisation of Cochabamba, Bolivia examined earlier, and World Bank/IMF structural adjustment programmes.

Leading up to 2003, Bechtel gave $1.3 million in campaign contributions, 59 per cent to Republicans. It is extraordinarily well connected to the Bush administration. George Schultz, former secretary of state and also former Bechtel CEO, was the head of the advisory board for the Committee for the Liberation of

Iraq, an openly pro-war group created by the Project for the New American Century, with close ties to the Bush White House. The committee was committed to 'work beyond the liberation of Iraq to the reconstruction of its economy'.[29]

In November 2006, Bechtel withdrew entirely from Iraq, leaving its contracts largely unfulfilled. At the time of its departure, the average Iraqi household received less than two hours of electricity per day. Sixty-eight per cent of Iraqis still did not have access to safe drinking water, and only 19 per cent had sewage service.[30]

SHELL OIL AND FLUOR

Philip Carrol, the CPA's first Oil Ministry 'adviser', was the former chief executive of both Shell Oil and Fluor, an engineering company. In September 2003, Fluor received a contract from the Army Corps of Engineers for up to $500 million, to be shared with two other companies, to repair electrical infrastructure.[31] Under Carroll, Shell had collaborated with the Nigerian dictatorship in the early 1990s in suppressing a popular non-violent uprising from the Ogoni people in the Niger Delta, where Shell's operations were based. Ogoni leader and internationally renowned author Ken Saro Wiwa was executed by the Nigerian military, and hundreds of innocent Ogoni people died. The other company that Carroll headed, Fluor, is the subject of a multibillion-dollar lawsuit claiming that it exploited and brutalised black workers in apartheid-era South Africa.[32] Shell, along with every other major oil company, has effectively sabotaged international efforts to address global climate change.

Fluor had given nearly $2 million in campaign contributions from 1996 to 2003, the majority to Republicans. Carroll receives more than $1 million in retirement funds from Fluor, a company that was competing directly for reconstruction bids.[33]

20
Locking Down Iraq: Post Sovereignty

With a heavy dose of fear and violence, and a lot of money for projects, I think we can convince these people that we are here to help them.

Lieutenant Colonel Nathan Sassaman, US 4th Infantry Division, December 2003[1]

Iraqis, along with international criticism, pressured the CPA into advancing the so-called handover of sovereignty to June 2004. 'Sovereignty' was not handed over to any democratically elected or recognised body, but to the CPA hand-picked Iraqi Governing Council, which then became the transitional government on 28 June 2004. Bremer, in particular, was instrumental in ensuring that former CIA agent Iyad Allawi would be selected as the interim prime minister. This transitional government then oversaw a complicated CPA-devised caucus system designed to ensure that only, or at least primarily, Coalition sympathisers would be allowed to run in the eventual elections and constitution processes demanded by Grand Ayatollah Sistani's *fatwa*.[2]

Even if Iraq's transitional government had the inclination to challenge the CPA orders, their hands were largely tied. The CPA economic orders were embedded in the post-sovereign process as the 'Transition Administration Laws', and to be overturned would require a two-thirds majority approval of any future legislative assembly, plus the individual approval of the prime minister, president, and both vice-presidents.[3] The CPA's neoliberal orders were incorporated as law in the passage of the October 2005 Iraqi Constitution. Article 26 of the US-drafted constitution renders the Bremer economic orders inviolable, and that subsequent democratically elected Iraqi governments are largely powerless to change them.[4] In addition, just as the British had done when installing King Faisal, over two hundred CPA advisers remained embedded to 'assist' the post-sovereign process, and to ensure that the CPA economic laws were being implemented.[5] The new government would not even have enough freedom to create its own budget; the 2004–06 transitional government budget had to be approved by the CPA.[6]

Literally hours before the official handover, Bremer signed CPA revised Order 17, guaranteeing that the Coalition military and foreign contractors would be immune from prosecution by the new Iraqi government.[7] And shortly after the UN established the Development Fund in May 2003, Bush issued Executive Order 13303 which decreed that 'any attachment, judgment, decree, lien, execution, garnishment, or other judicial process is prohibited, and shall be deemed null and void' with respect to the Development Fund for Iraq and 'all Iraqi petroleum and petroleum products, and interests therein'.[8] Companies like Halliburton and Bechtel would not be held accountable for environmental damage, employment practices, negligence, industrial accidents, pollution, or human rights abuses, etc.

One of the CPA's more effective means of embedding its economic and other orders into the political and institutional future of Iraq was CPA Order 96, which imposed a party slate system. This meant that these same political parties could be identified, nurtured, financed and subsequently controlled, while parties that did not fit the picture could be eliminated from ever participating. The US put almost half a billion dollars (US$458 million) towards identifying, creating, and then resourcing those parties most supportive of its agenda, and guaranteeing a favourable outcome.[9] It was through this process that the US ensured Iraqi politics would be determined on ethnic (Arab vs Kurd) and religious (Sunni vs Shia) lines. The ultimate guarantee was the presence of 150,000 Coalition troops.

The months leading up to and just after the handover saw the most brutal of all American military actions in Iraq. In April 2004, the Coalition attacked the resistance centres of Najaf, Fallujah and Baghdad's Sadr City. Fallujah's largely Sunni population had been particularly resistant to the occupation after US troops opened fire on a peaceful demonstration in April 2003, killing 17 people. The protest was against the military seizing a school to use as their base; three more people were killed by US troops at a protest two days later condemning the first killings. The late March 2004 assault on Fallujah escalated when the charred and mutilated bodies of four Blackwater private security guards were hung over the Euphrates River.[10]

Independent western journalists Dahr Jamail and Jo Wilding, along with journalists from Arab news service Al Jazeera, reported from Fallujah that American snipers were shooting dead anything that moved, including women and children, and were also denying ambulances access to the city. Iraqis responded with outrage, and huge food and medical aid convoys were soon making their way to the city from all over Iraq.[11] Despite the US military's overwhelming firepower, the attacks on Najaf and Fallujah ended in eventual truces.

While there were few if any reports of American snipers intentionally killing women and children in Fallujah in the American corporate media, the horrors of what the US was doing to large numbers of Iraqis at the Abu Ghraib prison was too big a story not to run, and it exploded in April 2004. Most victims were undoubtedly innocent; two months earlier, the Red Cross reported that American intelligence officers had admitted that between 70 and 90 per cent of all Iraqis detained were guilty of nothing more than being in the wrong place at the wrong time.[12]

When the US and Coalition forces returned to attack Fallujah a few months later in November 2004, it would be one of the most brutal in modern military history, and one which Noam Chomsky described as 'far more severe than the [Abu Ghraib] torture scandals'.[13] This second assault, codenamed Operation Phantom Fury, like the first, was to clear out suspected Sunni insurgents who were allegedly using the city as a base for attacks on coalition troops. Citizens were instructed to evacuate the city, population 250,000, before the attack began, but men aged 15–45 were prohibited from leaving.[14] Many family members chose to stay with their fathers and brothers. Once the bombing began in October 2004, all exits out of the city were sealed off. An estimated minimum 30,000–50,000 civilians were then trapped in Fallujah when the Coalition assault began.[15]

Planned and directed by Australian Major General Jim Molan, the list of war crime allegations committed by US and Coalition forces on the civilian population at Fallujah is staggering. Cutting off water and electricity, occupying the hospital and denying medical care, shooting families trying to surrender under a white flag, unleashing bunker-busting bombs and the confirmed horrific use of white phosphorous as a chemical weapon are a short summary of what the US unleashed on Fallujah.[16] As examined in Chapter 28, the attack on Fallujah has left a toxic legacy of rampant cancer and birth defects.

Rumsfeld made clear the intent of the January 2005 Iraqi elections, which would then determine the new national constitution: the US would 'consistently steer the process in ways that achieve stated US objectives. The Coalition will not let a thousand flowers bloom.'[17]

Predictably, the January 2005 national elections overseen by the US occupation saw Shia and Kurdish-dominated parties win the vast majority of seats. Equally predictably, most Sunnis and their parties boycotted the election in protest at the utter destruction of Fallujah and the increased targeting of Sunnis in general. The American military's house-to-house sweeps were focused primarily in Sunni areas, and three-quarters of all US detainees in 2005 were Sunnis, even though they comprised only about 20 per cent of the total population.[18]

With a very tight timeline from the January 2005 election to the US imposed deadline of August 15 to draft a constitution, there was little time for broader civil society consultation, or draft reviews. The process of drafting the constitution was controlled by the US and a few chosen leaders of the political parties that had won in the January electoral process orchestrated by the Coalition. The chief US negotiator was Ambassador Zalmay Khalizad, a signatory to the Project for the New American Century's 1998 letter calling for regime change. The end result was a highly flawed and very rushed document, with the content of earlier drafts emphasising social justice and sharing of wealth removed. Sunni representatives were invited to the draft meetings only at the last stages and were presented with it as a finished document. Nearly all Sunni leaders then refused to support the constitutional referendum, which took place on 15 October, and which saw overwhelming approval from Kurds and Shias, and outright rejection by Sunnis.[19]

The constitution deferred a number of crucial issues, such as the role of an upper legislative house and a Supreme Court, for future parliaments to decide. A UN advisory commission said that the constitution 'does not include all the powers that are necessary for a stable functioning of the State'.[20] The 'stable functioning of the State' would therefore continue to be provided by the US and 150,000 occupation troops.

This constitutional process institutionalised what would soon become the sectarian divisions and horrific violence that has so defined the post-invasion reality of the Iraqi state. Ethnic and religious identity would now dominate Iraq. Iraqi Federation of Oil Unions head Hassan Juma'a said, 'The first time Iraqis heard of ethnic divisions was when Iraq got invaded. We do not deal according to religion or ethnicity. I am 53 years old and never heard of these divisions before. If the US did not whip up divisions, they could not divide and rule.'[21]

In September 2004, Khalizad's predecessor as ambassador, John Negroponte, personally appointed Colonel James Steele to develop the Special Police Commandos (SPC), a 5,000-member counter-terrorism force. Their membership came from elite units of Saddam's Republican Guards and the hated *mukhabarat*, the secret police.[22]

The training of death squads was, alas, hardly a new policy for US intervention. Steele had previously led the US Military Advisory Group in El Salvador in the mid-1980s, where he had been responsible for training the infamous government death squads which terrorised and brutalised the mass civil-society resistance to the US-supported neoliberal government. Similar death-squad tactics were employed by the US-trained and supported Nicaraguan Contras, who favoured torture and targeting of schools and hospitals as part of a campaign of sheer terror aimed at eradicating civil-society support for the progressive gains of the Sandinista government. These covert operations were run out of Honduras, whose US ambassador at the time was none other than John Negroponte.[23] Similar US tactics were deployed with Operation Phoenix in Vietnam, and as part of the wave of terror deployed against any and all resistance to the neoliberal juntas in Chile and Argentina and throughout South America.

The SPC units were under the direct control of the Shia-dominated Ministry of the Interior, in whose basement secret SPC detainee prisons were uncovered in November and December 2005. A large number of detainees had been subjected to severe torture, with their fingernails ripped out, electric shocks to genitals, and savage beatings resulting in broken bones. Apparently, the SCP units were trained by the same US officials responsible for the widespread torture horrors of Abu Ghraib. Of the 1,100 bodies received in July 2005 at the Baghdad morgue, nearly three-quarters had been tortured or summarily executed.[24]

With political power now vested in ethnic and religious identity, the US assisted its parties in forming their own militias. Controlling territory now meant controlling those people who would vote and keep you in power. Baghdad became utterly Balkanised, with Sunni-majority neighbourhoods driving out Shias, and vice versa.[25] The violence escalated after the February 2006 bombing of the al-Askari shrine in Samarra; by the end of the year, civilian deaths would double to 3,000 a month and the country seemed to be on the verge of all-out sectarian civil war.[26]

Just before the Abu Ghraib mass torture story broke in April 2004, security expert John Pike told Britain's *Daily Telegraph*:

> The creation of a well-functioning local secret police, that in effect is a branch of the CIA, is part of the general handover strategy ...

The presence of a powerful secret police, loyal to the Americans, will mean that the new Iraqi political regime will not stray outside the parameters that the US wants to set.[27]

THE INTERNATIONAL MONETARY FUND: HEDGING ITS BETS

The CPA also ensured that Iraq's economy and political decisions would be directly accountable to the World Bank and International Monetary Fund. Within six months of the handover, the unelected CPA-appointed transition government headed by Allawi negotiated the elimination of 80 per cent of US$40 billion of the total US$120 billion Iraqi debt accrued under Saddam Hussein. The debt was primarily owed to Russia, Germany and France – countries that opposed the US-led invasion. The deal came with conditions, however. While the first 30 per cent was cancelled immediately, cancellation of the next 30 per cent was tied to an IMF neoliberal structural adjustment programme, and the final 20 per cent would be granted only after the IMF certified the success of Iraq's adherence to the IMF conditions.[28]

In December 2005, it became clear what type of conditions the IMF would impose on Iraq. In exchange for a US$685 million loan at that time, the IMF insisted that Iraq remove government subsidies on the price of domestic oil and further open the economy to private investment. Petrol and diesel – crucial for running the generators that provided individual sources of electricity – plus cooking fuel, kerosene, and public transportation costs all increased five-fold as a result, and protests ensued nationwide. Iraq's oil minister, Ibrahim Bahr al-Uloum, resigned in protest.[29]

As well as slashing fuel subsidies, another IMF condition was that Iraq pass a new oil law, setting out the legal and legislative framework for 'private investment in the sector'. Similar conditions were attached to the UN-negotiated March 2007 International Compact to provide further debt relief. In return for the Iraqi government's commitment to meet a long series of benchmarks, countries involved would alleviate an additional $38 billion in debt relief and aid, and the World Bank offered to loan Iraq an additional $2.5 billion. The key benchmark? Passage of the new oil law.[30] Thousands of public-sector employees marched in Baghdad on 19 October 2008 when the Finance Ministry announced salary and pension cutbacks as demanded by the IMF conditions.[31]

In dealing with a new Iraq, liberated from the oppression of Saddam Hussein, Iraqis would be subjected to the exact same neoliberal free market treatment the US and the First World has forced on the rest of the planet. Whether the occupation and troops remain doesn't matter in the long run; what matters is putting in place the mechanisms to ensure Iraq becomes and remains a neoliberal American-dependent client state.

21
Iraqi Oil: A New and Improved Saudi Arabia for the Twenty-first Century

Iraq's state-owned nationalised oil industry was excluded from the CPA's mass privatisation plans. The CPA's Oil Ministry's chief 'adviser' was Philip Carroll, former chief executive of Shell and Fluor. Carroll left the Iraq position in September 2003 and was replaced by Robert McKee III, an ex-ConocoPhillips executive with close ties to Halliburton.[1]

While the CPA felt it could pursue the pre-meditated sell-off of Iraq's economy, it was much more careful regarding the hugely politically sensitive issue of Iraq's oil. The Coalition knew that any attempts to privatise Iraq's nationalised oil industry would give even further impetus to the insurgency, and also be viewed by much of the world as an obvious attempt to seize Iraq's oil. Bush himself, as well as all the members of his administration, repeatedly stated that Iraq's oil belongs to the Iraqi people. British Prime Minister Tony Blair and Australian Prime Minister John Howard echoed this also.

But given the crucial importance of control of Iraq's oil to the neoliberal project, it is inconceivable that the US and its allies would relinquish that control. Through the invasion, occupation, the establishment of 14 'enduring' military bases, by creating dependency on the World Bank, IMF and WTO, and by embedding the Bremer laws into the constitutional process, the US was establishing what it believed would be long-term structural control over Iraq, and thus long-term *de facto* control over Iraq's oil.

The solution was production sharing agreements (PSAs), where the oil is still owned by the state, but foreign oil companies have access to production and refining. PSAs would last for 30–40 years, and would not be able to be renegotiated by any future government.[2] Shortly after the 28 June 2004 handover of sovereignty, the non-elected, CPA-appointed, former CIA agent head of Iraq's transitional government, Iyad Allawi, began negotiating the concept and terms of the PSAs.[3]

PSA terms are vastly favourable to multinational companies, in this case, oil companies. Proposals at the time were to allocate approximately 64 per cent of Iraq's oil reserves to PSAs, as outlined in a November 2005 report by the London NGO, Platform.[4] The report estimated that Iraq would stand to lose between US$74 billion to US$194 billion compared to leaving oil development in public hands, based on a very conservative US$40 a barrel. According to Platform, profits for the foreign oil companies would be guaranteed a 42 to 162 per cent rate of return.

THE OIL LAW

The key for the US was to gain control of Iraq's oil, while avoiding the controversial issue of actual privatisation. Once Iraq had a constitution and elections had been held, the focus was then on getting the Iraqis to do it themselves. In February 2007, the Iraqi Parliament began debating the passage of a new comprehensive oil law. The legislation was drafted in secret, and was not released publicly until March. It enabled a radical restructuring of the Iraqi oil industry and was the ultimate wish list for western oil companies. Its passage would mean American control of Iraqi oil for the indefinite future. Its ultimate defeat, despite the considerable efforts of the Bush administration, the US Congress, the military occupation, and the most powerful corporations in the world, is an inspiring story of David vs Goliath dimensions.

While not specified, the legislation[5] essentially allowed for the same type of contracts as the production-sharing agreements. The law would have allowed multinational companies the exclusive right to develop Iraq's 50 non-producing oil fields, both discovered and undiscovered, for contract periods of 30 years. The existing 27 producing fields would have remained under Iraqi national production, but as they became exhausted, the new fields under foreign control would take an ever-increasing share of production.

Contract terms included stabilisation clauses, which stipulate that no changes can be made to the terms over the life of the contract. If oil prices shot up to $300 a barrel, Iraq would be stuck with the same conditions as when the contracts were signed. And if an Iraqi Parliament in a few years' time wanted to pass a carbon tax, and take a percentage of oil companies' revenue to pay for renewable energy, the government would have to pay any and all compliance costs. There was also no requirement to hire Iraqi workers or services.

The legislation also included the crucial American neoliberal obsession with the investor–state resolution process, with foreign oil companies able to directly sue the Iraqi government if they felt their rights to full profits were being impeded in any way. The disputes would be settled by third-party arbitration tribunals who would be exclusively limited to only considering the commercial aspects. Iraqi courts would have no say, and if the Iraqi government chose to disregard the outcome, it would have to pay restitution. Crucial to Iraq's very fledgling democracy, the legislation would have allowed contracts to be signed without the Council of Representatives' (the Iraqi Parliament's) approval. The Ministry of Oil and regional government heads alone could approve them.

The law would have replaced the 1961 Law No. 80, in which Iraqis stood up to the exploitative terms of the Iraq Petroleum Company (IPC) and its US/British/French ownership as a result of the 1958 Revolution. It granted the rights to Iraq's considerable undeveloped fields to the newly formed and publicly owned Iraq National Oil Company, and allowed the existing fields to continue to be run by the IPC. The IPC and foreign control of its oil ended with the full nationalisation of the oil industry in 1972.

The draft of the legislation was initially kept secret from the Iraqi people, but it was not kept secret from US President George Bush. In December 2006, before it had even been presented to the Iraqi Parliament, known as the Council of Representatives, Bush publicly called on the Council of Representatives to pass the legislation.[6] Shortly thereafter, he requested an additional 21,000 troops for Iraq as part of the new 'surge' strategy.

Bush had seen the oil law draft because his administration helped write it. UK activist and oil analyst Greg Muttitt's excellent book, *Fuel on the Fire*, details the oil legislation and the Iraqi civil-society struggle to defeat it. Thanks to Muttitt's research, we now know that nine American and British oil companies, and numerous US, UK, and IMF officials, all gave input from the time the first draft was completed in July and long before the Council of Representatives, let alone the public or any civil-society groups, had access to it.[7]

CIVIL-SOCIETY RESISTANCE: THE DEFEAT OF THE US OIL LAW

Muttitt was able to obtain a copy of the legislation, and copies were quickly made available to Iraqi union leaders. When they read the bill, they were outraged, and quickly built a campaign to prevent the Council of Representatives from ever passing it. Iraq's five trade union federations, representing hundreds of thousands of workers across a range of industries, released a statement in December 2006 rejecting the 'handing of control over oil to foreign companies, whose aim is to make big profits at the expense of the Iraqi people, and to rob the national wealth, through long term, unfair contracts, that undermine the sovereignty of the state and the dignity of the Iraqi people'.[8]

The CPA's economic laws, mass privatisation plans, and the pseudo-privatisation of Iraq's oil have all met widespread opposition in Iraq, and civil-society resistance to these plans explains at least in part why they have all been put on hold. While the western media focuses on suicide bombers and other more militant opposition to the occupation, resistance to the US is diverse and multi-faceted.

One of the most effective organisations has been the Iraqi Federation of Oil Unions (IFOU) General Union of Oil Employees, representing over 23,000 Iraqi oil and gas industry workers. These workers had kept Iraq's oil flowing despite the sanctions and years of war. IFOU head Hassan Juma'a Awad was clear about the intention of the oil law: 'Iraq's resources and treasure [would be] stolen in front of the Iraqis' eyes. For decades, Iraqis [would] remain unable to respond to anything because the right of the investor is guaranteed.'[9] In another interview, he said that 'If those calling for production sharing agreements insist on acting against the will of Iraqis, we say to them that history will not forgive those who play recklessly with our people's wealth and destiny, and that the curse of heaven and the fury of Iraqis will not leave them.'[10]

The IFOU (then known as the Southern Oil Company Union) achieved an early and important win against the occupation, when it threatened a national strike against the CPA's wage law. That law set public-sector workers – which in Iraq's state-owned economy was more or less the entire country – at US$35 a month, whereas foreign workers were earning up to $1,000 a day. In January 2004, their three-month struggle succeeded in forcing the CPA to nearly double oil-sector wages. This was particularly impressive, given that the CPA had retained the Saddam-era law banning trade unions.[11] The union had also successfully protested at the Basra Refinery in June 2003 in order to get paid at all.[12] Another strike two months later forced Halliburton's Kellogg Brown and Root to use local Iraqi workers rather than imported labour from South Asia.[13]

Stopping the legislation from being passed was no easy matter, as the Council of Representatives had a party majority clearly beholden to the US and was working largely, but not exclusively, on the Bush administration's behalf. The sectarian violence was at its peak, and the US had just launched its surge of an additional 21,000 troops in part to re-establish some stability, particularly in Baghdad. It was also to give the government of Prime Minister Nuri al-Maliki enough stability to actually govern and be able to pass the oil law.

The pressure was not subtle. On 10 January 2007, Bush said in a nationally televised address that 'I've made it clear to the Prime Minister and Iraq's other leaders that America's commitment is not open ended. If the Iraqi government does not follow through on its promises, it will lose the support of the American people.'[14] The Associated Press reported in March that Bush had warned Maliki that continued support for his government was conditional on passage of the oil legislation.[15] That same month, the US Congress included satisfactory progress on the passage of the oil legislation as one of its key benchmarks for ensuring continued American aid and reconstruction funds for the Iraqi government.[16] This was no idle threat. Regardless of what one thought about the occupation, the reality is that the Iraqi government was utterly dependent on American aid and support for its day-to-day functioning.

Meanwhile, western corporate media did its part, regurgitating Bush administration and congressional rhetoric that the oil legislation was a revenue-sharing law that would ensure all Iraqis a just and equitable share of the nation's oil wealth. The slowness in passing it was due to internal squabbling between regional governments, particularly Kurdistan, and the national government over how large a slice of pie each were going to receive.

The reality was that the legislation was stalled because the Iraqi Federation of Oil Unions was succeeding in making it a major national issue within Iraq. In June 2007, with the legislation now a national issue, the IFOU escalated their strike against the oil law and partially shut off the flow of fuel at the Basra Refinery. Their primary demand was to be able to open the legislation up to debate and civil-society input, including their own. They also sought general improvements for workers and to be paid outstanding bonuses dating back two years.

As highlighted in Muttitt's *Fuel on the Fire*, Iraqi troops arrived under General Ali Hamadi, and after a tense stand-off, Hamadi agreed to meet with union leadership to try and resolve the strike. What happened next is, frankly, amazing: Hamadi was so convinced of the justice of the union's case that he said he would personally try to convince Maliki to ensure that the union and other civil-society opposition would be able to give input to the legislation. If he failed, he would resign from the army and join the strike. In return, the union suspended the strike for a week. Maliki agreed to the conditions, and on 11 June the IFOU declared victory.[17]

On 4 July, the Association of Muslim Scholars issued a *fatwa* stating that any Council of Representatives member who voted for the oil law 'will be damned with the wrath of God and must bear the consequences of the crime of collaborating with the enemy in stealing common wealth'. The *fatwa* was then a sermon topic for the AMS's 2,000 imams all over Iraq.[18] By this time, the injustice and American strong-armed tactics associated with the oil law had drawn considerable international attention. In July, six Nobel Peace Prize winners condemned the inclusion of the oil law as a US benchmark for the continuation of aid, as well as the oil law itself.[19]

By August, it was clear that the US was not going to be able to get enough votes in the Council of Representatives to meet its imposed deadline of September. In the midst of devastation and chaos, Iraqi civil society had succeeded in stopping what the full might of the US and its military occupation so desperately wanted: full neoliberal corporate control of Iraqi oil, under the cloak and legitimacy of a democratically elected Iraqi government. That the government had been established via a process that the US thought would enable it to always have control makes the victory only that much more remarkable.

IRAQ: SAUDI ARABIA FOR THE TWENTY-FIRST CENTURY

With no new national oil law and none in the foreseeable future, the Kurdistan Regional Government signed a number of PSAs in October and November 2007, infuriating the central government, which claimed it had exclusive authority.[20] As examined in Chapter 10, since that time the Iraqi Ministry of Oil has now signed contracts with foreign oil companies covering the next 20 years. The contracts are worth 60 billion barrels, by far the largest offering ever in the history of international oil deals, and cover over 60 per cent of Iraq's oil.[21] If realised, Iraq could be pumping an astounding 12 million barrels a day by 2017, and be in a position to completely eliminate OPEC as the world oil price fixer, or be able to manipulate and control OPEC from within, similar to what Saudi Arabia has done on behalf of the US. The implications for the continuation of the American empire are clear: as long as oil is priced in dollars, and as long as the US has *de facto* control over Iraq, this means a consolidation in American ability to maintain its dominance over the global economy.

As Muttitt's research highlights, the contracts actually encourage such a scenario. For example, if Iraq had to cut oil production as per a future OPEC quota requirement, the Iraqi government will have to pay full compensation for any lost production. In other words, companies are guaranteed profits regardless of whether they are actually producing oil or not, so the incentive for the government is to keep pumping. While not as generous as the terms stipulated in the failed oil legislation, these and other conditions make these contracts among the most profitable in the world.[22]

The original negotiating terms were that the contracts would be joint ventures, with existing Iraqi oil companies having a guaranteed majority stake of 51 per cent. By the time the first round of bidding occurred, this had been reduced to 25 per cent. Conditions requiring Iraqi labour are vague. And while it was somewhat surprising that many of the bids were won by state-owned oil companies like China's National Petroleum Corporation, BP, Shell and ExxonMobil also were winners. They would be returning for the first time since being banished when Iraq nationalised its oil in 1972 and rid itself of the exploitative Iraqi Petroleum Company (IPC). Analysts believe the returns on the contracts will be 20 per cent or more.[23]

As highlighted throughout this book, that the outcome would allow Iraq to possibly outrival Saudi Arabia should not have come as a surprise to anyone, and would have undoubtedly been the same outcome if the oil legislation had passed. Already on 27 February 2004, Fadhil Chalabi, former Iraqi oil minister under the Baathists and then adviser to the US government, said that Iraq was looking to withdraw from OPEC, citing the excuse that it would need to release more oil than was allowed under the OPEC quota to pay for reconstruction costs.[24]

In the absence of a new oil law, Oil Minister Hussain al-Shahristani, with Maliki's strong support, went ahead and negotiated the contracts under the executive branch authority. They are illegal, as the existing Iraqi 1961 Law No. 80 requires Council of Representatives' approval for any and all new oil production contracts. But since the US failed in its efforts to have its takeover of Iraqi oil legitimately passed by the Council of Representatives, it simply accomplished more or less the same thing via its tighter control of the executive branch, which includes Prime Minister Nuri al-Maliki, who had already been threatened with removal from office by Bush over the non-passage of the oil legislation. Perhaps in return for his support in the massive and illegal sell-off of Iraq's oil reserves, Bush allowed Maliki a show of strength in standing up to the US in negotiating the exit of all US combat troops by the end of 2011 as per the Status of Forces Agreement (SOFA).

Part VI

Expanding the Empire: A Neoliberal Free Trade Area for the Middle East

22
The US Middle East Free Trade Area

For many conservatives, Iraq is now the test case for whether the US can engender American-style free-market capitalism with the Arab world.

Neil King, Wall Street Journal, 1 May 2003[1]

In the end, what both the United States and Europe have missed is that many components of FTAs serve the interests of elites closely associated with unpopular Arab governments.

Riad al Khouri, Carnegie Institute, 2008[2]

On 9 May 2003, Bush announced that the United States was forming the US Middle East Free Trade Area (MEFTA). The countries included in the US MEFTA are Algeria, Bahrain, Cyprus, Egypt, the Gaza Strip/West Bank (Palestine), Iraq, Israel, Jordan, Lebanon, Libya, Morocco, Oman, Qatar, Saudi Arabia, Syria, Tunisia, the United Arab Emirates and Yemen.

In announcing the US MEFTA, Bush said:

Across the globe, free markets and trade have helped defeat poverty, and taught men and women the habits of liberty. So I propose the establishment of a U.S.-Middle East Free Trade Area within a decade, to bring the Middle East into an expanding circle of opportunity, to provide hope for the people who live in that region.[3]

He went on to say that 'The Middle East presents many obstacles to the advance of freedom ... Freedom in the Middle East', Bush argued, 'is in our national interest,' and that 'Progress will require increased trade, the engine of economic development.' By freedom, Bush meant the freedom of corporate individuals to eliminate obstacles to further capital penetration to the largely closed markets of the Middle East.

He certainly wasn't talking about human freedom and concern for democratic and human rights, as the US directly propped up the authoritarian regimes that dominated the Middle East and North Africa. The US also directly supported Israel and its suppression of

Arab Palestinians in Gaza. In early 2011, mass protests engulfed the region, leading to the collapse of the US-backed Tunisian and Egyptian dictatorships. Uprisings calling for a change of government occurred in Bahrain, Syria and Yemen, and major protests also swept through Algeria, Jordan, Morocco, Oman and Saudi Arabia, as well as Iraq. Nearly all were met with violent repression on the part of the authorities, with many arrests and deaths. An uprising in Libya quickly escalated into armed conflict.

While reasons for the protests were varied, nearly all called for democratic reforms, as well as direct improvement in living conditions to address the mass poverty, lack of rights and access to education, health care and employment that defined a region where authoritarian elites consolidated their wealth and controlled their people through repression. As highlighted earlier with Saudi Arabia, the tremendous petrodollar wealth generated by the oil-producing countries was recycled back into the United States rather than development and opportunities for their own people. The Arab world in general has the highest rate of unemployment and the widest spread in income distribution on earth.[4]

There was, of course, another commonality to the uprisings: nearly all of the countries where protests occurred were American client states. Egypt, along with Saudi Arabia, was a crucial US anchor. Tunisia, Algeria and Yemen were all in the US orbit. As were Jordan, Oman, Bahrain and Morocco, all of whom have signed Free Trade Agreements with the US. The two exceptions were Libya and Syria. What began as an uprising in Libya quickly spread to outright civil war, with the US and NATO providing air cover and military support for forces rebelling against long-term US nemesis Muammar al-Qaddafi. Libya also just happens to have the largest oil reserves in Africa.

In this dry tinderbox, the spark that helped ignite this mass resistance was the skyrocketing of world food prices, thanks to the US deregulation of commodity prices which allowed them to be subject to the same casino capitalism that brought on the housing bubble and subsequent global financial collapse in 2008. As we shall see, those countries which have reduced their agricultural tariffs as part of the Middle East Free Trade Area process had the least recourse to deal with the increased food costs.

In 2001, when Bush administration planning began in earnest for a Middle East-North Africa free trade area, the United States had not only had its 'freedom' impeded by being denied economic opportunities in Iraq post-sanctions, it was largely eliminated from opportunities in the Middle East in general. This was the last region of the world that had not been penetrated by the neoliberal debt-control mechanisms of the World Bank and the IMF, or market liberalisation via the WTO. The economies of the 13 oil-producing nations of the region were largely state-run, and in 2002, only two had any IMF debt.[5] While the US had succeeded in getting the rest of the world to strip public employment and services, nationalised industries, and restrictions on foreign capital, these were all distinguishing features of the Middle East oil-producing countries as of 2003.

In 2003, the IMF said that these economies were distinguished by 'lagging political and institutional reforms; large and costly public sectors ... [and] high trade restrictiveness', and that its 'regulatory burden' was much more restrictive than anywhere else in the world.[6]

The Middle East, in general, comprised a tiny percentage of US trade: less than 4 per cent of US exports, and less than 5 per cent of US imports, and perhaps more telling, only 1 per cent of US foreign direct investment.[7] There was also a noticeable dearth of western products and brand names available in the shopping districts of Oman, Saudi Arabia and other Arab countries. While Coca-Cola might be available in Beirut, Lebanon, it faced much stricter government control than most other countries in the world. The Arab oil-producing countries also had nationalised oil industries, eliminating the biggest and most lucrative investment opportunities available to the biggest and most predatory of multinational companies.

There certainly were exceptions, for example, Egypt and Jordan, that were not significant oil producers. Egypt was heavily indebted and had followed the US-prescribed and WTO, IMF and World Bank-administered neoliberal formula of privatisation, deregulation and government cutbacks to its detriment.

As we've seen, by 2002, when the propaganda began in earnest regarding the need to invade Iraq, neoliberalism as an effective policy instrument was met with large-scale protests around the world, most notably the WTO protests in Seattle in 1999. The US was meeting similar resistance to its efforts to form the Free Trade Area of the Americas (FTAA), a NAFTA-style Free Trade Agreement (FTA) for all the countries of North and South America, and which ultimately failed. It faced a great struggle to approve the much smaller Central American Free Trade Agreement.

In the face of such opposition, it changed strategies. Instead of problematic regional agreements, the US instead would focus on individual countries to sign bilateral agreements. These individual FTAs could be directly tailored to the specific country, and the US would have a major advantage in pressuring a single country to conform versus dealing with several countries at a time. It would also be an easier approach to what was clearly one of the ultimate jewels in the neoliberal crown: the investor–state provision that investors, that is, corporations, could directly sue governments if they believed their free trade investor rights to profit had been violated.

These disputes would be settled in 'neutral' third-party dispute courts, who would be bound to only consider commercial interests, essentially eliminating a country's ability to look after the welfare of its people. Instead, only the welfare of the allegedly wronged commercial interest could be taken into account. This was part of the 'WTO-plus' process for the US in signing individual FTAs, as it went beyond the WTO mechanism which allowed countries to sue other countries in neutral tribunals, as in the example where the US sued the European Union for blocking genetically modified (GMO) crops. Mass civil-society and global South opposition had defeated this 'investor–state' provision in the Multilateral Agreement on Investment (MAI) and had prevented it from being instituted in the WTO Doha Round.

Pursuing individual country FTAs was the approach the US took with the Middle East Free Trade Area. There is a four-stage process for countries to join the MEFTA. First, countries must join the World Trade Organization; the US would support WTO membership for countries that sought it. Secondly, the US would support the Generalised System of Preferences to certain products from MEFTA countries, granting them better access to the US market. Access to the world's largest market is a huge incentive for any country. Third, each country would need to sign a Trade and Investment Framework Agreement, and finally, a direct Free Trade Agreement with the US. Each of these individual FTAs would then form the broader US Middle East Free Trade Agreement by Bush's target date of 2013.[8]

The US also pursued signing Bilateral Investment Treaties (BITs) with individual countries. These treaties specifically address investor protection issues. For countries that had not signed a full FTA, a BIT was a means of getting countries to commit to full-investor NAFTA-style investor-protection provisions, including the third-party dispute settlement process. Of the countries that have not yet signed full FTAs with the US, Egypt and Tunisia have signed BITs.

Joining the WTO means an automatic reduction in tariffs, and agreement on intellectual property rights recognition and protection. Because it both sets the rules and then appoints itself as the enforcer for world trade, and because the rules are largely written by the US and other rich countries, there are few single greater tools for US neoliberal global hegemony than the WTO, and the US was eager to get remaining countries to join. When Bush proposed the MEFTA in May 2003, Algeria, Lebanon, Libya, Saudi Arabia, Syria, Yemen and Iraq were not WTO members.

Iraq was granted WTO observer status on 11 February 2004, despite being under military occupation and officially governed by a foreign power. The BearingPoint contract stipulated that Iraq begin its WTO membership process by February 2004.[9] Iraq continues to have observer status and refines its economic decisions and laws to conform to future WTO membership. The impetus to join the WTO as the first step towards entry to the MEFTA was significantly heightened by the willingness of the US to militarily invade a neighbouring nation to achieve its goals.

The United States also has a major carrot to entice countries to enter into the FTA process. The second stage after WTO membership is favoured access to the US market, by being included in the US Generalised System of Preferences (GSP). The GSP means tariff-free entry to the US market, and covers 4,650 products from 144 countries. Participating in the MEFTA means access to the GSP for at least some of a participating country's products. MEFTA participants Jordan, Morocco, Bahrain, Egypt, Lebanon, Algeria, Tunisia, Oman, Yemen, and now Iraq have GSP privileges.[10]

The next step is the signing of a Trade and Investment Framework Agreements (TIFA). In her book, *The Bush Agenda*, Antonia Juhasz summarises the intent of the TIFAs:

> The United States uses the TIFA to identify changes that it wants to see in the other country's laws. In most cases, these include privatisation of state-owned industries, new investment protections for foreign companies, the elimination of domestic content requirements and technology transfer, elimination of requirements for certain percentage of local investment by foreign companies, the elimination of tariffs and quotas, the elimination of local price support systems, opening all sectors to foreign investment, the elimination of rules requiring that foreign companies partner with local companies, and the like.[11]

The final stage of the US-MEFTA process is the signing of individual free trade agreements. These FTAs are designed as 'WTO plus'. They go beyond the WTO trade requirements in environmental and financial services, investment laws, national treatment, and intellectual property rights (IPR). While joining the WTO addresses trade with other WTO nations, individual FTAs are one-on-one with the United States. With each FTA, the US is able to increase pressure and leverage for the remaining countries to sign similar agreements, which will ultimately result in one large Middle East Free Trade Area. As of August 2011, so far Jordan, Israel, Morocco, Bahrain and Oman have signed FTAs.

The overall process is to engage these countries with the rest of the neoliberalised world in a race to the bottom, where each will try to out-compete their neighbours in lowering wages and labour rights, and opening their economies further to attract foreign investment.

THE PRIZE: CORPORATE ACCESS TO SAUDI OIL SERVICES

Focusing again on Saudi Arabia, the world's largest oil producer and long-term American ally, it had provided a key underpinning for US neoliberal hegemony for over 30 years. It worked with successive US governments to ensure OPEC price shocks did not occur, and in return it received considerable US military support and protection, particularly in 1991 when Iraq and its army of one million was massed on its border after invading Kuwait.

However, Saudi Arabia had a largely closed economy to US corporations, including access to providing services to its oil sector. The same applied to the other large oil producers included in the proposed MEFTA – Iraq, Kuwait, Iran and the United Arab Emirates. Oil and natural gas exploration for US companies, as well as repair, installation and distribution services, existed but in piecemeal and restricted fashion in the nationalised oil industries of those countries. Many MEFTA countries had high tariffs on various imports, and where US corporations are allowed to operate they were subject to many more restrictions. Tariffs on imports averaged at least 20 per cent higher than other areas of the world.[12]

Saudi Arabia and its relatively closed-off market of 28 million people had resisted efforts to join the WTO, which by definition would mean opening up its economy to foreign corporate penetration and control. For whatever reason, Saudi Arabia formally joined the

WTO in November 2005. As part of the requirements for WTO membership, Saudi Arabia was required to sign an accession agreement,[13] committing it to open its oil-services industry to foreign companies. While its oil remains nationalised and under government ownership, it must now allow foreign companies to compete for oil-service contracts. And it cannot give Saudi companies preference over foreign firms, identical to the national treatment provision in CPA Order 39. The accession agreement also committed Saudi Arabia to

> ... ensuring that state-owned or controlled enterprises or those with special or exclusive privileges will make purchases and sales of goods and services based on commercial considerations, and firms from WTO members will be allowed to compete for sales to, and purchases from, these Saudi enterprises on non-discriminatory terms.

'Non-discriminatory' means national treatment. The agreement even allows other WTO members, the United States, for example, to challenge Saudi Arabia if it suspects that it is limiting its oil exports or slowing down production for 'political' rather than 'commercial considerations'.

The agreement covered more than just oil-related services. It also included financial services, as established under the General Agreement on Trade in Services (GATS). Similar to the CPA's (Bremer's) order in Iraq, foreign banks can now establish direct, 100 per cent foreign-owned branches in Saudi Arabia. Previously, they had been limited to only a minority ownership, and it had to be with an existing Saudi bank. The agreement also included telecommunications and insurance, and a commitment for the country to 'liberalise' its 'environmental services market'. Saudi Arabia also committed to lowering its tariffs, and reducing its agricultural subsidies. 'Liberalising its environmental services market' is trade-speak meaning full or partial privatisation of water and sewage systems, among others.

The Saudis have been less enthusiastic about signing an actual Free Trade Agreement with the United States. They have been a leader in establishing the broader Gulf Cooperation Council (GCC) consisting of Bahrain, Kuwait, Oman, Qatar, Saudi Arabia and United Arab Emirates, and an individual FTA would impede efforts to negotiate more beneficial agreements for the broader region.

Saudi Arabia objected on that basis to the US-Bahrain and US-Oman FTAs. The six GCC members signed an agreement in 2001 to draw their policies and economic relations in a collective manner with non-GCC members. As the Saudis view it, this should prohibit GCC states from signing individual trade agreements.[14]

23
Case Studies: Jordan and Morocco

JORDAN

The first US Free Trade Agreement was signed in 1985 with Israel. The second in the Middle East was the US-Jordan Free Trade Agreement, which had been negotiated under Clinton and came into effect in December 2001 under Bush.

Much praised at the time for including provisions on the environment and labour, the first time ever in any free trade agreement, the US-Jordan FTA would eventually eliminate nearly all duties and other barriers to trade in goods and services. Investor rights – including the all-important investor–state international dispute mechanism – had already been covered in a Bilateral Investment Treaty signed previously.

In addition, the FTA strengthened the existing Qualifying Industrial Zones (QIZs) in Jordan, which had been established in 1996. Products manufactured in the QIZ were granted the much-coveted duty-free entry to the United States. There was a catch though: Israel. QIZs are an agreement between the US, Israel and another country, in this case Jordan. To qualify for duty-free entry to the US, at least 8 per cent of products emanating from the QIZ had to have an Israeli component.[1] The QIZ is essentially a massive bribe to force an Arab country to do business with and give direct financial support to Israel.

While the labour provisions seemed to be a substantial step forward in addressing criticisms about how free trade agreements often resulted in increased working hours while simultaneously reducing wages, job security and safety, in reality the labor provisions exacerbated an already bad situation and made it worse.

The FTA's Article 6 on Labor[2] states that 'The Parties reaffirm their obligations as members of the International Labor Organization', and that they 'strive to ensure that such labor principles and the internationally recognized labor rights … are recognized and protected by domestic law'. In terms of enforcement, it simply stated that 'A Party shall not fail to effectively enforce its labor laws.'

Article 6 identifies internationally recognised labour rights as '(a) the right of association, (b) the right to organize and bargain collectively, (c) a prohibition on the use of any form of forced or compulsory labor, (d) a minimum age for the employment of children, and (e) acceptable conditions of work with respect to minimum wages, hours of work, and occupational safety and health'.

The problem was that Jordan's labour laws were woefully inadequate. The General Federation of Jordanian Trade Unions estimates that 30 per cent of the workforce is unionised. The General Federation is the only legally allowed federation; thus 70 per cent of the population does not have the opportunity to join a union. Strikes and demonstrations can only occur with government permission, a serious negation of trade union rights. Mediation of labour disputes is conducted by the government, and is not voluntary on the part of union members. The official workweek is 48 hours, 54 in hospitality industries such as hotels and restaurants, well below its FTA partner, the US's, standards.[3]

But the real problem was that Jordan has an estimated 300,000 migrant workers, comprising approximately 20 per cent of the workforce in a country with only 7 million people. These workers are prohibited from joining or forming a union. Many are agricultural labourers from other Arab countries, in particular Egypt and Syria, as well as domestic workers from the Philippines and Sri Lanka.[4] The FTA would do little, if anything, to improve their working conditions.

In fact, the QIZ exacerbated the problem significantly. It was Chinese and other Asian apparel manufacturers, not Jordanians, who set up factories in the QIZ, thus allowing them to avoid internationally agreed individual-country manufacturing quotas. They imported their own, not Jordanian, textiles and materials, and also imported their own cheap and easily exploited near-slave labour from Bangladesh and other South Asian countries. It's now estimated that at least 66 per cent of the total employment in Jordan's QIZ factories are Asian migrant workers.[5]

A *New York Times* expose in 2006[6] reported that near slave-labour conditions and human trafficking were widespread in the QIZ. Based on a National Labor Committee (NLC) report 'US Jordan Free Trade Agreement Descends into Human Trafficking',[7] as well as its own investigating, the *Times* and the NLC found that the FTA had resulted in a major expansion in these hellish sweatshops, with the new owners having brought in an additional 25,000 foreigners to work in these factories, primarily from Pakistan and Bangladesh and other poor countries.[8]

The undercover investigations revealed that many workers had their passports confiscated when they arrived in the country. Without adequate identification, they were unable to even go out in the streets for fear of being jailed or deported. Workers were subjected to physical abuse, often were not paid, and forced to work 20-hour days. Workers were often beaten and or subjected to immediate deportation if they complained or sought help.

Most had become deeply indebted to labour brokers in their home countries. Workers from Bangladesh were quoted in the *Times* article that they had become indebted from $1,000 to $3,000 to work in Jordan. After arriving and having their passports confiscated, they found the jobs paid far less than they'd been promised, and nowhere near the country's minimum wage. 'We used to start at 8 in the morning, and we'd work until midnight, 1 or 2 am, seven days a week,' said Nargis Akhter, a 25 years old Bangladeshi. 'When we were in Bangladesh they promised us we would receive $120 a month, but in the five months I was there I only got one month's salary – and that was just $50.' Charles Kernaghan, executive director of the NLC, said, 'These are the worst conditions I've ever seen.' Target and Walmart were identified as major retailers who benefited from the low-cost clothing.

And this was a free trade agreement lauded for its labour provisions.

Thanks to the human trafficking spurred by the FTA, Jordan's apparel exports to the US soared 2,000 per cent between 2000 and 2005, reaching $1.1 billion in 2005, and over 30,000 new jobs were created.[9] GDP soared by 20 per cent in the first three years.[10] These are the types of statistics that the US government, the World Bank, the IMF, the WTO, and other proponents will cite as the tremendous benefits of neoliberal free trade, and why Jordan's Arab neighbours should all sign FTAs as soon as possible.

That few Jordanians benefited, and that the work was done essentially by human trafficking, is never reported. Nor will you find any mention on the US Trade Representative website that these 'newly created' jobs came at the direct expense of American textile workers. The great irony of Bush giving his speech launching the Middle East Free Trade Area in South Carolina in 2003 is that 57 textile plants in that state had closed and 70,000 people had lost their jobs since 2000.[11] This is not only the stark reality of neoliberal corporate globalisation; it is also its intention.

Despite Jordan's economy growing at an annual rate of 7 per cent or more for a year for the past decade, few Jordanians saw any benefits. An estimated third of the population lives in poverty, and the official unemployment rate is around 14 per cent while unofficially it is believed to be much higher. Thanks to Jordan opening up its services sector, eight of its top banks are now foreign owned, and American insurance companies dominate its insurance market.[12]

Meanwhile, there appears to be no power greater than the need for cheap labour to manufacture clothing for the remaining Americans who can afford it, and to get those increasing numbers who can't further hooked onto credit card and other forms of domestic debt.

Despite the international attention on the horrific labour abuses occurring in Jordan's export clothing factories, a June 2011 follow-up report by the National Labor Committee, now renamed the Institute for Global Labour and Human Rights, found that conditions had, if anything, deteriorated, especially for women workers. The report's title says it all: 'Sexual Predators and Serial Rapists Run Wild At Wal-Mart Supplier in Jordan'.[13] The investigation found that scores of young Sri Lankan women working in Classic, Jordan's largest export garment factory, 'suffered routine sexual abuse and repeated rapes, and in some cases even torture', and that those 'who refuse the sexual advances of Classic's managers are also beaten and deported'. US and Jordanian officials were made aware of the abuses as early as 2007 but nothing was done.

Classic's clothing is exported duty-free under the FTA for American mega-retailers Walmart, Hanes, Kohl's, Target and Macy's. The investigation found that the standard shift for the Sri Lankan, Bangladeshi, Indian and Nepalese workers was 13 hours a day, six and seven days a week, with shifts sometimes as long as 18½ hours, and that workers are 'routinely cursed at, hit and shortchanged of their 61 cent an hour wages for failing to reach their mandatory production goals'. The US Trade Representative Office website in 2011 stated that the US-Jordan FTA requires 'effective labour ... enforcement'.[14]

Thanks to the FTA's gradual phase-out of agricultural tariffs, as well as similar measures required by its membership in the WTO such as reducing its agricultural support programmes, Jordan has increased its food imports from the US and other countries. With a population of approximately 7 million, it imported $193 million worth of rice, nuts, wheat and corn from the US in 2009.[15]

On 15 January 2011, Jordanians launched the first of many protests to come, in their version of the Arab Spring. On the same day that saw Tunisian dictator and close US ally Zine El Abidine Ben Ali flee his country after weeks of unrest, thousands demonstrated throughout Jordan in a 'Day of Rage', protesting record-high food prices and high unemployment. King Abdullah II responded with a $500 million package of price cuts in fuel and staples, including sugar and rice. In response to further protests, King Abdullah even sacked his government.[16]

The Tunisian and Jordan protests would soon be joined by the Egyptian uprising and other major protests across the region, most of which had the issue of high food prices as a core issue. Food costs had hit a record high, surpassing the global crisis of 2008. Global averages for cereals, cooking oil, meat and dairy products and other foods had risen by 25 per cent from December 2009 to December 2010, according to the UN Food and Agriculture Organisation (FAO).[17] Jordan had experienced outright rioting in 1996 when the price of bread tripled after subsidies were cut in response to another IMF demand, and King Abdullah suspended Parliament when it refused to support the price hikes.[18]

MOROCCO

The US-Morocco FTA entered into force on 1 January 2006. It was the first FTA signed as part of the Bush push for the broader Middle East Free Trade Area. US Trade Representative Robert Zoellick, soon to leave to become president of the World Bank, made it clear that Morocco was just a stepping-stone on the US's route to a full Middle East (and North Africa) Free Trade Area: 'Our agreement with Morocco is not just a single announcement, but a vital step in creating a mosaic of U.S. free trade agreements across the Middle East and North Africa.'[19]

The US government's export promotion website, Export.gov, positively gushes that Morocco's immediate elimination of tariffs on nearly all US non-textile industrial exports was 'a record for an FTA signed with a developing country partner', and that US industry viewed the Agreement's intellectual property rights (IPR) chapter as 'the most advanced IPR chapter in any FTA negotiated so far' and 'a precedential agreement for future FTAs'.[20]

This, of course, is the point of each new FTA: to outstrip the provisions of the previous one.

The US-Morocco Free Trade Agreement[21] also guarantees protections and market domination for US pharmaceutical drug companies by stipulating that 'government marketing-approval agencies will not grant approval to patent-infringing pharmaceuticals.' This means Morocco cannot provide low-cost HIV and other crucial medicines unless it pays the full patented price. The right to profit trumps the right to life. It also provides protection for Monsanto and other mega-agribusiness firms specialising in genetically modified crops, singling out newly developed plant varieties and animals for protection. American farmers and ranchers, including poultry farmers, cattle producers and wheat farmers, have had increased access to Moroccan markets as tariffs were reduced by percentage points over a number of years. About half of all Moroccans are employed in agriculture.

The FTA specified that most US service providers, including banks and insurance companies, are to be treated equally with Moroccan companies. American investors will have almost unilateral rights 'to establish, acquire and operate investments in Morocco on an equal footing with Moroccan investors'. The Agreement expressly prohibits any possibility that ordinary Moroccans might actually benefit directly, such as requirements for US firms operating in Morocco to buy Moroccan rather than US inputs for goods manufactured in Morocco. Nor can the Moroccan government favour Moroccan firms over American ones when it comes to purchasing and contracts.

The environmental provisions require that each government enforce its own domestic environmental laws, but then adds that their enforcement should be 'married with provisions that promote voluntary, market-based mechanisms to protect the environment'. This is almost laughable, as one of the attractions of setting up FTAs with poor countries is to take advantage of the fact that their environmental laws are much weaker than those in the US. This was a major issue with NAFTA and the *maquiladoras* that sprang up in Mexico along the US border, with pollution and toxic waste issues.

Bowing to pressure from globalisation critics, the third-party dispute settlement allows public submissions and that the hearings are to be open to the public. Considering they would be held in a neutral third country, just exactly what public would be able to attend was not clarified.

Nor is it clear how such a lopsided agreement could possibly help contribute to greater freedom, democracy and economic opportunity, which were the much ballyhooed points of Bush's original announcement to establish a Free Trade Area for the region. The Morocco FTA has done nothing to further democracy in Morocco, a country whose King Mohammed VI enjoys virtual absolute rule, including being Morocco's supreme religious authority. Nor has it brought economic opportunity for average Moroccans – nor for average Americans, for that matter. Five years after its launch, half of all Moroccans are illiterate, a figure virtually unchanged over the past ten years. Morocco ranks 130 in the most recent United Nations Human Development Index, which is based on a composite score of health, literacy and overall standard of living.[22] One measure that has notably increased appears to be corruption, with 70 per cent of Moroccans now stating that it had become a major issue.[23] Corruption and neoliberalism go hand-in-hand, as witnessed by the CPA's tenure in Iraq.

What is clear is that Morocco's embracing of neoliberalism has exacerbated these problems. A Carnegie Institute report[24] found that 'the move to embrace a free trade economy has brought a sharp increase in the price of basic goods throughout Morocco. Prices of basic foods have gone up continuously since 2005, with, for example, sugar and meat rising about 30 percent in 2006–2007', and that Morocco's FTA with the US has required 'it to deregulate prices, which means increasing them to the same level as international ones'. This in turn directly contributed to the fact that 'more than 6 million Moroccans live under the poverty line out of a total population of 32 million.' Yet according to the US Trade Representative Office, the FTA has been a roaring success for both countries, highlighted by the increase in two-way trade to $2 billion in 2009.[25]

Generally considered to be one of the most stable of all Arab nations, Morocco exploded on 20 February 2011, with tens of thousands protesting throughout the country demanding democratic reforms. They were not the first; large-scale protests had occurred in September 2007, with protesters, angered by rising prices, set government buildings on fire.[26]

Similar to Jordan, the protests did not go so far as to demand the king abdicate the throne. The focus has been on real and meaningful constitutional reform, driven in part by the same increase in food prices that ignited other protests throughout the region. The government responded by nearly doubling its food subsidies for 2011.[27]

24
Case Studies: Oman and Bahrain

OMAN

The US-Oman FTA was signed into law in September 2006, but did not become active until January 2009. It eliminated all tariffs on industrial and consumer products, and nearly all agricultural tariffs. US Trade Representative Susan Schwab summarised that

> On the first day this agreement goes into effect, 100 percent of consumer and industrial products will flow without tariffs. In addition, Oman will offer substantial market access across its entire services regime, provide a secure, predictable legal framework for US investors operating in Oman, ensure effective enforcement of labour and environmental laws, and protect intellectual property.[1]

For Schwab to state that Oman will ensure effective enforcement of labour laws is particularly interesting, since forming or joining an independent labour union in Oman is illegal.[2] As Oman's only obligation under the FTA is to adhere to its own labour laws, even by neoliberal globalisation standard, the Oman FTA set an exceptionally low bar.

Compared to Oman, Jordan's foreign guest-worker issue is minuscule. An incredible 80 per cent of Oman's workforce – some 600,000 of Oman's 3 million people – are guest workers from China, Bangladesh and other poor countries.[3] And according to the US State Department in 2006, Oman 'does not fully comply with the minimum standards for the elimination of [human] trafficking'.[4] And like Jordan, many of these guest workers were promised good paying jobs in Oman in return for placing themselves in deep debt to labour brokers. Upon arriving, their passports were taken and they became virtual slaves with the same abuses found in Jordan's Qualifying Industrial Zone factories.

Much to its credit, in May 2006, the US Senate Finance Committee approved an amendment to the then-pending US-Oman FTA that would 'prohibit goods made with slave labor, forced labor or labor from human trafficking from receiving preferential duty-free access'. The Bush administration stripped the amendment out of the text before sending it back to Congress, which eventually approved it.[5]

While workers have no recourse under the FTA for abuses that occur in factories set up to benefit from the FTA's beneficial access to the US market, investors have a great deal. Like the Morocco FTA and as covered in the Jordan Bilateral Investment Treaty, it contains the NAFTA investor–state provisions. If an American multinational company believes that the Omani government – whose economy, as Public Citizen pointed out at the time, was about the same size as Worcester, Massachusetts – is impeding their right to make a profit because of an affirmative law protecting the environment, public health, or labour right (highly unlikely), it can sue before an international third-party panel. Oman is prohibited from prioritising local firms or products over US ones. Monopoly and patent rights for US pharmaceutical firms are also guaranteed protection.[6]

Long considered to be politically stable and loyal to the ruling Sultan Qaboos Bin Saeed, who has been in power for 40 years, Omanis protested in never-before-seen numbers in their part of the Arab Spring. Relatively smaller in numbers than many of their neighbours, the protests mainly called for an end to corruption amongst Omani government officials, and a more effective distribution of Oman's considerable oil wealth. Qaboos Bin Saeed responded almost immediately by promising to create 50,000 jobs, although considering 10,000 of these would be for law enforcement, it was a mixed benefit. He also promised to raise minimum wages, and establish unemployment benefits and a consumer protection authority.[7]

BAHRAIN

Lying just off the east coast of Saudi Arabia, the tiny island nation of Bahrain, population 1.2 million, signed a Free Trade Agreement with the US that went into effect 11 January 2006. Bahrain is less than 60 kilometres long and only 17 kilometres wide. As much as half the population are foreign guest workers.[8] Bahrain is one of the staunchest of America's Arab allies, and serves as the headquarters of the US Navy's Fifth Fleet. It has also become a primary financial services hub in the Middle East. The Sunni minority royal family's response to the Shiite majority population's mass protests has been arguably the most brutal of all the Arab Spring uprisings.

The FTA immediately eliminated tariffs on 98 per cent of US agricultural products, and 100 per cent of bilateral trade in consumer and industrial products became duty free. According to the US Trade Representative Office:

> Bahrain opened its services market wider than any previous FTA partner, creating important new opportunities for US financial service providers and companies that offer telecommunications, audiovisual, express delivery, distribution, healthcare, architecture, and engineering services.[9]

These opportunities include the right to establish subsidiaries, joint ventures, or branches for banks and insurance companies. And like other FTA's, these companies must receive the same treatment as Bahraini firms, and the Bahraini government cannot 'discriminate' against US firms in purchasing in excess of certain monetary thresholds. Petty cash expenditure apparently is okay.

Speaking again for US industry as a whole, Export.gov states that 'U.S. industry supports the IPR provisions of the Agreement noting that it maintains many of the key characteristics of the IPR chapter of the U.S.-Morocco FTA, which the U.S. industry considers a benchmark for all FTAs.'[10]

Opportunities for Bahrain to utilise its foreign guest workers as potential slave labour are also available. Textiles and apparels became immediately duty free. The FTA does address what the US obviously believed to be a flaw in the Jordan FTA, which was that materials came from China and other countries, rather than originating from Jordan. It specifies that qualifying textiles and apparel had to contain either US or Bahraini yarn and fabric, with a transition time built in to allow this to be adhered to.[11]

The FTA's Chapter 15 on Labor says that 'each Party shall strive to ensure that its laws provide for labor standards consistent with the internationally recognized labor rights', and 'shall strive to improve those standards'. Both parties agreed to 'establish priorities and develop specific cooperative activities' to address the worst labour abuses, such as child labour. The strongest provision is for each government to provide access for workers and employers to 'fair, equitable and transparent labor tribunals or courts'.[12] This sounds fine, but considering that foreign guest workers have no rights at all, and ordinary Bahrainis have few at best, access to these labour tribunals or courts is highly questionable.

The June 2011 US State Department Trafficking in Persons Report summarises the current situation for Bahrain's' foreign 'guest' workers:

> Bahrain is a destination country for men and women subjected to forced labor and sex trafficking. Men and women from India, Pakistan, Nepal, Sri Lanka, Bangladesh, Indonesia, Thailand, the Philippines, Ethiopia, and Eritrea migrate voluntarily to Bahrain to work as domestic workers or as unskilled labourers in the construction and service industries. Some, however, face conditions of forced labor after arriving in Bahrain, through use of such practices as unlawful withholding of passports, restrictions on movement, contract substitution, nonpayment of wages, threats, and physical or sexual abuse.[13]

Bahrain had been hailed a leader in labour rights reform when it abolished its requirement that all guest workers have official sponsors, the first Gulf state to do so. This sponsorship requirement, known as *kafala*, was viewed as the root cause of much of the Gulf state's exploitation of workers, as it meant workers were utterly indebted to their sponsors. The new law gave migrants the fundamental right to leave their jobs and seek other employment without the employer's consent. In June 2011, *kafala* was reinstated by King Hamad Al Khalifa, meaning migrant workers were forbidden from leaving their employer within the first year of employment.[14] As is the case in Jordan and the State Department report, it means many workers can't leave, period.

As with Morocco, the Bahrain FTA dispute settlement process is presented as open and transparent, with opportunities for public submissions, but with zero ability to actually effect the outcome.

REPRESSION IN BAHRAIN

Of all the protests and uprisings that have comprised the Arab Spring, Bahrain's has been amongst the most impressive, both for the sheer size of those involved, and also for their courage and commitment in the face of what has been arguably the most repressive and violent of state responses.

Bahrain's long-dominant Al Khalifa royal family is Sunni. The majority of indigenous Bahrainis are Shia, approximately 70 per cent of the population. As well as having made itself into a regional financial hub, Bahrain also has oil and natural gas, and its national revenues have tripled over the last seven years thanks to high oil prices. Yet many Bahrainis live in squalid poverty, with few opportunities for employment in the booming financial sector, or highly industrialised oil fields. Housing is a particularly big issue. Official reports show that at least 50,000 families are on housing waiting lists, and some have waited for 20 years or more. The result is that many Bahrainis live in overcrowded conditions with poor services and sanitation.[15]

Meanwhile, the high-rise buildings, shopping malls and five-star hotels built for foreign investors and the local elite stand in stark contrast. In a country so small, much of the land for the new economy has been reclaimed from the ocean, which in turn has ruined much of the ocean ecology and fish stocks that Bahrainis traditionally depended upon to make a living.[16] These displaced people then must compete with the hordes of foreign guest workers for jobs. It is the pattern of neoliberal capitalism repeated over and over; traditional economies like fishing and community-based agriculture are forcibly replaced by ones focused exclusively on economic growth and profit.

On 25 February 2011, the *New York Times* reported that up to 200,000 of Bahrain's 1.2 million people marched in the capital, Manama.[17] This followed on the heels of other protests beginning 14 February, which had drawn tens of thousands, and which had seen seven civilians killed amid widespread repression by security forces. The daily protests choked the island's main roads, severely disrupting the high-rise business district and government institutions.[18]

Despite state repression, the large-scale peaceful protests and calls for democratic reform continued for four weeks. On 14 March, at the invitation of the Bahraini royal family, thousands of Saudi Arabian troops crossed the 25-kilometre bridge connecting the two countries over the Gulf of Bahrain. These military troops then launched an assault on the thousands of peaceful protestors gathered around Manama's Pearl Square, the monument to Bahrain's now largely destroyed pearling industry.[19] Clearly, the ruling Saudi family could not tolerate the possibility of even the whiff of democracy being instituted in such a close neighbour.

Nor, apparently, could the United States. In an unscheduled visit, Secretary of Defense Robert Gates was in Bahrain on 12 March, two days before the Saudi invasion. Gates's unannounced visit came within days of the UK's top national security adviser's closed meeting with the monarch.[20] Two days after Gates's meeting, Saudi troops had arrived at the king's invitation.

It is inconceivable that a client state like Saudi Arabia would take such belligerent action without the approval of the American government, regardless of whether it had been requested to do so by the Bahraini king. Clearly, Gates's visit was to give the Obama administration's green light to the operation, and to ensure the status quo of Arab rule and suppression would continue. The *Asia Times'* Middle East analyst Pepe Escobar wrote on 2 April:

> Two diplomatic sources at the United Nations independently confirmed that Washington, via secretary of state Hillary Clinton, gave the go-ahead for Saudi Arabia to invade Bahrain and crush the pro-democracy movement in their neighbor in exchange for a 'yes' vote by the Arab League for a no-fly zone over Libya – the main rationale that led to United Nations Security Council resolution 1973.[21]

The Bahraini government then declared martial law. Yet despite at least 40 people having died, and thousands more injured, jailed, fired, and/or tortured as of September 2011, and the relative lack of western media coverage, especially compared to Egypt, the protests continued. And while the US and its allies were all over the human rights abuses committed in Libya by supporting a military assault and no-fly zone, and in Syria by launching sanctions – their support for the Bahraini dictator Al Khalifa was never in question. Nor was the fact that in 2010 the US supplied Bahrain with $19.5 million of military aid, as much per capita as it gave to Egypt.[22]

The very largest of America's corporations had lobbied hard for approval of the Bahrain and Oman FTAs, including Boeing, Dow, ChevronTexaco, ExxonMobil, Motorola and Intel. The Pharmaceutical Researchers and Manufacturers lobby group said 'a trade agreement with Oman would provide life saving medicines to the region and protect IPR standards that make new drug R and D possible.' Susan Kling Finston, PhRMA's associate vice-president for Middle Eastern/North African affairs, put it succinctly: 'The standards will promote an attractive environment for foreign investment.'[23]

They were hardly alone. As with other US-driven FTAs and neoliberalism in general, it is American corporations who have been the most vociferous, and active, in promoting the US Middle East Free Trade Area. In October 2004, the National Foreign Trade Council (NFTC) and the Business Council for International Understanding formed the US Middle East Free Trade Coalition to lobby for the MEFTA. Both organisations are comprised of some of the largest corporate entities in the world. The NFTC has four hundred member companies, and executives from Bechtel, Chevron, Halliburton and Walmart serve on its company board of directors.[24] The Business Council for International Understanding, despite its name, is a focused lobby group seeking to increase US business opportunities overseas. It also has a large list of powerful corporate members, including every major US oil company, Citigroup and JP Morgan financial services providers, as well as Coca-Cola and Ford.[25]

Privatisation, the strengthening of intellectual property rights, and allowing competition in nationalised services like water, sewage, electricity and education were listed as top priorities for MEFTA negotiations by the US Middle East Free Trade Coalition. It sent a letter to every member of Congress encouraging quick action on the Bahrain deal, and lobbied extensively for the Oman agreement.[26]

25
Egypt and How to Make a Fortune from Hunger and Misery

I really consider President and Mrs. Mubarak to be friends of my family.

US Secretary of State Hillary Clinton, 2009[1]

What for a poor man is a crust, for a rich man is a securitized asset class.

Futures trader Ann Berg, 2011[2]

EGYPT

Of all the uprisings that swept through North Africa and the Middle East in 2011, Egypt received the most attention and commentary by western media and governments. A massive uprising of demonstrations, marches, non-violent civil disobedience and labour strikes began on 25 January in response to the Tunisian uprising, which saw US ally and ruthless dictator Zine El Abidine Ben Ali flee the country. Millions of Egyptians coalesced around the demand for the removal of the blatantly corrupt US-supported regime of Hosni Mubarak. Daily images of a dense sea of Egyptians converging on Cairo's Tahrir Square were met with overwhelming global public support for the Egyptian people. Such support made it seemingly impossible for the US to continue to back Mubarak, and instead the Obama administration focused on calling for a peaceful transition to democracy – democracy that would keep Egypt beholden to the neoliberal dictates of the World Bank, the IMF and the WTO, and locked into its proper place in the broader vision of a Free Trade Area for the Middle East/North Africa region. After much prevarication, Mubarak resigned from office on 11 February. While the protests were predominantly peaceful, there were numerous clashes and as of July 2011 an estimated 846 people had been killed and thousands injured.[3]

The US has not succeeded in signing a Free Trade Agreement with Egypt, in part because it hasn't needed to. Few countries in the world have been closer allies, and few governments greater advocates of US-driven neoliberal globalisation, with greater consequences to its own people, than Egypt. It is no mystery why the Egyptian people had had enough. The immediate statistics of the utter pillage of Egypt is stunning. Mubarak's family fortune is estimated to be as much as $70 billion.[4] Nearly half of all Egyptians – some 40 million people – live on less than $2 a day, which meant that when food prices increased to record levels, many Egyptians literally could not afford to eat. Thirty per cent are illiterate.[5]

Nor did ordinary Egyptians ever consent to their government's collaboration with the US in Israel's ongoing repression of their fellow Arab Palestinians in Gaza, or to Mubarak's ongoing role of kowtowing to Israel and the US in the lamentable Middle East peace process between Palestinians and Israel.

Most Egyptians understand that their nation's wealth has been stolen. Each year, US$3 billion flowed out of the pockets of ordinary Egyptians to pay off the government's external debt, which as of 2011 was a massive $35 billion. From 2000 to 2009, Egypt had actually paid $3.4 billion more than the original value of what it had borrowed, thanks to interest.[6] This, of course, is the point of free market, neoliberal capitalism: manoeuvring countries into and keeping them in debt, forcing them to open up their economies while cutting government programmes for the poor, and selling off their nationalised industries so that wealth is extracted from the poor to make the already rich much much richer.

In more recent years, Egypt had made itself even more attractive for foreign capital by eliminating restrictions on foreign investment and repatriation of profits. Related taxes on dividends and capital gains were also cut to zero. Egypt's nationalised banks were partially or entirely privatised. As a result, $42 billion of foreign money flooded the country between 2004 and 2009.[7] While this hot money helped make international investors and Mubarak and his cronies even richer, it resulted in no benefits to ordinary Egyptians. Instead, as with allowing food commodities to be subject to the casino capitalism of Wall Street speculation, poverty was exacerbated.

Yet Egypt was touted as an economic success story. In April 2010, the IMF lavished praise on Mubarak's wonderful progress, and Egypt consistently ranked high on the World Bank's top reformers list in the five years leading up to 2011.[8] And since their definition of success consists almost entirely of a country's ability to increase economic growth regardless of how many people suffer as a result, Egypt was a success. Deregulation and privatisation on the scale of Mubarak's looting definitely increases economic growth, although usually for the short amount of time before global capital moves onto the next country which has disembowelled itself to appease Wall Street's relentless seeking-out of easy, short-term profit speculation. Egyptian GDP growth had averaged 6 per cent for the six years up to and including 2009.[9] But also, according to World Bank statistics, Egypt's top earners increased their share of income since the 1990s, while the country's poorest has seen their portion decrease.[10] Similar statistics tell the same story for the US itself, and for every other country that has followed the neoliberal debt-restructuring path.

In Egypt, the system had been kept in place since 1978, with $35 billion in military aid from Washington, and with repression. The approximate $1.7 billion it received in total aid in 2010 was exceeded only by the $2.4 billion the US gave to Israel.[11] No one knows exactly how many political prisoners are in Egyptian jails; estimates run from 6,000 to 17,000. Egypt was the Bush administration's first choice for suspects arbitrarily seized under its extraordinary rendition programme, which was overseen by Omar Suleiman, Mubarak's former head of intelligence.[12]

As highlighted in Chapter 16, Colin Powell had cited false information gained under torture from Ibn al-Shaykh al-Libi, who the US had sent to Egypt for torture, to convince the UN Security Council of the imminent need to invade Iraq. Yet it was Suleiman, appointed by Mubarak as vice-president, who Obama wanted to replace Mubarak.[13]

The crystal-clear message was that it would be business as usual, regardless of who resided in the White House.

It's no wonder that Egyptians have such clear distrust for the US. Consistent polls have shown that roughly 80 per cent of the population has a negative opinion of the United States, including polls since Mubarak's departure. Egyptians, as well as the majority of their Arab neighbours, believe that the US and Israel are far more of a threat to the world's well-being than Iran's nuclear programme.[14]

THE IMF/WORLD BANK RESPONSE: MORE OF THE SAME

Triggered in part by the record rise in food prices, the protests almost immediately became political, with a sharp focus on the need for Mubarak to leave, but also for systemic reform. Consistently, these demands were for the return of the wealth that had been so obviously stolen from the people, and that the state should support and provide services to the poor, and renationalise the numerous industries that had been privatised.

Yet for the US and its neoliberal agents, the World Bank and the IMF, the obvious cause of Egypt's meltdown was that it had not pursued its economic liberalisation far enough. The IMF's advice to the G8 summit in May 2011 regarding the Egyptian crisis was that:

> Overcoming high unemployment will require a substantial increase in the pace of economic growth ... Achieving such growth rates will entail both additional investment and improved productivity. The key role will have to be played by the private sector, including by attracting foreign direct investment. Thus, government policies should support an enabling environment in which the private sector flourishes.[15]

In other words, an acceleration of the policies which had created the crisis in the first place. This is clearly what the Obama administration was referring to in its relentless soundbite of its support for an 'orderly transition' to democracy. Implicit in this is that by not going far enough, the Mubarak dictatorship had blocked the democratic aspirations of the Egyptian people to further dismantle their own ability to live in peace and prosperity. The reality, of course, is just the opposite – by further chaining Egypt to the World Bank, the IMF, the WTO and potentially a Free Trade Agreement, it would make no difference whether Egypt's system of governance was a democracy or a dictatorship. As it was so blatantly displayed for all to see in Iraq, so-called democracies are just as potentially controllable as dictatorships.

New billions were promised to help the Egyptian people weather the financial storm and to not default on their massive debt. This in turn would ensure Egyptians would get even deeper into debt to the same neoliberal institutions that had been responsible for creating the debt in the first place. The key is that this cycle of the very poor paying over and over to the very rich continues unabated and unchallenged. The fact that much of the debt was odious – loaned to a dictator who clearly enriched himself and his cronies with little benefit to the Egyptian people – was not sufficient reason to cancel it outright.

Much to its credit, the Higher Council of the Armed Forces, Egypt's interim government, rejected offers of new loans from the IMF because they would 'burden future generations'. Funds were instead supplied by Saudi Arabia and Qatar.[16] Much to its discredit, however, in May 2011 a spokesperson for the same interim government said in response to promised funds from the

European Bank for Reconstruction and Development that 'the current transition government remains committed to the open market approach, which Egypt will further pursue at an accelerated rate following upcoming election.'[17]

That the military interim government could go ahead and speak for a yet-to-be elected government that it would 'pursue at an accelerated rate' 'the open market approach' is astounding. Astounding, but honest. Once a country is entrenched as deeply as Egypt is to the World Bank and IMF, it doesn't matter what type of government it has. The reality is that it is beholden to these agents of neoliberal capitalism, and hence to American hegemony, and what is in the best interests of its people is at best a secondary consideration.

Egypt signed an agreement with the US in 2005 to bring in Qualifying Industrial Zones (QIZ). As was the case with Jordan, Egypt's QIZs must have an 11.8 per cent Israeli component to receive duty-free entry into the US. In 2005, clothing and textile exports dominated Egypt's economy, and amounted to $600 million a year.[18] Faced with the rabid competition from Jordan's QIZs, Egypt also faced the phase-out of its guaranteed-country export quota on textiles and apparel. This was coming to an end thanks to a WTO agreement that applied to all member countries; as a result, Egypt would be competing directly with China and India for export entry to America and other markets. It faced the potential loss of an estimated 150,000 jobs as a result.[19] Unlike Jordan though, Egyptian textile and garment workers were actually from Egypt itself, not imported foreign guest workers who could be manipulated and exploited.

The potent one-two combination of the WTO and possible loss of access to the American market displays the tools the United States has available to manipulate countries into agreeing to neoliberal free trade deals. Despite considerable opposition to the deal from an Egyptian public appalled at doing such direct and beneficial business with Israel, Mubarak agreed.

A Free Trade Agreement with the US probably would have resulted in more benefits to Egypt's export capacity to American markets. As we've seen, Egypt had already opened up its services and fulfilled most of the criteria the US required for an FTA, decimating its poor while further enriching Mubarak and other elites. But FTA talks were suspended when Egypt, in a rare example, refused to support the US's crusade against Europe's moratorium on GMO crops in the WTO.[20]

And what about Tunisia, whose uprising had catalysed the Arab Spring? The same wealth inequality, high unemployment and poverty were evident there as in Egypt. Tunisia had allowed more than 67 per cent of its publicly owned firms to be privatised, and had eliminated most restrictions on foreign investment. And like Egypt, the benefits went to the ruling family, in this case close US ally Zine El Abidine Ben Ali. The IMF had praised Tunisia's embracing of these neoliberal reforms as 'prudent macroeconomic management'. At the same time, American diplomats referred to Tunisia as a 'police state' in cables released by Wikileaks.[21]

But according to World Bank President Robert Zoellick, it was not these conditions that Mohammed Bouazizi, the young street vendor who set himself on fire 17 December, sparking the Tunisian uprising that drove Ben Ali out of the country, was objecting to. Zoellick remarked:

> ... the key point I have also been emphasizing and I emphasized in this speech is that it is not just a question of money. It is a question of policy ... keep in mind, the late Mr. Bouazizi was basically driven to burn himself alive because he was harassed with red tape ... one starting point is to quit harassing those people and let them have a chance to start some small businesses.[22]

In other words, Bouazizi committed suicide because Tunisia's commitment to neoliberal reform and deregulation had not gone far enough.

PROFITING FROM HUNGER AND MISERY: SPECULATING ON GLOBAL FOOD PRICES

While the Arab Spring was in large part a revolt of the region's population against the autocratic rule that had kept the vast majority of them impoverished, the actual trigger was the skyrocketing cost of food.

Egypt is the world's largest importer of wheat. Combined with the fact that roughly 40 per cent of Egyptians struggle to get by on $2 a day or less in an economy that's been wrenched open to international finance, any rise in the cost of imported food has a discernible effect. A Credit Suisse survey observes that Egypt's food inflation in 2010–11 was 20 per cent – among the highest in the world.[23] Even with the food subsidies that the Egyptian government provides to 70 per cent of the population, rising food prices hit Egypt's poor particularly hard.

But it wasn't just Egypt. According to the UN Food and Agriculture Organisation (FAO), the average cost of buying food increased by nearly a third globally from June to December 2010.[24] The price of wheat increased 70 per cent during the same period, maize 74 per cent and sugar 77 per cent. The January 2011 FAO food index had increased by 3.4 per cent, the highest increase since it began monitoring global food prices in 1990. Yet according to the FAO, there had been no major change in either global demand or supply in that six-month period.

So what happened? Wall Street and neoliberal deregulation happened. Olivier de Schutter, UN Rapporteur on the Right to Food, said, 'Prices of wheat, maize and rice have increased very significantly but this is not linked to low stock levels or harvests, but rather to traders reacting to information and speculating on the markets.'[25] Food commodities were now subject to the same casino roulette-wheel of international speculation that had created the subprime mortgage crisis, the record high prices in oil in 2008, and now, thanks to the semi-religious obsession with the ideology of neoliberal deregulation regardless of the consequence as long as it generates profit, the food crisis.

SPECULATING ON HUNGER: THE NEXT BIG THING

The repeal of the Glass-Steagall Act in 1999 had allowed investment firms and banks to speculate with people's mortgages; similarly, a near simultaneous push by the same hedge funds and other speculators resulted in the deregulation of how food was traded. In 1999, the Commodities Futures Trading Commission deregulated futures markets, eliminating previous restrictions that had limited speculation to those who actually had a connection with food production.[26] Like Glass-Steagall, these protections had been in place as part of the New Deal to prevent the excesses that triggered the stock market crash and Great Depression.

The new mega-investment bank firms, led by Goldman Sachs, were now free to create commodities indexes, which included oil and gas. These new investments allowed food commodities such as wheat and rice to be traded in a way similar to regular stocks. Buying low and selling high became the name of the game. The higher the price of food, the more investors profited. And when the subprime crisis led to the global financial crisis in 2008, and when previously safe US government investments like Treasury Bills were now offering practically nothing, investors of all stripes, including pension funds, put their money in what looked to be the next big thing: food commodities. From 2003 to 2008, commodity index fund speculation went from $13 billion to $318 billion.[27] As Frederick Kaufman, who has written extensively on the issue, explains:

> Spearheaded by oil and gas prices (the dominant commodities of the index funds) the new investment products ignited the markets of all the other indexed commodities, which led to a problem familiar to those versed in the history of tulips, dot-coms, and cheap real estate: a food bubble. Hard red spring wheat, which usually trades in the $4 to $6 dollar range per 60-pound bushel, broke all previous records as the futures contract climbed into the teens and kept on going until it topped $25. And so, from 2005 to 2008, the worldwide price of food rose 80 percent – and has kept rising.[28]

Hedge-fund manager Michael Masters stated that on the regulated exchanges in the US in 2008, an estimated 64 per cent of all wheat contracts were held by speculators with no interest whatsoever in actual wheat production or consumption. They owned it solely in anticipation of price inflation and resale. But it wasn't just wheat. Maize nearly doubled rising by 90 per cent, and rice tripled.[29] Billionaire financier George Soros said it was 'just like secretly hoarding food during a hunger crisis in order to make profits from increasing prices'.[30]

The food crisis that resulted in 2008 effected a hundred countries, and riots broke out in at least 30. The UN Food and Agriculture Organisation estimates that in poorer countries, 60–80 per cent of people's incomes are spent on food, and that approximately two billion people spend 50 per cent or more of their income on food.[31] The 2008 food crisis saw at least 200 million face malnutrition and starvation, and for the first time, the number of people in the world who are food insecure hit the 1 billion mark. Jean Ziegler, the UN Special Rapporteur on the Right to Food from 2000 to 2008, has called this 'a silent mass murder', entirely due to 'man-made actions'.[32] Olivier De Schutter, Ziegler's successor, stated that 'a significant portion of the price spike was due to the emergence of a speculative bubble.'[33]

There were undoubtedly factors other than just international investor speculation. During this same time, millions of acres of

US farmland had been taken out of food production to grow corn for ethanol and other biofuels, and droughts and floods linked to global climate change had reduced crop production in some countries. Climate change is another area that American leadership has refused to adequately deal with. Reducing global emissions would mean reforming the global neoliberal economic system which is so dependent on oil, and reducing dependency on oil when it is priced in dollars is not something the US is going to agree to any time soon.

And while there certainly was an increase in catastrophic weather patterns in 2010 – Russia's wheat crop was devastated by a record drought, and Australian wheat production was similarly devastated by record flooding – the FAO categorically states that events in Russia, Australia and elsewhere were not factors in the huge 32 per cent rise in global food prices in the last six months of 2010. What was a factor was the deregulation of control over who could profit from food production.

And with the right to profit, comes the right to exploit. *The Observer*'s John Vidal highlights that in 2010

London hedge fund Armajaro bought 240,000 tonnes, or more than seven per cent, of the world's stocks of cocoa beans, helping to drive chocolate to its highest price in 33 years. Meanwhile, the price of coffee shot up 20 per cent in just three days as a direct result of hedge funds betting on the price of coffee falling.[34]

Legislation that Obama signed as part of Wall Street reform legislation in July 2010[35] did nothing to prevent the global price of food hitting record highs in December 2010. The legislation was supposed to close the regulatory loopholes that allows major investment and financial firms to speculate in agricultural commodities. But without real reform, traders will just figure out new ways to exploit new loopholes.

Subjecting basic human needs like housing, food and water to investor speculation occurred hand-in-hand with the assault by neoliberal globalisation on forcing countries to eliminate the agricultural tariffs that protected their food sovereignty. Combined with an emphasis on growing luxury crops for export, such as coffee and cocoa, to pay off national debt meant a country's ability to feed itself was severely undermined, while their dependence on the highly subsidised crops of the United States and other developed countries was significantly increased. Recognising that dependency, there are few reasons other than sheer greed and exploitation to explain the conscious deregulation of agricultural commodities – commodities that much of the now-globalised world is dependent upon to feed itself.

Agriculture is clearly a challenge for many of the arid nations of North Africa and the Middle East. But not for Iraq. What the US did there under the CPA and ongoing military occupation is a case study for how the US and its major corporations intend to someday control the entire world's ability to feed itself.

Part VII

Sowing the Seeds of Democracy: A Case Study of Iraqi Agriculture

26
Neoliberal Authority: Iraqi Agriculture

The ability to provide food security for its people is at the very heart of a nation's sovereignty. With the blatant disregard for the welfare of the Iraqi people so evident in the CPA's desire to establish Iraq as a neoliberal client state, it should come as no surprise that the US and its allies prioritised their own agricultural exports to Iraq while sabotaging Iraq's ability to develop its own food security.

A broader examination of US agricultural policy, though, tells a much larger and more sinister story. There is no bigger market in the world than food: everyone must eat. Just as neoliberal deregulation in the name of increased profits led to commodity-price increases, hunger and political upheaval throughout the Middle East, control of agricultural production – particularly the seeds that grow the world's staple crops – is ultimately control of life itself. Through the same free market neoliberal institutions that have embedded and increased its hegemony over the last 30 years, the US and its mega-agribusiness corporations have sought to expand and ultimately control the entirety of humankind's food supply.

In that context, American efforts to revitalise Iraqi agriculture have been sadly predictable. The intent is clear: to establish a western-style agriculture based on large-scale mono-crops that can be owned and manipulated by western agricultural giants such as Monsanto and Cargill, while creating a dependency on western fertilisers, tractors and other carbon-intense practices. They have been stymied by the same issues that have slowed down US efforts in Iraq in general – the sectarian violence, lack of Iraqi government oversight, and, not least of all, a drought of historic proportions.

Iraq is the ancient birthplace of agriculture, and its wheat, legumes and other seed-crop varieties have been developed and refined for local conditions over a period of 10,000 years. It is also unique among Middle Eastern countries because of its water resources, and hence its potential to be self-sufficient in food production, which it was up through the 1970s. Approximately 27 per cent of the country is available for agriculture; half of that is from extensive irrigation of the Euphrates and Tigris rivers.[1] Traditionally, wheat is the country's most important crop, followed by barley and chickpeas.

Control of Iraq's water might soon be as strategically important as control of oil in the arid Middle East. Part of the US push for Free Trade Agreements, and implicit in WTO rules, is water privatisation. By opening up a country's services to competition, corporations like Bechtel have been able to privatise this crucial human need for private profit. And just as every human being must eat, every human being also must drink, as well as have water for crops and livestock.

Iraqi agriculture, like nearly everything else in the country, had been devastated by the Gulf War, ensuing sanctions, and the 'Shock and Awe' of the 2003 invasion. The US had intentionally bombed the extensive canals and irrigation systems on which Iraqi agriculture depended, as well as poultry farms, fertiliser and pesticide-production facilities, and pumping stations. As examined in Chapter 8, the sanctions were specifically designed to exacerbate hardship and to reduce, if not outright eliminate, Iraq's ability to feed itself. With the exception of the Kurdistan region, the UN Oil for Food programme was prohibited from purchasing Iraqi-produced food, creating food dependency on imports. Iraq was also prohibited from importing spare parts or fertilisers. Its 1990–91 agricultural output was 80 per cent smaller than the previous pre-sanctions 1989 output, and by 1999, one in four children aged 1–4 suffered from chronic malnutrition, among a host of other food-related health issues.[2]

But back in the 1980s, when America was supplying Iraq with the infrastructure to build chemical weapons, Iraq was also a major agricultural market for the US. It accounted for 90 per cent of American rice exports, and wheat exports were worth half a billion dollars a year. The Prevention of Genocide Act, which would have enacted sanctions against Iraq because of Saddam Hussein's use of chemical weapons against the Kurds, was blocked in part by legislators from rice- and wheat-growing areas.[3]

NEOLIBERAL AUTHORITY: IRAQI AGRICULTURE

The Bush administration picked Daniel Amstutz to oversee Iraq's agricultural reconstruction. By picking Amstutz, the US made it very clear exactly what type of agricultural reconstruction they envisioned for Iraq. Amstutz was already infamous for being the chief US negotiator at the Uruguay Round of GATT talks in 1987–89, which led to the founding of the World Trade Organization. It was Amstutz who led the American insistence that food and agriculture be included in global trade rules, and was the lead author for the controversial WTO Agreement on Agriculture. He had also been a top executive at Cargill, the conglomerate which controls much of the world's grain trading, and CEO of the North American Export Grain Association. He started off as a partner at Goldman Sachs where, according to his biography, he initiated the firm's commodities-trading and futures-brokerage businesses. His biography goes on to state that 'He played a key role in helping achieve more trade liberalisation for agriculture than in all preceding multilateral trade rounds.'[4]

Amstutz also was behind the Freedom to Farm Bill in the first Bush administration, which, similar to what lay in store for Iraq, eliminated tariffs and slashed federal price supports for small American farmers. Thousands of American farmers went bankrupt and their farms were consolidated into ever-larger corporate enterprises, and mega-grain traders like Cargill reaped increased profits.[5] As we are about to see, he has also arguably done more than anyone else to force highly controversial genetically modified seeds onto a very resistant world.

Oxfam's policy director Kevin Watkins said at the time:

> Putting Dan Amstutz in charge of agriculture reconstruction in Iraq is like putting Saddam Hussein in the chair of a human rights commission. This guy is uniquely well placed to advance the commercial interests of American grain companies and bust open the Iraqi market, but singularly ill equipped to lead a reconstruction effort in a developing country.[6]

Settling into his new position, Amstutz announced that

> Iraqi farmers have had little incentive to increase production because of price controls that have kept food very inexpensive. With a transition to a market economy, we can see health returning to agriculture and incentives to employ good farming practices and modern techniques.[7]

According to Amstutz, the point of a country's agricultural system is not to keep food inexpensive and affordable for its citizens. And by health, Amstutz is referring to profit. Based on his track record, it wasn't generating profits for Iraqi farmers that was his primary concern.

In addition to Amstutz's agribusiness ties, the Bush administration also had a number of significant connections to Monsanto, the world's dominant purveyor of controversial genetically modified organisms (GMOs). Department of Agriculture Secretary Ann Veneman had served on the board of directors of Calgene, a Monsanto subsidiary, and Rumsfeld had spent eight years as CEO of Monsanto subsidiary Searle. Supreme Court Justice Clarence Thomas had been a top corporate lawyer for Monsanto in the 1970s.[8]

Technically, Amstutz shared responsibility with Australian Wheat Board (AWB) Chairman Trevor Flugge. As highlighted earlier, it would later be revealed that AWB under Flugge, with apparent Australian government complicity, had paid Saddam Hussein's regime nearly A$300 million in kickbacks under the UN's Oil for Food programme. The evidence is compelling that Australia participated in military action against Saddam Hussein in return for assurances that its lucrative wheat exports under the Oil for Food programme would continue.

Flugge was paid almost A$1 million for approximately eight months' work in Iraq. His salary was paid out of Australian aid relief to Iraq, as part of the country's 'humanitarian contribution to the Iraqi people'. Responding to criticism when Flugge's salary details were exposed in early 2006, Australian Prime Minister John Howard was unapologetic. 'I will tell you why we sought his involvement,' he said. 'It was because our principal concern at that time was to stop American wheat growers from getting our markets. We thought Mr. Flugge would fight hard for the Australian wheat industry.'[9]

It is instructive that Howard admitted the truth regarding Flugge. For an ideology that professes to be about freedom of the individual, it is rare, if at all, that any human individuals – in this case, Iraqis – get to have a say regarding whether they want a neoliberal regime governing them or not. Howard also admitted that agricultural reconstruction had nothing to do with ensuring food security to Iraq's devastated population, but about who was going to profit from exporting wheat to Iraq.

When the war started in March 2003, AWB had over $300 million worth of outstanding contracts with Iraq under the Oil for Food programme, and was eager – as was the Howard government – to ensure the contracts would be honoured under the new CPA occupation government.[10] These contracts, we now know, were laden with illegal kickbacks to the Hussein government. AWB was the biggest single supplier of food under the Oil for Food programme, and sold 12 million tonnes of wheat valued at A$2.6 billion under the programme.[11]

Amazingly, one of Flugge's duties with the CPA was to review the previous AWB wheat contracts under the Oil for Food programme, and help determine whether they should be honoured by the new CPA administration. Unsurprisingly, the CPA honoured the kickback-laden wheat contracts in September 2003.[12] Flugge also ensured that long-term Iraqi Grains Board head, Yosif Abdul Rahman, received a top position in the Ministry of Trade despite the CPA's purging of top Baathists from government positions. Rahman had been AWB's chief contact in Iraq for the kickbacks.[13] That Bush allowed the former head of AWB to be appointed to such a position can only be viewed as a reward for Australia's military participation in the invasion.

Amstutz and Flugge immediately began to eliminate as quickly as possible the price supports and other agricultural subsidies that Iraqi farmers had enjoyed under the Hussein government. *Washington Post* writer, Ariana Eunjung Cha, outlined the government assistance for Iraqi farmers before the invasion:

> Farming inputs such as seeds, fertilizer, pesticides, sprinklers, and ... tractors ... were subsidised often at a third or even a fourth of the market price. The government leased land for one cent per donam, about six-tenths of an acre, a year. It bought the country's main crops, wheat and barley, at a fixed price, whether they were useable or not. And it ground up the grain and provided it free as flour to the people each month as part of the guaranteed food program in which every family received a basket of flour, sugar, tea, and other necessities.[14]

Invoking a classic neoliberal mantra, Flugge explained to Cha in the same article that subsidising farming supplies is 'all wrong'. The CPA would provide assistance in the form of technology and education and the market would take care of the rest.

The CPA had already mandated the elimination of all tariffs, duties and other taxes on imports. This led to the flooding of Iraq with foreign foodstuffs, and instantly created a new and substantial agricultural market for American wheat farmers. In a market dominated by Australia during the sanctions, the US exported $190 million worth of wheat in the first year after the invasion, compared to zero before the invasion.[15] Australia was rewarded appropriately with contracts in 2004 and 2005 for over two million tonnes of wheat to Iraq.[16]

27
Order 81 and the Genetically Modified Seeds of Democracy

The reason we are in Iraq is to plant the seeds of democracy so they flourish there and spread to the entire region of authoritarianism.

George W. Bush[1]

Amstutz and Flugge were also directly responsible for one of the most extreme of the CPA economic laws, Order 81, which introduced a system of monopoly patent rights over seeds. Crucial to Order 81 was the Plant Variety Protection (PVP) provision: 'Farmers shall be prohibited from re-using seeds of protected varieties or any variety mentioned.'[2] Any Iraqi farmer who knowingly or unknowingly uses these 'protected varieties' of seeds is required to pay an annual license fee. Under Order 81, it would now be illegal for farmers to use these 'patented' seeds, even if taken from their own harvest, without paying a royalty to the seed-patent owners.

As farmers do throughout the world, Iraqis saved their seeds from one harvest to plant for the next. Order 81 was referring to seeds that had been genetically modified, and which had been patented by mega-agribusiness corporations like Monsanto, Dupont and Dow. Getting farmers hooked on these seeds and the requisite fertilisers and pesticides is a huge industry – both in terms of profits and controversy. These seeds had been banned under the Baathists.[3]

Genetically modified crops often do provide a higher crop yield than traditional seeds. But in addition to the issue of corporate dependency and debt, there are a number of other problems. While some GMO crops are resistant to various pests and weeds, often they are genetically modified to simply be more tolerant to higher levels of insecticide, like Monsanto's Roundup Ready. Weeds and insects inevitably adapt, requiring greater amounts of insecticides, and lower crop yields. Aerial spraying often wipes out neighbouring crops that are not genetically modified. But farmers must pay the patent fee regardless of how good a crop they have. If GMO seeds are blown into a neighbouring non-GMO field, the non-GMO farmer will still have to pay the patent fee on any crops grown as a result. And with Monsanto's infamous 'terminator' seeds, which stop crops from actually producing new seeds, farmers have no choice but to pay for new seeds each crop cycle. There is also the issue of GMO technology and how its lack of seed diversity impacts on broader biodiversity, as well as ongoing concerns regarding GMOs' health effects on both humans and livestock.

The history of US corporations developing GMOs and then forcing the technology onto the developing world, with US government support, is well documented. In *Seeds of Destruction*, F. William Engdahl details one of the first and most well-known examples when, in 1998, a Texas biotechnology company, RiceTec, took out a patent on its genetically modified basmati rice.[4] The governor of Texas at the time was one George Bush Jr. Regular basmati rice has been grown for thousands of years and is the main staple for India, Pakistan and other parts of South Asia. RiceTec then sold its GMO-patented version in the US as regular basmati rice. Because of Daniel Amstutz's efforts, under WTO rules regarding barriers to free trade, countries were prohibited from requiring that food containing GMOs be labelled. As a result, people buying the genetically modified RiceTec product had no idea it had been patented.

RiceTec had obtained the vast repository of traditional knowledge and variety of basmati seeds thanks to the corporate-funded International Rice Research Institute (IRRI) in the Philippines. IRRI had allowed duplicate basmati germplasms to be stored in a seed bank in Fort Collins, Colorado. RiceTec was able to illegally access the Fort Collins gene bank and then simply patented the genetic code of Filipino basmati rice. Because the Philippines had approved GMO crops, its farmers would now have to pay RiceTec a patent and annual fee to grow what had been freely available to them and thousands of other farmers throughout the region.

Thousands of Filipino small farmers went out of business, because they couldn't afford the seeds, or the fertiliser and pesticides necessary for the GMO basmati rice seeds to work. The inevitable result was that small farms had to consolidate into bigger ones in order to afford to stay in business. In the late 1990s, at least 4,000 Filipino rice farmers had died from chemical pesticides, either from misuse of the new deadly poison, or intentionally via suicide.[5]

This was followed by the famous 'Golden Rice', which claimed that because it had been genetically modified to contain beta-carotene (Vitamin A), eating just one bowl a day could prevent blindness and other Vitamin A deficiencies that afflicted much of the Third

World. They neglected to mention the bowl would need to contain nine kilograms of golden rice to have any possible effect.[6]

In India, 200,000 farmers have committed suicide over the last 13 years after falling into deep debt when their genetically modified crops failed. The majority were cotton farmers, who had become indebted via GMO patent fees and the purchase of expensive chemicals for growing Monsanto's bt cotton. 'The combination is unpayable debt, and it's the day the farmer is going to lose his land for chemicals and seeds, that is the day the farmer drinks pesticide,' renowned Indian activist Vandana Shiva said. 'And it's totally related to a negative economy, of an agriculture that costs more in production than the farmer can ever earn.'[7] This is why Shiva and other critics refer to the neoliberal policies that force genetically modified seeds and chemicals onto the poor as the 'suicide economy of corporate globalisation'.

The introduction of genetically modified crop technology has been fought against, ever since it was first introduced in 1996. At the time of the 2003 Iraqi invasion, few countries had approved GMO crops for production, despite considerable efforts by the US for them to do so. In the entire Middle East and North Africa, not a single country had approved the planting of GMO crops.[8] By 2010, Egypt had approved GMO corn, but was growing only half-a-million hectares, putting it far down the list of GMO crop producers.[9]

Only 29 countries allowed GMO production in 2010, and many of these had not adopted the technology willingly. The GMO industry's International Service for the Acquisition of Agro-Biotec Applications states that

> It was the spectacular success of illegally planted GM cotton seeds in India that eventually forced national regulators in that country to permit the legal planting of GM cotton in some regions in 2002. It was the wide spread of illegally planted GM soybeans in Brazil that finally forced the government of that country to legalize the technology in 2003.[10]

It doesn't take a great deal of imagination to guess who was doing the illegal planting. This is the problem – once introduced, GMOs are very difficult to eradicate. That's why most countries focus on not allowing them to be planted in the first place.

The rest of the world took a major step in blocking the spread of US-backed GMO crops with the 2000 Cartagena Protocol on Biosafety, which came into effect in September 2003. Signatories could block the importation of GMO food based on the long-established precautionary principle, and did not need to provide any scientific backing or proven evidence of risk. They were also free to place tighter regulations or to outright ban GMO crops within their borders.[11] The Cartagena Protocol was a direct challenge to the WTO's Agreement on Agriculture, which as we will see below had been a major tool to open up countries to GMO trade.

Just as Iraq could provide a new era of neoliberal hegemony at a time when so much of the world was resisting it, Iraq could also provide a launching pad for American agribusiness that could then spread to the rest of the anti-GMO Middle East and North Africa. By ensuring recognition and protection of intellectual property rights (IPRs) in the individual Free Trade Agreements, the US was clearly trying to pave the way for further adoption of GMO crops throughout the region.

After gobbling up other, smaller companies, by the time Order 81 was passed in 2004, three American companies – Monsanto, DuPont and Dow – and one Swiss company, Syngenta, dominated the global GMO seed market. Of these, Monsanto was by far the largest, providing the seed technology for 90 per cent of all genetically engineered crops.[12] By 2004, the majority of the US soybean crop and nearly half its corn crop was genetically modified.[13] Monsanto, Dow and Dupont are also famous for their role in developing napalm, Agent Orange, and other horrors unleashed by the American military in Vietnam.

In 2002, the UN's Special Rapporteur on the Right to Food, Jean Ziegler, summed up US efforts to push GMOs on the rest of the world: 'There is absolutely no justification to produce genetically modified food except the profit motive and the domination of the multinational corporations.'[14]

But in 2001, the US Supreme Court upheld that plant and other life forms indeed can be patented. Despite having worked as a Monsanto lawyer in the 1970s, Justice Clarence Thomas was not required to recuse himself from the case; he actually wrote the majority decision.[15] The full might of the US government and its neoliberal free trade agenda ensured that these patents would also be protected under international law, and that the rest of the world would accept GMO agriculture whether they wanted it or not.

The WTO was the perfect vehicle for doing so. And Dan Amstutz was the perfect man to push it through the WTO.

THE WTO AGREEMENT ON AGRICULTURE

Amstutz, with ample assistance from Cargill, Monsanto and the other dominant entities in the trillion-dollar-a-year global agribusiness market, largely wrote the WTO's Agreement on Agriculture, and, as the US's main negotiator, helped ram it through despite the strenuous objections of other countries to having agriculture covered at all in a global trade agreement. The Agreement became binding when the WTO was launched in January 1995.

In a nutshell, the Agreement on Agriculture views any government support for agriculture to be an unfair barrier to free trade.[16] Under a complicated schedule, the agreement severely reduces, with the ultimate aim of altogether eliminating, government farm programmes and price supports. And as highlighted in the individual Middle East Free Trade Agreements, it does the same with a country's tariffs and other import controls. Amstutz was careful to ensure there were major loopholes which allowed for the huge subsidies that underpin US and European corporate agriculture to continue.

Crucially, as we saw earlier, GMO patents are protected under the WTO's Trade Related Aspects of Intellectual Property Rights (TRIPS), which requires all members to pass rigid intellectual property laws. These laws then recognise GMO patents, and that Monsanto and other patent holders have the indisputable legal standing to require farmers using GMO seeds to pay patent fees and sign legally binding contracts.[17] Countries are prohibited from requiring labelling, or from using their own national standards or testing, of GMO products under WTO rules regarding 'Technical Barriers to Trade'. Under the WTO, a country's ability to maintain the health and well-being of its citizens is always subordinate to the corporate right to profit, and such barriers to neoliberal free trade are not allowed.

The Cartagena Protocol established the right to ban GMOs. But for those countries who have either approved GMO crop production, and or allow the importation of GMO food products, the WTO is a major tool to further prise open their food security to GMO infiltration.

When Saudi Arabia joined the WTO in 2005, it meant that it had to abandon its GMO labelling law, which had been in effect since December 2001. Previously, any company that exported GMO products without clearly identifying them as genetically modified, would be banned from any further business in the future.[18] Once it became a member of the WTO, such labelling requirements were viewed as barriers to trade, and Saudi Arabia would most certainly be subject to sanctions if it continued the policy.

While subsidies for poor countries' agriculture are, in the words of Flugge, 'all wrong', just before the Iraq invasion, the 2002 US Farm Bill initiated $180 billion in new subsidies over ten years, the bulk of which were designated for the large-scale monocrop export agriculture, which has decimated small American family farms.[19] Thanks to these subsidies, US export crops are often sold well below the cost of producing them. This in turn allows the mega-grain trading giants Cargill, Archer Daniels Midland, and Bunge – who between them control 90 per cent of global grain trade[20] – to dump their excess commodities onto the world market. In turn, local farmers are undercut, more small farmers lose their land, more land is converted to monocrop agriculture to be competitive in the neoliberal corporatised system, and more desperate people are available to undercut the wages of other desperate people in the urban sweatshops that inevitably accompany the process. Everyone loses in this race to the bottom – everyone except for the mega-corporations and their shareholders.

Often the excess food is dumped as part of American government relief aid, and as with the majority of the US food chain, much of the content has been genetically modified. In May 2003, the same month that Bush announced the US would be bringing neoliberal freedom to the Middle East via the US Middle East Free Trade Area (MEFTA), he also expressed his concern for the world's poor. According to Bush, Europe's outright refusal to allow GMO crops was a primary cause of mass starvation in Africa. It was this European resistance to GMOs that had in turn resulted in a number of African nations like Zambia, Zimbabwe and Mozambique to refuse US famine relief that was comprised largely of genetically modified food.[21] These countries viewed the risk of contaminating their indigenous agriculture and long-term food security with GMOs outweighed the short-term benefit of famine relief. Once the US took over Iraq, there would be no refusal of Iraqis accepting GMO food.

Genetically modified seeds have also been widely distributed as part of these US aid programmes. Farmers often don't know what they are, and then suddenly find themselves unable to pay the patent and royalty fees, nor can they afford the required fertiliser and chemicals that GMOs won't work without. Getting the entire world hooked on GMO seeds – meaning that every single thing grown for consumption would be patented – would mean profits, as well as control, beyond even Milton Friedman's reckoning.

As well as setting Iraq up as a laboratory for corporate agriculture, Order 81 dropped any and all pretence that America was there to facilitate democracy, explicitly stating that its primary aim is Iraq's 'transition from a non-transparent centrally planned economy to a free-market economy'. Equally undemocratic, Order 81 was also enacted to ensure that Iraq's legal system would be compatible to joining the World Trade Organization, which would ensure future Iraqi governments would be willing contributors to the global system that underpinned American hegemony, regardless of whether US troops were still in the country or not. It was an unelected unaccountable American occupation government that was making these decisions, not Iraqis.

28
Seeds in the Ground

Amstutz oversaw the USAID's Agriculture Reconstruction and Development Program for Iraq (ARDI).[1] The actual work was contracted to Development Alternatives (DAI), and was for 'the transition from a command-and-control production and marketing system to a market-driven economy where farmers and agribusinesses are able to take risks and realize profits'.[2] The immediate focus was on expanding Iraq's wheat crop via high-grade imported certified wheat seed. Fifty-six demonstration sites were set up in the pro-US Kurdistan region, with the intention of 'introducing and demonstrating the value of improved wheat seeds'.[3]

The virtues of the programme, as well as the general benevolence of the American government helping poor backwards Iraqi farmers, are written up in countless military websites and US farm journals. The following was published in *Prairie Grain* in the spring of 2005:

> Working with the U.S. Army, officials from Texas A&M University, Kansas State University, Colorado State University and the Arizona-based World Wide Wheat Company began to look at U.S. wheat varieties that could survive the intense heat and arid climate of Iraq … After months of research, the scientists from Texas A&M, KSU, CSU and WWW selected a mix of wheat and barley lines that could theoretically survive in Iraq. 'We selected several cultivars adapted to varied production methods and end use qualities, not knowing the specifics of Iraq production as to soils, rainfall and or irrigation,' said Rex Thompson, a researcher at Word Wide Wheat.[4]

Rather than utilising Iraqi seeds that had been developed to the conditions of Mesopotamia over the last 10,000 years, or assisting Iraqis in ensuring their indigenous wheat-seed supply was protected and could be regenerated, wheat and barley seed was imported that could 'theoretically' survive in Iraq. The arrogance is astounding – the seeds were selected despite 'not knowing the specifics of Iraq production as to soils, rainfall and or irrigation'. What *was* known is that World Wide Wheat's seeds would not work at all without dependency on pesticides, herbicides, fungicides and fertilisers so readily available from Monsanto, Dow, and DuPont.

It gets worse. Of the six distinct wheat seeds chosen, three were for durum wheat – durum is exclusively grown for pasta production. Pasta had never been grown in Iraq, and is hardly a staple of the Iraqi diet. Which means that over half of the entire project was designed to grow wheat for export. After the devastating effects of the first Gulf War, the sanctions, and the 'Shock and Awe' of the 2003 military invasion, Iraq was now being turned into a vast experiment in agribusiness exploitation.

Despite considerable efforts on the part of Monsanto, genetically modified wheat has not yet been approved for commercial release. That does not mean that it doesn't exist. The imminent launch of Monsanto's GMO wheat in 2004 was met with a global campaign to stop its introduction. Under a mass consumer campaign led by international NGOs, grain buyers in Europe and Japan threatened to boycott all American and Canadian wheat imports if GMO wheat was commercially introduced. As a result, Monsanto had to cancel what it believed would be the highly profitable genetically modified release of the world's other staple grain.[5]

Once a GMO crop is commercially grown, it is very difficult to put the genie back in the bottle. What Monsanto and other seed developers like World Wide Wheat needed was a test site big enough to experiment with its suitability for commercial release. Monsanto could not have dreamt of a better opportunity than Iraq, where under a US military occupation, GMO wheat or other GMO crops could potentially be grown without impediment. And considering US foreign policy had dedicated itself to forcing countries to adopt GMOs, it does not require much imagination to identify what they would do in a country under their military obligation, and which they had carte blanche rule over agriculture. Especially with Dan Amstutz there to oversee the initial stages.

Neither USAID, the USDA, nor the US military has allowed independent scientists to determine whether the seed had been genetically modified. World Wide Wheat describes itself as specialising in 'proprietary varieties' of cereal seeds, which means its clients – that is, farmers – pay a licensing fee.[6] So while World Wide Wheat's website emphasises that its proprietary varieties are not genetically modified, by having farmers pay a license fee it essentially hooks them into the same dependency as if their crops *were* genetically modified. Texas A&M's Agriculture Program's website describes itself as 'a recognised world leader in using biotechnology'.[7] Biotechnology is a buzzword for genetic modification.

Despite doubling the area sown, over the project's three years, Iraq's national wheat production dropped from 2.6 million tonnes in 2002 to 2.2 million tonnes in 2006. Even worse, the national average for yields per hectare went from 1.6 tonnes to 0.6 tonnes.[8]

In 2006, USAID introduced the $343 million Inma Agribusiness Program[9] and Izdihar, or the Iraq Private Sector Growth and Employment Generation, with the contracts awarded carried out by development conglomerate Louis Berger Group. Again not big on subtlety, Inma means 'growth' in Arabic. Much of Inma's work is done by placing agricultural advisers in the Ministry of Agriculture, and as part of Provincial Reconstruction Teams (PRTs), that operate on the local level throughout the country. The majority of personnel on any PRT are US military personnel.[10]

Amongst its activities, Inma is establishing large US-style cattle feedlots in Iraq, and, via the PRTs, distributing more seeds – 200 tons of wheat seeds in Kurdistan to help alleviate the drought in 2007 and 2008,[11] and 776 tons of wheat and barley seeds were also distributed in western Ninewa during the drought. Inma also initiated a micro-loan system to help farmers pay for its programmes, ranging between $500 to $25,000. It emphasised that the wheat and barley seeds it distributed in Ninewa were also distributed to those farmers 'unable to obtain the loans needed to buy seeds'.[12]

How the PRTs actually worked on the ground is encapsulated in a February 2010 USDA Foreign Agricultural Services press release titled 'Hybrid Seed Corn Quality Amazes Iraqi Farmers, Expansion in Al Anbar Province Planned'.[13] It highlights how a PRT agriculture adviser with the US Marine Corps Battalion 1/7 helped Iraqi farmers in the Fallujah area grow a bumper crop of Monsanto's DeKalb-brand hybrid corn. The release emphasised that previous corn harvests had been limited due to 'poor genetics'. Now Iraqi farmers could 'experience the gains in production seen by other farmers using the [hybrid seed] technology around the world'. The six-and-a-half tonnes of seeds yielded 150 bushels per acre, five times the yield of locally grown seed corn. It then said that 'In a study conducted in Iraq, hybrid seed produced 500 percent more yield than traditional seed corn', and that 'Applying additional fertilizer to the hybrid corn fields increased production to 600 percent.' Thanks to the agricultural adviser's and the Marines' efforts, the corn was sold via distributors in the Fallujah area. The Foreign Agricultural Service (FAS) of the US Department of

Agriculture was assisting in showcasing the Monsanto hybrid seed at demonstration plots throughout Al Anbar Province and was facilitating 'a Province-wide launch of the product'.

Dekalb hybrid seed corn is not genetically modified. But hybrid seeds still hook farmers on the promise of higher yields, and get them to indenture themselves to the seemingly endless cycle of 'Applying additional fertilizer to the hybrid corn fields' in order to further increase yields.

Whether providing them the seeds and fertiliser for free, or by loaning the farmers money, the US is hooking Iraqi farmers on a path of corporate dependence that facilitates the consolidation of small farms into larger agribusiness entities specialising in mono-crops – the same pattern of agriculture that has occurred everywhere the US and its neoliberal free market agenda has had influence, including America itself.

But there is another subtext. As we saw earlier, Fallujah was brutally attacked by US forces in April and November 2004, with the documented use of chemical weapons, depleted uranium munitions, and a host of other war crime allegations. The assault on Fallujah did not end with the city being militarily subdued. An extensive peer-reviewed study released in July 2010 found higher rates of cancer, leukaemia, and infant mortality in Fallujah from 2005 to 2009 than corresponding rates for survivors in the years following the atomic bombs dropped on Hiroshima and Nagasaki in 1945. The epidemiological study, 'Cancer, Infant Mortality and Birth Sex-Ratio in Fallujah, Iraq 2005–2009',[14] surveyed 711 houses and 4,843 individuals and found a four-fold increase in cancer rates since the Coalition assault.

The types of cancer were similar to the cancers resulting from radiation fallout at Hiroshima and Nagasaki. The study also found heightened levels of birth defects, and infant mortality rates of 80 deaths out of 1,000 births; eight times higher than in neighbouring Kuwait. Leukaemia rates were 38 times higher, cancer in children 12 times more frequent, breast cancer 10 times more common than in nearby Arab countries of Jordan, Egypt and Kuwait.

The assault on Fallujah was led by US Marines. Now that they had largely decimated the area and its people, the Marines' new role was apparently to finish it off.

The PRTs and other on-the-ground American entities could easily redistribute GMO seeds each year, with the intention to simply wait until Iraq is stable enough to demand the Iraqi government adhere to its international legal obligations and pay the patent and royalty fees due to Monsanto and other patent holders. No one, including the Iraqi government, knows how many GMO crops are being grown in Iraq, or the extent of the problem.

In a 2009 interview with *Baghdad Bulletin* author David Enders, the Iraqi Minister of Agriculture Ali Bahedeli openly acknowledged his concerns that GMOs were being introduced to Iraq by the American occupation without his department's permission or knowledge. 'We have a committee for registering seeds and pesticides in Iraq,' he said. 'Until now, we find some of these organisations and the [US reconstruction teams] bringing seeds from farmers from abroad. We ask them, if you want to help the Iraqi farmers, let us know what you are planning to do.'[15]

This seed-registration process existed prior to the invasion, and similar to the oil law, remains the law of the land until a new seed law is passed. At present, it takes up to two years for imported seeds to be approved for sale in Iraq, and technically this has prohibited mass import and distribution of US agribusiness seeds.[16] But Emma Piper Burket, coordinator of the US-based Iraqi Seed Project, says that at least in the north in Kurdistan, many seeds are imported. In conducting research for a documentary on the subject, she found in June 2011 that many of the seeds in Kurdistan were imported from Iran, Syria, Holland and the US. These imported seeds were prevalent at a seed-market bazaar; what were *not* prevalent were Iraqi seeds.[17] While Kurdistan in general enjoys more autonomy from the central government in Baghdad than the rest of the country, in theory it is still under the same seed-registration restrictions as the rest of Iraq.

Another critical institution that the US did not protect from the 2003 post-invasion looting was Iraq's national gene bank, ironically located in the town of Abu Ghraib. It was in the Abu Ghraib prison that the US military abused, tortured and murdered Iraqi detainees. Iraq's national collection of plant genetic resources was almost totally lost, either outright stolen during the looting, or destroyed when the cold-storage equipment was looted. According to the UN's Food and Agriculture Organisation, 'Iraq had a relatively stable and functioning public-sector controlled seed industry before the war in 2003.'[18]

Decimating Iraq's ability to replenish its own seed stocks of course meant that new seeds would have to be imported. With so much missing, and the US having access to what remains, the possibility exists that a patent could be taken out on a particular seed from

Iraq's rich genetic material developed over centuries, similar to what RiceTec did with Filipino basmati rice.

Iraq's genetic heritage might have been completely lost if not for the efforts of Sanaa Abdul Wahab Al Sheick, of the Iraqi National Gene Bank in the town of Abu Ghraib. At great personal risk, she personally took large numbers of seed germplasms and hid them. Some she buried in the backyard of her house or in the grounds of the seed bank. During the worst of the sectarian violence, and with the crucial electricity needed to keep the genetic resources cool in the midst of Iraq's brutal summer heat, and at great risk to herself, she succeeded in preserving a substantial amount that would have otherwise been lost forever.[19]

29
Hunger and Misery:
A Profitable Occupation

A country with two great rivers should have been the biggest exporter in the world, but now we beg for food from those who participated in killing us.

Iraqi Um Muthanna, 2007[1]

Despite US-focused efforts at improving Iraq's wheat yield with its wonder seeds, wheat production for 2010 was 1.86 million tonnes, a stunning drop from the 2.6 million tonnes Iraqi farmers produced under the severe limitations they endured under the sanctions in 2002.[2]

And despite the clear intent of the CPA's policies, the Iraqi government has continued to subsidise farmers via state-supported crop pricing and other means. Iraqi agriculture faces the same problems as the rest of the Iraqi economy, with crippling shortages of electricity, fuel and continuing security problems.

If there is a single word to sum up the numerous trumpeted plans, announcements and press releases from various Iraqi government officials since the invasion, that word would be 'competitive'. In December 2004, Iraq's interim Agriculture Minister Sawsan Ali Magid al-Sharifi, said 'We need Iraqi farmers to be competitive, so we decided to subsidise inputs like pesticides, fertilisers, improved seeds and so on. We cut down on the other subsidies, but we have to become competitive.'[3]

Iraqi agriculture would have to be very competitive indeed to compete with the highly subsidised GMO-laden commodity foods from the US, or vegetables and fruits from its neighbours, all of whom were profiting from the CPA's elimination of tariffs. In a country that had been largely self-sufficient in food production as recently as the 1970s, Iraq was now importing an incredible 80 per cent of its food.[4]

'A country with two great rivers should have been the biggest exporter in the world, but now we beg for food from those who participated in killing us.' This is how 60-year-old Um Muthanna put it in an interview with independent journalist Dahr Jamail in 2007, in response to the lack of local Iraqi produce at a Baghdad market.[5]

Despite the continuation of government support, and despite the considerable effort the US has spent on agricultural development since the invasion, Iraqi agriculture is nowhere near a level of self-sufficiency. The sectarian violence and insurgency has affected agriculture just as it has affected every other aspect of Iraqi life. Farmer Haji Jassim, in a November 2006 interview, said the biggest obstacle was simply a lack of available farmers and labourers 'since most of our young men who were not killed by US and Iraqi troops are in jail or missing'.[6] 'Local agricultural production is almost nil,' stated Majid al-Dulaymi from the Iraqi Ministry of Agriculture in an interview with the Inter Press Service in February 2007. 'Now the private sector is importing everything, and the prices are too high to afford.'[7]

In addition to having to compete with subsidised imports, Iraq has also suffered a prolonged drought that has severely impacted production. This combination of factors has meant that many Iraqi farmers have gone bankrupt. By 2008, an estimated 90 per cent of farmers in Diyala Governate had abandoned their farms due to the shortage of water and inability to compete with cheap imports.[8]

The drought has been severe, with annual rainfall in Iraq down by 50 per cent in recent years. The UN Food and Agriculture Organization (FAO) attributes the drought in part to the disruption of traditional weather patterns due to global climate change. Equally severe to the country's dependency on irrigation has been the reduced flow in the Tigris and Euphrates rivers due to the construction of dams in Turkey and Syria, which will lead to a water shortage of 33 million cubic metres by 2015.[9]

The water issues have also effected one of the success stories of post-invasion Iraq: the restoration of the Iraqi marshes. These extensive wetlands in Iraq's south were once double the size of the Florida Everglades, and equally renowned for the biodiversity and wildlife that lived there. But anti-government guerillas used them as a hideout, and Saddam Hussein had them drained. Their restoration by the Arab Marsh People themselves, along with considerable international aid since 2003, saw more than half of the area restored by early 2007. Then came the drought, and the increase of water being diverted from the Tigris and Euphrates by Iraq's northern neighbours.[10]

It's not only the quantity of water that is impacting Iraqi agriculture, it's the quality. Despite the billions handed out to

Bechtel and others, at least two-thirds of the sewage produced by Baghdad's population of 6 million is dumped untreated into the Tigris and Euphrates.[11]

And then there is the land itself. A 2010 Iraqi government report found at least 40 sites around the country that were contaminated with extremely high levels of radiation and dioxins.[12] Communities near these sites, particularly Najaf and Fallujah, were found to have increased rates of cancer and birth defects over the past five years. It had been five years previously that the American military had brutally attacked Najaf and Fallujah. High levels of ionising radiation were also found, believed to be from the widespread application of depleted uranium in US munitions during the Gulf War and the invasion.

High levels of dioxins were found in the agricultural fields throughout southern Iraq. Narmin Othman, Iraq's environment minister, said 'The soil has ended up in people's lungs and has been on food that people have eaten. Dioxins have been very high in those areas. All of this has caused systemic problems on a very large scale for both ecology and overall health.'[13]

But according to the US Department of Agriculture in 2010, Iraq's relative lack of Iraqi agricultural production was because 'Iraqi government policies distort markets and undermine productivity', and because Iraqi farmers are using 'inferior seed varieties'.[14]

The US Department of Agriculture has done some positive work at the local level of getting Iraqi agriculture functional. Agriculture adviser John Ellerman oversaw a two-year project to establish a farmer-owned cooperative in Madain Qadaa, a district just east of Baghdad, beginning in 2009.[15] Working with the US military, who provided security, the project helped clear irrigation canals and repair pumping stations, much of it done with local farmers' labour. The farms were family owned, and small – between two to five hectares. Of the approximately 4,000 farmers in the district, 1,000 joined the co-op. USDA provided grants to buy 15 tractors and two combines, which the co-op then made available not only to its members for ploughing, planting and harvesting, but to any farmers who requested the services. Ellerman and his team tried to convince the co-op to charge an extra fee to non-members for the use of the co-op's services, but discriminating against fellow farmers in any way is 'just not part of their culture'.

The area went from roughly 20 per cent of land in wheat and barley production to nearly full production in two years. The farmers used their own seeds, and no seeds were provided by the USDA. Ellerman believes the same is true for the rest of Iraq, with 99 per cent of all seeds the same ones Iraq farmers have been using for decades, if not centuries. While the US would very much like to get GMO and hybrid seeds directly imported, the seed-registration law has stymied these efforts. He emphasised that the US is putting a great deal of pressure on the Iraqi government to allow the direct importation of hybrid and other seeds without the two-year approvals and testing process.

When I suggested that America had the capacity to have widely distributed GMOs and other seeds, Ellerman replied, 'We don't do that stuff. We're not over there to dominate or control things. Our tactic is to try to work with them to maybe change the regulation. We don't dictate how their government should run. We're there to support the development of their government, not to dominate.'

Unfortunately, Ellerman was the only person employed by the USDA to help establish Iraqi farmer cooperatives. He also helped start two other co-ops in the Abu Ghraib area west of Baghdad. These projects lacked the $6 million funding base of the Madain Qadaa co-op, and with the army no longer in the area as part of the general pullback of US troops, their success was not as clear. Other USDA agricultural advisers have helped form farmer associations, more or less getting area farmers to work together but without the cooperative business model or level of funding.

Ellerman also emphasised that because of the huge electricity costs involved with the pumping stations inherent in the irrigation needed for Iraq's agriculture, that it was cheaper for the country to import grain than to grow it. For countries like the US, that can grow grain without irrigation, combined with the economies of scale of the massive American and Australian farms versus the very small 2–5-hectare farms of Iraq, it was almost impossible for Iraq to realistically compete.

John Ellerman is clearly one of the good guys working for the US in Iraq. If the US would have employed thousands of Ellermans to help facilitate a grass-roots revival of Iraqi agriculture with aid money that clearly benefited people on the ground, Iraqi agriculture would be a much heralded success story rather than the dismal failure that has been highlighted thus far. And while he is right about it being cheaper to import grain than to grow it in Iraq, it is not because of any nonsense about economies of scale. It is because the American government heavily subsidises its agribusiness model of agriculture, while it simultaneously eliminated any and all import protections that would have allowed Iraqi agriculture to recover from nearly 30 years of wars and sanctions, which included the very intentional destruction of those canals and pumping stations that Ellerman helped repair. And the reason fuel and electricity costs are so prohibitively expensive is the exact reason why US grain exports are so cheap: subsidies, or rather the lack of them. As we've seen, Iraq had to cut its fuel and diesel subsidies as part of a structural adjustment programme forced upon it by a military occupation government.

As highlighted earlier, the reason Iraqi farms are so small is because the Iraqis fought a revolution in 1958 and overthrew its British puppet monarchy. It then instituted land reform, and broke up the large landholdings of the British-imposed elites and redistributed the land back to the people whose ancestors had farmed the land for literally thousands of years. It is clear that the majority of Iraqis are very proud of their revolutionary heritage and the social benefits it brought, just as they are proud that their country threw out the US, British and French owners of the Iraqi Petroleum Company when Iraq nationalised its oil industry in 1972. Saddam's dictatorship, as well as the US invasion and occupation, are viewed as anathema to that heritage by most Iraqis.

HUNGER AND MISERY: A PROFITABLE OCCUPATION

Decimating Iraq's agriculture through sanctions, deliberately destroying its irrigation and infrastructure via targeted bombing, and then invading and eliminating tariffs and other import protection has proved immensely profitable for American agribusiness. In a market that didn't exist in 2002 under the sanctions, US exports to Iraq have averaged at least $1.5 billion a year since 2005, dominated by agriculture-related products.[16] Iraq is now one of the top five export markets for US hard red winter wheat, rice and poultry.

And with such a ready-made and militarily controlled market, there is apparently no reason to export high-quality commodities. In July 2006, thousands of tonnes of imported food were found to be contaminated and/or past their expiry date, and caused widespread poisoning. Australian wheat shipments had previously been found to contain steel fragments, rendering it inedible.[17]

In June 2010, USDA shamelessly announced that it had 'adjusted its strategy to focus more on market development and market access for U.S. products', and to 'expand the range of U.S. food and agricultural products exported to Iraq, promote joint ventures, and boost investment in Iraq's developing agricultural sector'.[18]

Regarding the need to 'boost investment', almost on cue, in March 2011, Agriculture Minister Ezzeddin al-Dawla announced that Iraq was seeking foreign investment in agriculture to help the country become self-sufficient in grains within three years. 'We are offering incentives for farmers to speed up the process and we welcome foreign investors,' he said.[19]

The net result of eight years of US enforced agricultural 'reconstruction' is summarised in a June 2011 essay by Layth Mahdi, an agricultural adviser to the Iraqi government:

Prior to 2003, Iraq had imported about 30 percent of its food needs annually. The decline in agricultural production after this period, created the need for importing 90 percent of the food at a cost estimated at more than $12 billion annually. Due to the sudden shift in the agricultural policy from subsidized assistance to an immediate shift to a free market policy, the outcomes led to a decline in production. The observed outcome resulted in many farmers abandoning the land and agriculture. The impact on natural resources results in an exploited and degraded environment leaving the land destitute and the people impoverished, unemployed [and] experiencing a sense of losing their human dignity.[20]

Part VIII

Conclusion: Iraq and the Corporate Capture of the Democratic State

30
The Corporate Capture of the Democratic State

I think the economic logic behind dumping a load of toxic waste in the lowest wage country is impeccable and we should face up to that … I've always thought that under-populated countries in Africa are vastly underpolluted.

Larry Summers, President Barack Obama's first National
Economic Council chief, writing in 1991[1]

THE IRAQ INVASION: SUCCESS?

This book has argued that the invasion of Iraq was to guarantee the continuation of American neoliberal hegemony. Relative to that, the US had five primary motivations to militarily seize control of Iraq:

1) Eliminate the threat a post-sanctions Iraq posed to the stability of Saudi Arabia and its petrodollar financing of the US economy, and the Saudi state's willingness to serve American interests via its dominant oil-producer status;

2) Remove Iraq's prohibition on US companies from developing Iraqi oil or any other markets once the UN sanctions ended;

3) Eliminate the euro as Iraq's currency payment for oil, and restore the dollar as the unchallenged global oil currency;

4) Seize the opportunity to create a free market, neoliberal, US client state in Iraq where none had existed before, and

5) Seize the even larger opportunity to expand global capital penetration into the largely closed-off Middle East via the US-Middle East Free Trade Area. Iraq would also allow the potential expansion of the American agribusiness model of corporate agriculture.

Based on the premise that the United States, with British and Australian support, invaded Iraq to preserve and extend American neoliberal hegemony, the invasion and subsequent occupation has been a success. This is in contrast to the widely accepted perception that Iraq has been a disaster for the United States and for the policies of President George Bush, who at the close of his presidency in 2008 had the lowest approval ratings of any US president in history, in large part, although by no means exclusively, due to Iraq.

Iraq's potential capacity to pump 12 million barrels of oil by 2017, combined with existing US influence over Saudi Arabia, means American hegemony can theoretically extend into the next several decades. This will be dependent on the US successfully retaining the dollar as the global oil currency in the face of renewed efforts to eliminate or erode it. Based on its actions in Iraq, it is safe to predict that guaranteeing the dollar's oil dominance will be a very intense focus of US foreign and military policy. It is also safe to predict that it will continue to try to secure further Free Trade Agreements and other neoliberal tethering to the remainder of the Middle East and North Africa.

American efforts will now be focused on ensuring that Iraq has the legal, administrative, security and physical infrastructure capacity to enable this level of production. This will be no easy task, particularly given the inherent corruption of successive post-invasion Iraqi governments, the vehement resistance of the Iraqi people to the selling-off of their oil, and the dilapidated state of much of the country's oil infrastructure. But with Iraq now tethered to the IMF, the World Bank and the WTO, and with an electoral system that guarantees any elected government will be dependent on American aid and support in order to govern, American influence will remain strong regardless of how many troops are actually withdrawn.

Analysts who simply look at the civil strife and the relative lack of direct US or Iraqi-elected government control are looking at only one small aspect of the broader picture of American intentions. While America does not have the level of military or political control over Iraq it desires, neither does any other nation. The US has thus ensured that no other rival will have control of Iraq, or be in position to threaten the hegemony of the United States. This is consistent with stances taken by Bush administration officials beginning in 1991 with the Wolfowitz and Cheney Defense Guidelines document, the Project for New American Century and the Bush 2002 National Security Strategy.

It has not been, however, an unqualified success.

America did not succeed in forcing the Iraqi legislature to pass the US-sponsored oil legislation, and instead had to rely on clearly illegal actions on the part of the Iraqi government to open up oil production. It also did not succeed in imposing Bremer's mandate to privatise the Iraqi economy. As evidenced in Chapter 17, this particular failure can be blamed in large part on American arrogance and incompetence, as well as the effective resistance of Iraqi civil society. It *did* succeed in expanding free market neoliberalism into the broader Middle East and North Africa region as a whole, but it is nowhere close to realising Bush's goal of having a Free Trade Area Agreement for the entire region by 2013.

While wholesale privatisation under the CPA failed, the other elements of the CPA's neoliberal economic orders were implemented, in particular, the elimination of tariffs and other protections. It was the CPA that committed Iraq to WTO membership, and it was when Iraq was under the CPA occupation that Bush announced the US Middle East Free Trade Area Agreement. Similar to how dictators locked their countries into odious debt that the United States then demanded to be paid back by subsequently elected democracies, so the US has tied the Iraqi people to the neoliberal mechanisms of the World Bank, IMF and the WTO, regardless of what government they have in place.

It must also be emphasised that this suggestion of 'success' is within the very narrow definitions of US hegemony and the expansion of neoliberalism. This 'success' should be placed in the broader context of the illegality of the invasion itself, the illegality of Bremer's economic orders and the oil-expansion contracts, the mass-torture scandals of Abu Ghraib and Guantánamo Bay, and the ongoing violence that has resulted in as many as 1.2 million deaths directly attributable to the invasion,[2] and which has displaced nearly 5 million Iraqis.[3] Violence and torture have been the hallmarks of the US in Iraq, not democracy and the rule of law.

For a war that was supposedly to stop the killing fields of Saddam Hussein, America has now added 'Shock and Awe', Abu Ghraib, Guantánamo Bay and Fallujah to the list of words synonymous with horror and repression. Like Saddam's victims, the majority of Iraqis tortured or outright murdered by US forces were innocent of any crime. It is a shameful, shameful, legacy.

Despite its best and horrific efforts to break the spirit of the Iraqi people and force them to acquiesce and accept their fate as a neoliberal client state, the United States has failed miserably. Iraqis have fought back and will continue to do so. Ongoing opposition to American influence will no doubt continue to be militant, as well as the civil-society mobilisation that, against overwhelming odds, stopped the oil law, and forced the US to agree to withdraw its occupation troops.

And so, at a time when neoliberalism was being openly challenged and was in disrepute, US capital has succeeded in securing, however tentatively, a new area of conquest. The cost, though, has been exorbitant; ironically, it is the trillions spent on wars and bailouts protecting its neoliberal hegemony that will very likely lead to America's collapse.

NEOLIBERALISM: INTENT

Neoliberalism has clearly been a deliberate attempt to restore the class power to the uber-wealthy and take back the gains they had lost under Keynesianism and its government-focused policies of wealth distribution. The Iraq invasion was to guarantee the success of the global version of this system: a system where the rich have become much richer, while the poor have become poorer.

The widespread application since the early 1980s of neoliberal policies at the domestic and international levels have successfully restored economic wealth to the pre-Depression, pre-Keynesian New Deal era of the 1920s. In the United States, the top 1 per cent of income earners had a 16 per cent share of the nation's wealth before the 1930s New Deal. By the end of the Second World War, that figure was less than 8 per cent, where it stayed for over three decades.[4] By 2004, the top 1 per cent of the US population controlled 40 per cent of the country's wealth. At the time of Bush's presidency in 2001 and as the ability of the United States to maintain its neoliberal hegemony was facing a number of challenges, the richest 1 per cent of Americans had more money to spend after taxes than the entire bottom 40 per cent of the US population. The gap between rich and poor more than doubled from 1979 to 2000.[5]

As highlighted in Chapter 10, these trends have continued, with hourly wages increasing just over a dollar from 1973 to 2009 for most workers, while the hourly wage for those at the top increased by 30 per cent. And for those at the very top 1 per cent from 1979 to 2007, income skyrocketed by 275 per cent, but only 18 per cent for the bottom 20 per cent. And in an ongoing struggle for most Americans dealing with the worst financial crisis since the Great Depression, corporate profits increased by 36.8 per cent in 2010, the biggest gain since 1950.[6]

Even more conspicuous is the gap in incomes of those living in rich countries versus those living in poor countries, an area that neoliberalism and its emphasis on economic growth was supposed to rectify. In 1960, the income gap was 30:1; by 1997, arguably the peak of the application of neoliberalism, it had more than doubled to 74:1.[7] In 2006, the United Nations found that the world's richest 1 per cent of people owned over 40 per cent of all global wealth.[8]

Writing in 2002, in the midst of the build-up and intensifying propaganda for the need for regime change in Iraq, Indian writer Arundhati Roy summarised the state of the neoliberalised world:

> In the last ten years of unbridled Corporate Globalisation [neoliberalism], the world's total income has increased by an average of 2.5 per cent a year. And yet the numbers of the poor in the world has increased by 100 million. Of the top hundred biggest economies, 51 are corporations, not countries. The top 1 per cent of the world has the same combined income as the bottom 57 per cent and the disparity is growing. Now, under the spreading canopy of the War Against Terror, this process is being hustled along. The men in suits are in an unseemly hurry. While bombs rain down on us, and cruise missiles skid across the skies, while nuclear weapons are stockpiled to make the world a safer place, contracts are being signed, patents are being registered, oil pipelines are being laid, natural resources are being plundered, water is being privatised and democracies are being undermined.[9]

In their pursuit of neoliberalism and modern capitalism, successive American governments have shown remarkably little concern for the well-being – material, spiritual, or cultural – of other nations and peoples, including their own. What they have shown concern for is ensuring they have access to other nation's markets, and that neoliberal capitalism is allowed to flourish unimpeded regardless of whether the country is a democracy or a dictatorship.

As we've seen, this American neoliberal hegemony had resulted in so-called 'developing' countries paying $602 billion in debt repayments to rich countries in 2008, primarily the United States, off a total debt of $3.7 trillion.[10] From 1980 to 2004, they paid an estimated $4.6 trillion.[11] This is the immensely unfair and undemocratic system of wealth redistribution and neoliberal corporate control that the United States invaded Iraq to fight for and defend.

THE CORPORATE CAPTURE OF THE DEMOCRATIC STATE

A reasonable question, given the evidence, is how has neoliberalism been allowed to continue? Apart from the obvious answer of coups, military invasions and the debt weapon, how has the United States and its western allies been able to continue to justify these policies to their own people? And to justify the invasion of Iraq when evidence at the time to warrant such action was practically non-existent?

As we have seen, the very intentional corporate supported rise of right-wing think tanks, talkback radio, and Fox News has ensured there is a relentless and loud media voice justifying US neoliberal policies, both domestic and international. Mainstream media did little to challenge the Bush administration's lies about Iraq. Leaders like Venezuela's Hugo Chavez, who openly oppose US influence, are demonised; Chavez is consistently referred to in the media as a dictator, despite being democratically elected. If covered at all, media coverage of structural adjustment programmes or other neoliberal programmes inevitably focus on the failure of Third World countries to adequately manage their economies.

Mass media organisations such as newspapers, magazines and commercial radio and television stations are also, with few exceptions, corporations. Media corporations exist first and foremost to generate profit and returns to their shareholders, who are by and large other large institutional corporate investors. They also depend on other large corporations for their advertising revenue. Media corporations therefore have a vested interest in maintaining the status quo and the uninterrupted expansion of the global market economy. They are therefore often unquestioned supporters of neoliberalism and other policies that have at their heart increased economic growth and, in particular, deregulation, which has facilitated massive media consolidation in the United States, Britain and Australia. This in turn has led to the corporate media becoming a propaganda arm for an American government that is largely controlled by corporations.

This corporate control is all pervasive. Recalling Kinzer's observation that 'As the twentieth century progressed, titans of industry and their advocates went a step beyond influencing policy makers; they became the policy makers', key US government policy makers are now drawn directly from the ranks of finance and speculation. Present (2011) United States Treasury Secretary Timothy Geithner was director of the Policy Development and Review Department (2001–03) at the International Monetary Fund.[12] His predecessor, Henry Paulson, was CEO of Goldman Sachs before becoming the head of Treasury, as was Robert Rubin, treasury secretary under Clinton. Paulson also was a member of the International Monetary Fund's Board of Governors.[13] US trade representative under Bush and neoliberal zealot, Robert Zoellick, is now head of the World Bank.

Larry Summers, Obama's first National Economic Council chief, was also treasury secretary under Clinton, and was personally responsible for pushing the hard-line neoliberal policies in Russia's disastrous transition to free market neoliberal capitalism. He also was the chief economist at the World Bank 1991–93. It was during this time that a memo written by Summers was leaked to the press: 'I think the economic logic behind dumping a load of toxic waste in the lowest wage country is impeccable and we should face up to that ... I've always thought that under-populated countries in Africa are vastly underpolluted.'[14]

Obama also named Paul Volcker, former head of the US Federal Reserve and neoliberal architect under Reagan, to chair his newly formed Economic Recovery Advisory Board. The Bush administration officials and their direct relationships with some of the largest, most powerful corporations have been addressed throughout this book. Obama has continued this, and has also retained the same Bush military leadership that invaded Afghanistan and Iraq. He has escalated the Afghanistan conflict, tripled the number of drones dropping bombs in Pakistan, a country the US is not at war with, and launched his own bombing campaign against Libya. Goldman Sachs and JP Morgan were his two biggest corporate political action committee campaign contributors.[15]

And as we saw in Chapter 3, the push for neoliberal investment policies around Friedman's three-part formula of government deregulation, cutbacks and privatisation has, since the early 1970s, been met with an extraordinarily united, well-funded, focused corporate agenda. Political parties now depend on these corporations for campaign donations.

Thus the right of corporations to operate in society, and in the market, with the same 'freedom' guaranteed to human individuals via the Bill of Rights, has facilitated the ultimate rise of neoliberalism and hegemonic control. It is the biggest and wealthiest individuals that are the beneficiaries of neoliberalism, facilitated by the corporate 'right' to access the political system.

This corporate access has resulted in the ultimate consolidation of American society. For those Americans who still have retirement or pension plans, these investments are tied to the stock market. Many others have mutual fund or other stock market-related investments. When these investments drop in performance, investors – in this case, ordinary people, not predatory Wall Street speculators – will very quickly pick up the phone and demand that their financial adviser find a better return on their investment. This in turn places more pressure on corporations to lobby and infiltrate government to facilitate laws which will do so – like deregulating mortgage and food speculation, blocking climate-change legislation, enabling human trafficking in free trade agreements, invading Iraq, and countless other examples. Many of these same people will in the same breath condemn 'corporate greed' without fully comprehending how tied they are to the shareholder returns of these very same corporations.

But that does not explain why the American people, well beyond the example of any other so-called 'developed' country, have so readily accepted the very worst and most damaging aspects of corporate neoliberalism. The same system the US has forced on the rest of the world Americans have accepted for themselves, with little coercion by their government.

That doesn't meant there isn't any resistance, and millions of Americans are fighting every day for a more just and equitable society, and by extension, world. It was, after all, the social justice movements of the 1960s and their victories that compelled corporate America to go all out to establish neoliberalism as the guiding ideology for the nation. It was also American activists who shut down the WTO meeting in Seattle in 1999. And, as of October 2011, the Occupy Wall Street movement had exploded into a nationwide protest against the 1 per cent of the population having wealth and income well beyond any reasonable amount of the other 99 per cent.

But since the Reagan administration, the majority of Americans seem to have accepted the relentless corporate message that government is bad, and that the private sector can provide social needs more efficiently and better. As a result, prisons, health care and education are all now largely run for profit. Since the establishment of neoliberalism as America's guiding ideological and policy prescription, the United States now has the world's largest prison population, both in total numbers and per capita. Up to 50 million of its people have no health coverage, and its college graduates' life choices have now been reduced to what sort of job will best pay off their crippling student debts. Its food supply is contaminated with genetically modified organisms and chemicals more so than any other country. Real wages have barely increased since the 1970s. Americans work longer hours, for less pay, with fewer and shorter holidays, than they did in the 1970s. These statistics distinguish it from other First World beneficiaries of neoliberalism, particularly Europe. And the United States has done more than any other nation to block carbon emissions reductions to address arguably the true global crisis, climate change.

The predatory capitalism displayed throughout this book led to the subprime crisis and the near-collapse of the system itself. By invading Iraq, America displayed its military resolve to guarantee the continuation of the system. By bailing out the very institutions that created the financial crisis a few short years later, the US again clearly showed that it will stop at nothing to guarantee the continuation of a system that has so blatantly transferred massive wealth from the working and middle classes to the richest of the rich. The record number of people who have lost their jobs and homes as a result of the most recent financial crisis are not going to be bailed out, even though they did nothing to create the circumstances that they are now suffering for. Those same banks and large corporations, bailed out with trillions of dollars of public money, are now posting record profits and rewarding themselves with billions in bonuses. And it is these same banks and corporations, led by a Tea Party cheerleading squad, that are now demanding that Social Security and Medicare and what little government protection there is left be eviscerated, if not outright eliminated.

Yet Americans for the most part seem to feel this is a completely acceptable model for the rest of the world to follow. Enough Americans provide the unequivocal social and political support for the United States to have the world's largest military several times over, and to support the nonsense that America invaded Iraq to bring it democracy and freedom. The US military exists for one reason, and it is the reason it invaded Iraq: to preserve the same neoliberal hegemony that is so clearly decimating its own country.

But as we've seen, the rest of the world is fighting back: the tremendous and courageous resistance of the Iraqi people, the uprisings throughout the Middle East, the South American countries' mass departure of the World Bank and the IMF, the large-scale protests throughout Europe. At their heart, they have all been in condemnation of the US-driven neoliberal agenda that we've explored throughout this book, the exclamation point of which was the Iraq invasion and occupation.

WAYS FORWARD: REMOVING CORPORATIONS FROM THE DEMOCRATIC PROCESS

Milton Friedman argued that in a democracy, it is government that determines the parameters in which corporations operate, and that citizens are able to remedy corporate injustice via the democratic process. What Friedman neglected to address is that corporations have the ability to influence and access the democratic process in ways that ordinary citizens do not, and for entirely different motivations. As corporate influence on the political process has increased, so too has their ability to determine the policy and legislative framework governing them. This ability is motivated by one sole factor: profit. To quote Friedman, 'the social responsibility of business is to increase its profits.'[16] It is also their legal responsibility.

As seen throughout this book, it is large corporate 'individuals' who enjoy the same 'rights' as flesh-and-blood people that have benefited from neoliberalism. It has been American and other rich countries' corporations that have reaped billions upon billions of dollars from the ruthless application of Friedman's three-part formula. It has been corporate individuals, not human ones, who have bought up privatised public assets and replaced public services with ones dedicated to private profit rather than the public good, and who have benefited from opening up markets, stripping corporate regulations, and hiring the resulting cheap sweatshop labour in the utterly unwinnable race to the bottom.

According to the predatory form of neoliberal capitalism promulgated by the United States, the role of government is no longer to ensure its citizens have food, shelter, water and health care; these are now things to be commodified from which new corporate profit can be extracted. Economic growth and private profit are the correct ways to measure social well-being.

In the year 2012, anyone reading this book is either living in a corporate-dominated society, or is in one that the most powerful nation in the history of the world is attempting to make into one.

Yet that nation, the United States of America, is a democracy. Its citizens are supposed to be protected by their Constitution's Bill of Rights, and decisions like invading another sovereign country supposedly can only be done with the approval of its citizens' representatives. This is, of course, no longer the case, if it ever was. Because corporations have achieved the same legal rights and protections as those citizens, they have political power well beyond the ability of any flesh-and-blood citizen or citizens' groups. Congressional representatives and senators represent corporations, not their citizen constituents. The millions given in campaign donations, the thousands of K Street lobbyists in Washington DC, the money poured into controlling the mainstream corporate media and its messaging – this is what controls America, and what determines major decisions like whether or not to invade Iraq.

Artificial entities created for the exclusive purpose of generating profit should not be allowed to be part of the democratic process. As a society, we have long recognised and acted on the need to remove some individuals from the market because of their behaviour. For example, convicted paedophiles are prohibited from entering the labour market as childcare workers. Just as paedophiles prey on children, so do corporations prey on democracy, to find new means to generate ever-increasing profit, regardless of the broader damage to society.

Removing corporations from the democratic process is now not only important, it is a necessity. In response to the 2010 *Citizens' United* Supreme Court decision, which allowed even more corporate money into the political system, there is now a small but dedicated movement to rescind the 1886 *Santa Clara* decision and restore the Bill of Rights for the exclusive protection of flesh-and-blood citizens.[17]

If successful, it will be what the American people will be most remembered for. If not, their legacy will be to have allowed a horrendously destructive and predatory form of neoliberal capitalism to have flourished. The invasion and occupation of Iraq will be amongst the very worst of, unfortunately, countless other examples.

Notes

CHAPTER 1   INTRODUCTION: MAKING SENSE OF IRAQ

1. Howard Zinn, *A People's History of the United States: 1492 to Present*, New York: HarperCollins, 2010 (1st edn 1980), pp. 361–4.
2. William Cleveland, *A History of the Modern Middle East*, Boulder, CO: Westview Press, 2000, p. 468.
3. David Harvey, *A Brief History of Neoliberalism*, Oxford: Oxford University Press, 2005, p. 193.
4. Anne Reifenberg and James Tanner, 'Left in the Dust? US Oil Companies Fret Over Losing Out On Any Jobs in Iraq', *Wall Street Journal*, 17 April 1995.
5. Rajiv Chandrasekaran, *Imperial Life In The Emerald City: Inside Iraq's Green Zone*, New York: Alfred Knopf, 2006, pp. 162–3.
6. 'The Costs of War Since 2001: Iraq, Afghanistan, and Pakistan', Executive Summary, Eisenhower Study Group, Brown University, June 2011, p. 7.

CHAPTER 2   IRAQ: A DEVASTATED COUNTRY

1. Email interview with author, 5 September 2011.
2. Pepe Escobar, 'Bremer's Quick Study in Colony Building', *Asia Times*, 12 July 2004.
3. 'Iraq Ministry of Planning Confirms 23% Poverty Rate', *CurrencyNewshound. com*, 18 April 2011 <http://thecurrencynewshound.com/2011/04/18/iraq-ministry-of-planning-confirms-23-poverty-rate>.
4. Special Inspector General for Iraq Reconstruction, 'Quarterly Report and Semiannual Report to the United States Congress', 30 January 2009, p. 9.
5. Opinion Research Business, 'More than 1,000,000 Iraqis Murdered', 14 September 2007.
6. UN High Commissioner for Refugees, 'Iraq Refugee Emergency', 2008.
7. Institute for Economics and Peace, *Global Peace Index 2011*.
8. Democracy Index, 2010, A report from the Economist [Magazine] Intelligence Unit, November <http://graphics.eiu.com/PDF/Democracy_Index_2010_web. pdf>.
9. Transparency International, *Corruption Perceptions Index 2010 Results*.
10. Freedom House, 2011, *Iraq Country Report*, 2011.

CHAPTER 3   A FULL SCALE ECONOMIC OVERHAUL: THE RISE OF FREE MARKET NEOLIBERALISM

1. Mont Pelerin Society, 'Founding Statement', 1947 <www.montpelerin.org>.
2. Harvey, *Brief Introduction to Neoliberalism*, pp. 2–3.
3. Naomi Klein, *The Shock Doctrine*, London: Penguin Books, 2007, pp. 53–7.

4. Steve Hanke, 'We were all Keynesians – then', *Forbes.com*, 22 February 1999 <http://www.forbes.com/global/1999/0222/0204077a.html>.

5. Harvey, *Brief Introduction to Neoliberalism*, p. 11.

6. David Yogel, *Fluctuating Fortunes: The Political Power of Business in America*, New York: Basic Books, 1989, p. 59.

7. David Burks, 'Disenchantment with Business: A Mandate for Christian Ethics', *The Entrepreneur*, August 1977.

8. *US News and World Report*, 'Why Business Finds It Tough to Polish Its Own Image', 19 September 1977.

9. Lewis Powell Jr, 'Confidential Memorandum: Attack of American Free Enterprise System', 23 August 1971 <http://reclaimdemocracy.org/corporate_ accountability/powell_memo_lewis.html>.

10. Ibid.

11. Sharon Beder, *Suiting Themselves: How Corporations Drive the Global Agenda*, London: Earthscan, 2006, p. 13.

12. Ibid.

13. Harvey, *Brief Introduction to Neoliberalism*, p. 93.

14. Ted Nace, *Gangs of America: The Rise of Corporate Power and the Disabling of Democracy*, San Francisco, CA: Berret-Kohler, 2003, p. 148.

15. Jennifer Rockne, 'The Biggest Obstacle to Equal Representation for Women in Congress Isn't Sexism, It's Money', March 2001 <http://reclaimdemocracy. org/political_reform/women_in_congress.html>.

16. Reclaim Democracy, List and details of relevant Supreme Court decisions recognising corporate personhood, 2010 <http://reclaimdemocracy.org/ personhood/>.

17. Nobel Prize Foundation. List of all Nobel Prize winners <http://nobelprize. org>.

CHAPTER 4   CHILE AND THE BLUEPRINT FOR IRAQ

1. Klein, *Shock Doctrine*, pp. 54–5.

2. Harvey, *Brief Introduction to Neoliberalism*, p. 8.

3. Seymour Hersh, *The Price of Power: Kissinger in the Nixon White House*, New York: Summit Books, 1983, pp. 258–60.

4. Church Report, 1975. Quote is from Helm's 15 September 1970 meeting notes with Nixon, as documented in the Church Report, 'Covert Action in Chile 1963–1973', Select Committee to Study Governmental Operations with Respect to Intelligence Activities, Department of State, United States Senate, 18 December 1975. The full report is contained in <http://foia.state.gov/Reports/ ChurchReport.asp>.

5. Beder, *Suiting Themselves*, p. 44.

6. Orlando Letelier, 'The Chicago Boys In Chile: Economic Freedom's Awful Toll, *The Nation*, 28 August 1976.

7. Institute for Policy Studies. Webpage dedicated to Orlando Letelier <http:// lm.ips-dc.org/>.

8. Letelier, 'Chicago Boys in Chile'.

9. Harvey, *Brief Introduction to Neoliberalism*, p. 8.

10. Letelier, 'Chicago Boys in Chile'.

11. Ibid.

12. Ibid.

13. Klein, *Shock Doctrine*, p. 97.
14. Church Report.
15. Klein, *Shock Doctrine*, p. 86.
16. Ibid.
17. Joseph Stiglitz, *Globalisation and Its Discontents*, New York: W.W. Norton & Company, 2002, p. 8.
18. Thomas Friedman, *The Lexus and the Olive Tree: Understanding Globalization*, New York: HarperCollins, 1999, p. 464.

CHAPTER 5   NIXON, SAUDI ARABIA AND THE GEOPOLITICAL ROOTS OF THE IRAQ INVASION

1. David Hammes and Douglas Wills, 'Black Gold: The End of Bretton Woods and the Oil-Price Shocks of the 1970s', *The Independent Review*, vol. IX, no. 4, Spring, 2005, pp. 501–11.
2. David Korten, *When Corporations Rule the World*, San Francisco, CA: Kumarian Press and Berrett-Koehler Publishers, 2001 (2nd edn), pp. 161–2.
3. Ibid., pp. 178–9.
4. Peter Gowan, *The Global Gamble: Washington's Faustian Bid for World Dominance*, London: Verso, 1998, p. 19.
5. Beder, *Suiting Themselves*, pp. 48–9.
6. Gowan, *Global Gamble*, pp. 21–3.
7. Cleveland, *History of the Modern Middle East*, p. 468.
8. John Perkins, *Confessions of an Economic Hit Man*, San Francisco, CA: Berrett Kohler Publishers, 2004, p. 97.
9. Ibid., pp. 102–3.
10. Ibid., pp. 99–100.
11. Edward Morse, and James Richard, 'The Battle for Energy Dominance', *Foreign Affairs*, March/April, 2002, p. 20.
12. IMF, 'Monetary Matters, An IMF Exhibit – The Importance of Global Cooperation, Reinventing the System (1972–1981)', Part 4 of 7 <http://www.imf.org/external/np/exr/center/mm/eng/mm_rs_01.htm>.

CHAPTER 6   PETRODOLLAR RECYCLING, THIRD WORLD DEBT AND THE WASHINGTON CONSENSUS

1. Harvey, *Brief Introduction to Neoliberalism*, p. 52.
2. Charles Derber, 2004. *Regime Change Begins at Home*, San Francisco, CA: Berrett Kohler Publishers, p. 294.
3. Klein, *Shock Doctrine*, p. 141.
4. Beder, *Suiting Themselves*, pp. 25–7.
5. Ibid.
6. IMF, 'Monetary Matters'.
7. Harvey, *Brief Introduction to Neoliberalism*, p. 193.
8. World Bank, 'About Us', History of World Bank and Bretton Woods, 2010. <www.worldbank.org/about>.
9. John Cavanaugh and Jerry Mander (eds), *Alternatives to Economic Globalization: A Better World Is Possible*, 2nd edn, San Francisco, CA: Berrett Koehler Publishers, 2004, p. 56.

10. Stiglitz, *Globalization and Its Discontents*, p. 13.
11. Ibid., p. 99.
12. Ibid., p. 98.
13. C. Lomnitz-Adler, 'The Depreciation of Life During Mexico City's Transition into "The Crisis"', in J. Schneider and I. Susser (eds), *Wounded Cities*, New York: Berg, 2003, pp. 4–70, cited in Harvey, *Brief Introduction to Neoliberalism*, 2005, p. 100.
14. John Williamson, 'What Washington Means by Policy Reform', in Williamson (ed.), *Latin American Readjustment: How Much has Happened*, Washington, DC: Institute for International Economics, 1989.
15. Beder, *Suiting Themselves*, p. 97.
16. John Weeks, 'Credit Where Discredit is Due', *Third World Resurgence*, April, 1994.
17. Davison Budhoo, *Enough is Enough: Dear Mr. Camdessus ... Open Letter of Resignation to the Managing Director of the International Monetary Fund*, New York: New Horizons Press, 1990, p. 102.
18. Letelier, 'Chicago Boys in Chile'.

CHAPTER 7   NEOLIBERALISM, DEBT AND AMERICAN EMPIRE

1. Klein, *Shock Doctrine*, pp. 157–8.
2. Ibid.
3. Korten, *When Corporations Rule the World*, pp. 192–5.
4. Ibid., p. 195.
5. Harvey, *Brief Introduction to Neoliberalism*, p. 103.
6. Ibid., p.75.
7. Ibid.
8. Klein, *Shock Doctrine*, pp. 143–59.
9. Stiglitz, *Globalization and Its Discontents*, p. 95, 119.
10. These and other sad stories of neoliberal globalisation are detailed in Harvey's *A Brief Introduction to Neoliberalism* and Klein's *Shock Doctrine*.
11. Jubilee Debt Campaign, 'How big is the debt of poor countries?', 2011; available at <http://www.jubileedebtcampaign.org.uk>.
12. Islamic Relief International, 'Debt and Islam' Information Paper, November 2008 <http://www.jubileedebtcampaign.org.uk/Debt3720and3720Islam+4662.twl>.
13. Jubilee Debt Campaign, 'Why should we drop the debt?', 2011; available at <http://www.jubileedebtcampaign.org.uk>.
14. *MercoPress*, 'South American leaders sign agreement creating South Bank', 27 September 2009 <http://en.mercopress.com/2009/09/27/south-american-leaders-sign-agreement-creating-south-bank>.
15. Vince McElhinny, 'Bank of the South' Info Brief, Bank Information Center, November 2007 <www.globalexchange.org/sites/default/files/BankoftheSouth.pdf>.
16. Jubilee Debt Campaign, Ecuador, Country Information <www.jubileedebtcampaign.org.uk/Ecuador+4044.twl>.
17. Anthony Faiola, 'Calling Foreign Debt "Immoral," Leader Allows Ecuador to Default', *Washington Post*, 13 December 2008.
18. Mark Tran, 'Venezuela quits IMF and World Bank', *Guardian*, 1 May 2007.

19. Heather Stewart, 'Can the IMF Now Feed the World?', *Observer*, 26 April 2009.

20. Mark Weisbrot, 'IMF Shouldn't Get Money Without Reform', *New York Times*, 24 April 2009.

21. Christian Aid, 'Lifeline or Death-knell: What Will the IMF Offer?', April 2009 <www.christianaid.org.uk/images/imfbriefing.pdf>.

22. Weisbrot, 'IMF Shouldn't Get Money'.

CHAPTER 8   CONTAINING IRAQ: THE GULF WAR AND SANCTIONS

1. Michel Moushabeck, 'Iraq: Years of Turbulence', in Michel Moushabeck and Phyllis Bennis (eds), *Beyond the Storm: Gulf Crisis Reader*, Edinburgh: Canongate Books, 1992, p. 29.

2. Kanan Makiya, *Republic of Fear: Saddam's Iraq*, Berkeley: University of California Press, 1998 edn; originally published under the pseudonym Samir al-Khalil.

3. *Middle East Report*, 'Interview with Samih Farsoun', January 1991, pp. 5–6; cited in Gowan, *Global Gamble*, p. 160.

4. Perkins, *Confessions of an Economic Hit Man*, pp. 215, 217.

5. Gowan, *Global Gamble*, p. 160.

6. Lawrence Everest, *Oil, Power and Empire: Iraq and the US Global Agenda*, Monroe, ME: Common Courage Press, 2004, pp. 44–8.

7. Fred Halliday, *The Middle East in International Relations: Power, Politics and Ideology*, Cambridge: Cambridge University Press, 2005, p. 144.

8. United Nations, Security Council Resolution 661, August 1990.

9. George Bush Sr, 'The Liberation of Kuwait has Begun', Speech, in Micah Sifry and Christopher Cerf (eds), *Gulf War Reader*, New York: Three Rivers Press, 1991, p. 313.

10. Jean Heller, 'Photos Don't Show Buildup', *St Petersburg Times*, 6 January 1991.

11. Everest, *Oil, Power and Empire*, pp. 134–6.

12. Thomas Nagy, 'The Secret Behind the Sanctions: How the US Intentionally Destroyed Iraq's Water Supply', *The Progressive*, September 2001.

13. Ibid.

14. Paul Lewis, 'After The War; U.N. Survey Calls Iraq's War Damage Near-Apocalyptic', *New York Times*, 22 March 1991.

15. Everest, *Oil, Power and Empire*, p. 145.

16. Gowan, *Global Gamble*, pp. 154–6.

17. Dilip Hiro, *Iraq in the Eye of the Storm*, New York: Thunder's Mouth Press, 2002, pp. 38–40.

18. Robert Collier, 'Iraq Links Cancers to Uranium Weapons', *San Francisco Chronicle*, 13 January 2003.

19. UN Security Council Resolution 687, 6 April 1991.

20. Fairness and Accuracy in Reporting, 'Common Myths in Iraq Coverage', 27 November 2002 <www.fair.org/activism/iraq-myths.html>.

21. Hiro, *Iraq in the Eye of the Storm*, p. 77.

22. Looney's quote is from the *Washington Post*, 30 August 1999; cited in William Blum, *Rogue State*, Monroe, ME: Common Courage Press, 2005, p. 159.

23. Peter Baker, 'Iraq's Shortage of Medicine May Grow More Severe,' *Washington Post*, 19 December 2002.

24. 'Autopsy of a Disaster: The US Sanctions Policy on Iraq', Institute for Public Accuracy, 13 November 1998 <www.accuracy.org/44-autopsy-of-a-disaster-the-u-s-sanctions-policy>.
25. Seymour Hersh, 'Saddam's Best Friend: How the CIA Made It a Lot Easier for the Iraqi leader to Return', *The New Yorker*, 5 April 1999.
26. Everest, *Oil, Power and Empire*, p. 180.
27. Marian Wilkinson, and Phil Coorey, 'The Dirty Dozen', *Sydney Morning Herald*, 28 November 2006.
28. UNICEF, 'Child and Maternal Mortality Survey 1999: Preliminary Report', July 1999 <www.fas.org/news/iraq/1999/08/990812-unicef.htm>.
29. Ibid.
30. *Revolutionary Worker*, 'US Genocide in Iraq: A Conversation with Denis Halliday', 28 March 1999.
31. '60 Minutes', 'Punishing Saddam' Transcript, *CBS*, 12 May 1996.
32. *Wall Street Journal*, 'Smarting Over Iraq', Editorial, 5 July 2001.
33. Paul Lewis, 'Iraq Now Admits a Secret Program to Enrich Uranium', *New York Times*, 9 July 1991.
34. Scott Ritter, *Endgame: Solving the Iraq Crisis*, New York: Simon & Schuster, 2002.
35. Hersh, 'Saddam's Best Friend'.
36. Tim Weiner, 'The Case of the Spies Without a Country', *New York Times*, 17 January 1999.

CHAPTER 9   THREAT TO THE DOLLAR: IRAQ, THE EURO AND DOLLAR DOMINANCE

1. John Chapman, 'The Real Reasons Bush went to War', *Guardian*, 27 July 2004.
2. Richard Benson, 'Oil, the Dollar, and US Prosperity', 8 August 2003 <www.informationclearinghouse.info/article4404.htm>.
3. George Monbiot, 'The Bottom Dollar', *Guardian*, 22 April 2003.
4. US National Debt Clock, 2011 <http://www.brillig.com/debt_clock>.
5. William Clark, *Petrodollar Warfare: Oil, Iraq and the Future of the Dollar*, Vancouver: New Society Publishers, 2005.
6. Gowan, *Global Gamble*, p. 19.
7. Perkins, *Confessions of an Economic Hit Man*, pp. 250–51.
8. European Parliament, 'Resolution on the Communication from the Commission on the European Union's Oil Supply', 14 June 2001 <www.europarl.europa.eu/meetdocs/committees/itre/20011203/455711EN.pdf>.
9. Robin Newbold, 'EU urges Russia to Swap Dollar for Euro', *Asia Times*, 19 May 2001.
10. Faisal Islam, 'When Will We Buy Oil in Euros?', *Observer*, 22 February 2003.
11. Ibid.
12. Clark, *Petrodollar Warfare*, p. 117.
13. Stan Goff, 'The War for Saudi Arabia', 9 August 2004 <www.freedomroad.org/milmatters_30_saudiarabia.html>.
14. Chalmers Johnson, *Sorrows of Empire: Militarism, Secrecy, and the End of the Republic*, New York: Metropolitan Books, 2004, pp. 5–6.
15. William Drozdiak, 'Even Allies Resent U.S. Dominance', *Washington Post*, 4 November 1997.

16. Dan Morgan and David Ottaway, 'U.S. Drillers Eye Huge Petroleum Pool', *Washington Post*, 15 September 2002.
17. Islam, 'When Will We Buy Oil in Euros?'.
18. Ibid.
19. Ibid.
20. Clark, *Petrodollar Warfare*, p. 20.
21. David Spiro, *The Hidden Hand of American Hegemony: Petrodollar Recycling and International Markets*, Ithaca, NY: Cornell University Press, 1999, pp. 121–3.
22. Ibid., p. 125.
23. Daniel Yergin, *The Prize: The Epic Quest for Oil, Money and Power*, New York: Simon and Schuster, 1991, pp. 413–16.
24. Agence France-Presse, 'US World leader in Arms Sales, Saudi Arabia No 1 Buyer', 15 October 2003.
25. Oliver Morgan and Faisal Islam, 'Saudi Dove in the Oil Slick', *Observer*, 13 January 2001.

CHAPTER 10   DOLLAR CHALLENGE REDUX: THE GLOBAL FINANCIAL CRISIS AND IRAQI OIL

1. Carol Hoyos and Kevin Morrison, 'Iraq Returns to the International Oil Market', *Financial Times*, 5 June 2003.
2. Cyrus Sanati, '10 Years Later, Looking at Repeal of Glass-Steagall', *New York Times,* 12 November 2009.
3. US Senator Bernie Sanders, 'The Fed Audit', 21 July 2011. Senator Sanders' summary, as well as the full audit of the Federal Reserve, are available on his website <www.sanders.senate.gov/newsroom>.
4. 'The Costs of War Since 2001', p. 7.
5. *The Australian*, 'UN's Currency Call', 7 October 2009.
6. World Bank, 'Emerging Market Growth Poles are Redefining Global Economic Structure, Says World Bank Report', Press Release No:2011/483/DEC, 17 May 2011.
7. John Vinocur, 'Making Sense of Sarkozy's Currency Proposal', *New York Times*, 14 December 2009.
8. Robert Fisk, 'Arab States Launch Secret Moves to Stop Using the US Dollar for Oil Trading', *Independent*, 6 October 2009.
9. *Asia Pulse*, 'Dollar Supremacy to Continue as There's No Alternative: Reddy', 16 August 2011.
10. Fisk, 'Arab States Launch Secret Moves'.
11. Ibid.
12. John Pilger, 'The CIA is Behind the Rebellion', *Global Research*, 8 April 2011 <http://globalresearch.ca/index.php?context=va&aid=24225>.
13. *Economist*, 'The Disappearing Dollar', 2 December 2004.
14. Half in Ten Campaign, 'Restoring Shared Prosperity: Strategies to Cut Poverty and Expand Economic Growth', Report, October 2011 <http://halfinten.org/indicators/publications/2010report>; Congressional Budget Office, 'Trends in the Distribution of Household Income Between 1979 and 2007', Summary, October 2011 <www.cbo.gov/doc.cfm?index=12485>.

15. 'Petrodollar Recycling and Global Imbalances', Presentation by Saleh Nsouli, Director, IMF Europe, CESifo's International Spring Conference, Berlin, 23–24 March 2006.
16. Ibid.
17. Rachel Ziemba, 'Petrodollar Recycling: Focus on the Banks, RGE Analysts', *EconoMonitor*, 9 April 2008 <http://www.economonitor.com/analysts/2008/04/09/petrodollar-recycling-focus-on-the-banks/>.
18. Matthew Higgins, Thomas Klitgaard and Robert Lerman, 'Recycling Petrodollars', *Current Issues in Economics and Finance*, December 2006, vol. 12, no. 9.
19. Ibid.
20. Clark, *Petrodollar Warfare*, p. 63.
21. Geoff Hissock, 'Iraq's Oil Industry Looks for OPEC Growth Role', *The Australian*, 7 June 2011.
22. Margot Habiby, 'Saudi Arabia's 2010 Oil Production Exceeded OPEC Quota by 4.3%, U.S. Says', Bloomberg.com, 4 January 2011 <http://www.bloomberg.com/news/2011-01-05/saudi-arabia-s-2010-oil-production-exceeded-opec-quota-by-4-3-u-s-says.html>.
23. Clifford Krauss, 'Saudi Arabia, Defying OPEC, Will Raise Its Oil Output', *New York Times*, 10 June 2011.
24. John Vidal, 'WikiLeaks Cables: Saudi Arabia Cannot Pump Enough Oil to Keep a Lid on Prices', *Guardian*, 8 February 2011.
25. Greg Palast, 'OPEC on the March: Why Iraq Still Sells its Oil à la Cartel', *Harper's Magazine*, April 2005.

CHAPTER 11   CONTAINING IRAQ: OIL, IMPERIALISM AND THE RISE OF CORPORATE RULE

1. David Fromkin, *A Peace to End All Peace: The Fall of the Ottoman Empire and the Creation of the Modern Middle East*, New York: Owl Press, 1989, pp. 285–9.
2. Hugh Pope and Peter Waldman, 'Past Mideast Invasions Faced Unexpected Perils', *Wall Street Journal*, 19 March 2003.
3. Geoff Simons, *From Sumer to Saddam*, 2nd edn, New York: St Martin's Press, 1994, pp. 177–8.
4. Jonathan Glancey, 'Our Last Occupation: Gas, Chemicals, Bombs – Britain Has Used Them All Before in Iraq', *Guardian*, 19 April 2003.
5. Simons, *From Sumer to Saddam*, p. 147.
6. Everest, *Oil, Power and Empire*, pp. 44–8.
7. Cleveland, *History of the Modern Middle East*, p. 204.
8. Simons, *From Sumer to Saddam*, p. 153.
9. Yergin, *The Prize*, p. 401.
10. Joe Stork and Ann Lesch, 'Why War', *Middle East Report*, November–December 1990.
11. Steven Kinzer, *Overthrow: America's Century of Regime Change from Hawaii to Iraq*, New York: Henry Holt and Company, 2006, p. 4.
12. Ibid., p. 64.
13. Roger Morgan, *The United States and West Germany, 1945–1973: A Study in Alliance Politics*, Oxford: Oxford University Press, 1974, p. 54.

14. Kinzer, *Overthrow*, pp. 118–24.
15. Mostafa Zahrani, 'The Coup that Changed the Middle East – Mossadeq v. the CIA in Retrospect', *World Policy Journal*, Summer 2002.
16. Kinzer, *Overthrow*, pp. 58–9.
17. Ibid., p. 3.
18. Ibid., pp. 1–2.
19. United States Constitution, 14th Amendment, Section 1.
20. For an excellent overview, see William Meyers, 'The Santa Clara Blues: Corporate Personhood Versus Democracy', Redwood Alliance for Democracy, 2001 <www.iiipublishing.com/afd/santaclara.html>.
21. Archer Shaw, 1950. 'Letter from Abraham Lincoln to Colonel William F. Elkins, Nov. 21, 1864', *The Lincoln Encyclopedia*, New York: Macmillan, p. 40.
22. For a more in-depth examination, see Ted Nace, *Gangs of America: The Rise of Corporate Power and the Disabling of Democracy*, San Francisco, CA: Berret-Kohler, 2003, and Thom Hartmann, *Unequal Protection: The Rise of Corporate Dominance and the Theft of Human Rights*, New York: Rodale Books, 2002.
23. Charles Beard, *The Idea of National Interest: An Analytical Study in American Foreign Policy*, Chicago, IL: Quadrangle, 1934, p. 74.
24. Letelier, 'The Chicago Boys In Chile'.
25. Rhett A. Butler, 'Corporations Among Largest Economic Entities', Mongabay. com, 18 July 2005 <http://news.mongabay.com/2005/0718-worlds_largest. html>. Based on data July 2005 from *Fortune* magazine and the World Bank.

CHAPTER 12   IRAQ: RESISTANCE AND REVOLUTION

1. Cleveland, *History of the Modern Middle East*, pp. 317–18; cited in Everest, *Oil, Power and Empire*, pp. 61–2.
2. Marion Farouk-Sluglett and Peter Sluglett, *Iraq Since 1958: From Revolution to Dictatorship*, London: I.B. Tauris, 2001, pp. 31–4.
3. Richard Becker, 'The US and Iraq in Historical Perspective', International Action Center, 2003 <www.iacenter.org>.
4. Everest, *Oil, Power and Empire*, pp. 63–5.
5. Dana Schmidt, 'West to Keep Out of Iraq Unless Oil Is Threatened', *New York Times*, 17 July 1958.
6. Moushabeck, 'Iraq: Years of Turbulence', p. 29.
7. Simons, *From Sumer to Saddam*, p. 234.
8. Everest, *Oil, Power, and Empire*, pp. 69–72.
9. Said Aburish, *Saddam Hussein: The Politics of Revenge*, New York: Bloomsbury, 1999, pp. 57–9.
10. Antonia Juhasz, *The Bush Agenda: Invading the World One Economy at a Time*, New York: Regan Books, 2006, p. 152.
11. Makiya, *Republic of Fear*.
12. Gowan, *Global Gamble*, p. 158.
13. Halliday, *Middle East in International Relations*, p. 179.
14. Howard Teicher and Gayle Teicher, *Twin Pillars to Desert Storm: America's Flawed Vision in the Middle East from Nixon to Bush*, New York: William Morrow and Company, 1993, p. 103.
15. Dilip Hiro, *The Longest War: The Iran–Iraq Military Conflict*, New York: Routledge, 1990 pp. 42, 72.

16. Murray Waas, 'What Washington Gave Saddam for Christmas', in Micah Sifry and Christopher Cerf (eds), *The Gulf War Reader*, New York: Three Rivers Press, 1991, pp. 85–96.

17. William Blum, 'Chemical Weapons, the US, and Iraq: What the New York Times Left Out', *Counterpunch*, 20 August 2002.

18. Everest, *Oil, Power and Empire*, pp. 112–13.

19. Ibid., pp. 105–6.

20. Jim Valette, 'Crude Vision: How Oil Interests Obscured U.S. Government Focus on Chemical Weapons Use By Saddam Hussein', *Sustainable Energy and Education Network*, March 2003 <www.ips-dc.org/files/245/Crude_Vision2.pdf>.

21. Jim Vallette, 'Letter to the Bechtel Corporation', in 'Bechtel: Profiting from Destruction', A Collaborative Report by Corpwatch, Global Exchange, and Public Citizen, June 2003 <http://corpwatch.org/article.php?id=6975>.

22. Philip Shenon, 'Declaration Lists Companies that Sold Chemicals to Iraq', *New York Times*, 21 December 2002.

23. Andreas Zumach, 'Top Secret Iraq Report Reveals US Corporations, Gov't Agencies and Nuclear Labs Helped Illegally Arm Iraq', *Die Tageszeitung* (Germany), 17 December 2002.

24. Stephen Engelberg, 'Keeping Either Side From Winning the Persian Gulf War', *New York Times*, 12 January 1987.

25. Everest, *Oil, Power and Empire*, pp. 89–91.

26. Ibid., pp. 108–11.

CHAPTER 13   STATE OF PLAY: NEOLIBERALISM WOUNDED, US HEGEMONY CHALLENGED

1. Gabriel Kolko, 'Ravaging the Poor: IMF Indicted by Its Own Data', *Multinational Monitor*, June 1998 <http://www.thirdworldtraveler.com/IMF_WB/RavagingPoorIMF.html>.

2. Stiglitz, *Globalization and Its Discontents*, p. 3.

3. David C. Korten is the author of the groundbreaking work *When Corporations Rule the World*, West Hartford, CT: Kumarian Press, 2001.

4. Public Citizen, 'Multilateral Agreement on Investment', 2009 <www.citizen.org/trade/issues>.

5. Ibid.

6. Martin Khor, *The Need to Oppose the Emergence of an MAI in the WTO*, Penang: Third World Network, 1998.

7. World Trade Organization, 'What Is the WTO?' <www.wto.org>.

8. Peter Montague, 'The WTO and Free Trade', *Rachel's Environment and Health Weekly*, 21 October 1999.

9. 'EU GMO Ban was Illegal, WTO Rules,' *EU News* <www.EurActiv.com>, 12 May 2006 (updated 21 May 2007).

10. Beder, *Suiting Themselves*, pp. 158–9.

11. Erik Wesselius, 'Behind GATS 2000: Corporate Power at Work', Transnational Institute, May 2002 <http://www.tni.org/briefing/behind-gats-2000>.

12. Beder, *Suiting Themselves*, p. 86.

13. Lori Wallach, 'Obama's Choice', *The Nation*, 21 December 2009.

14. Juhasz, *Bush Agenda*, p. 211.

15. Stiglitz, *Globalization and Its Discontents*, p. 6.
16. Harvey, *Brief Introduction to Neoliberalism*, p. 193.
17. Public Citizen, 'Close Vote on Tiny Oman Free Trade Agreement Exposes Shifts in U.S. Trade Politics', Press Release, 1 August 2006.
18. Ibid.

CHAPTER 14   LOSING OUT: THE GEOPOLITICAL SIGNIFICANCE OF IRAQ'S OIL

1. Cheney's quote is from his speech at the Cato Institute's Collateral Damage Conference, 23 June 1998 <www.cato.org/speeches/sp-dc062398.html>.
2. Reifenberg and Tanner, 'Left in the Dust?'.
3. Warren Vieth and Elizabeth Douglass, 'Gauging Promise of Iraqi Oil', *Los Angeles Times*, 17 March 2003.
4. Sabrina Tavernise, 'Oil Prize Past and Present', *New York Times*, 17 October 2002.
5. Morgan and Ottaway, 'U.S. Drillers Eye Huge Petroleum Pool'.
6. Randy Schnepf, 'Iraq's Agricultural Sector', US Congressional Research Service, last updated 16 May 2003 <www.cnie.org/nle/crsreports/briefingbooks/Agriculture/Iraq%27s%20Agricultural%20Sector.htm>.
7. National Energy Policy Report (Cheney Report), National Energy Policy Development Group, 2001 <www.whitehouse.gov/energy/national-energy-policy.pdf>. For an excellent overview, see Michael Klare, 'Bush-Cheney Energy Strategy: Procuring the Rest of the World's Oil', *Foreign Policy in Focus*, January, 2004.
8. Klare, 'Bush-Cheney Energy Strategy'.
9. National Energy Policy Report (Cheney Report).
10. Michael Renner, 'Fueling Conflict', *Foreign Policy in Focus*, January, 2004.
11. United States Energy Information Administration, 'Persian Gulf Oil and Gas Exports', Fact Sheet, April 2003.
12. *Forbes*, 'Gusher: The Post-Saddam Premium', 28 October 2002.
13. Michael Renner, 'The Other Looting', *Guerrilla News Network*, 23 July 2003.
14. Klare, 'Bush-Cheney Energy Strategy'.
15. Paul McGeough, 'What the White House Really Wants', *Sydney Morning Herald*, 28 September 2002.
16. Spiro, *The Hidden Hand of American Hegemony*, p. 121.
17. Baker Report, 'Strategic Energy Policy Challenges for the 21st Century', Report of an Independent Task Force, sponsored by the James A. Baker Institute for Public Policy of Rice University and the Council on Foreign Relations, 2002, p. 42 <www.bakerinstitute.org>.

CHAPTER 15   THE PUSH FOR WAR

1. National Security Strategy (United States), 2002.
2. Harvey, *Brief Introduction to Neoliberalism*, p. 82.
3. Project for a New American Century, 'Rebuilding America's Defenses: Strategy, Forces and Resources for a New Century', 2000, p. 51 <www.newamericancentury.org/RebuildingAmericasDefenses.pdf>.

4. William Rivers Pitt, 'Blood Money', *Truthout*, 27 February 2003 <http://archive.truthout.org/article/william-rivers-pitt-blood-money>.

5. *New York Times*, 'Excerpts from Pentagon's Plan: "Prevent the Re-Emergence of a New Rival"', 8 March 1992.

6. Center for Responsive Politics, 2000, 2002, 2004 <www.opensecrets.org>.

7. Michael Moran and Alex Johnson, 'Oil After Saddam: All Bets Are In', *MSNBC*, 7 November 2003.

8. ExxonMobil's 2002 financial support statistics taken from 'Public Information and Policy Research' <www.exxonmobil.com>, accessed 9 July 2008.

9. Competitive Enterprise Institute, 2002 <www.cei.org>.

10. Danielle Pletka, 'Act Now To Get Rid of Saddam' *USA Today*, 15 January 2003.

11. ChevronTexaco's 2002 financial support statistics taken from 'Civic and Community Overview' <www.chevrontexaco.com>, accessed 10 July 2008.

12. Baker Spring and Jack Spencer, 'Post-War Iraq, Use Military Forces to Secure Vital U.S. Interests, Not for Nation-Building', Backgrounder #1589, 25 September 2002 <http://www.heritage.org/research/reports/2002/09/in-post-war-iraq-use-military-forces-to-secure-vital-us-interests>.

13. Anthony Cordesman, 'Iraq and America's Foreign Policy Crisis in the Middle East', Prepared Testimony before the Senate Foreign Relations Committee, 1 March 2001.

CHAPTER 16   INVADING IRAQ: BUSH AGENDA FROM DAY ONE

1. Jane Mayer, 'What Did the Vice-President Do For Halliburton?', *The New Yorker*, 16 February 2004.

2. Ron Suskind, *The Price of Loyalty: George W. Bush, the White House, and the Education of Paul O'Neill*, New York: Simon & Schuster, 2004, p. 38.

3. '60 Minutes', 'Punishing Saddam' Transcript, *CBS*, 12 May 1996.

4. Elaine Sciolino and Patrick Tyler, 'A Nation Challenged: Saddam Hussein; Some Pentagon Officials and Advisers Seek to Oust Iraq's Leader in War's Next Phase', *New York Times*, 12 October 2001.

5. James Risen, 'Terror Acts by Baghdad Have Waned, US Aides Say', *New York Times*, 6 February 2002.

6. *UPI*, 'Commissioner: Bush Deliberately Delayed Inquiry Report Until After Iraq War', 26 July 2003.

7. Bryan Bender, 'Spy Report Saw No Proof of Iraq Arms', *Boston Globe*, 7 June 2003.

8. Joseph Wilson, 'What I Didn't Find in Africa', *New York Times*, 6 July 2003.

9. George Bush Jr, 'Saddam Hussein Has Made The Case Against Himself', prepared text of speech to the UN General Assembly, *Wall Street Journal*, 12 September 2002.

10. George Bush Jr, 'State of the Union Speech', 27 January 2003.

11. Wilson, 'What I Didn't Find in Africa'.

12. US Department of State, press remarks with Egypt's Foreign Minister Amre Moussa, Cairo, Egypt, 24 February 2001, cited in Clark, *Petrodollar Warfare*, p. 95.

13. Full text of Powell's Address to the United Nations Assembly is available at <http://abcnews.go.com/US/story?id=90885&page=1>.

14. Marjorie Cohn, 'Egypt was a Common Destination for Torture of Detainees sent by U.S.', *Global Research*, 16 February 2011 <www.globalresearch.ca/index.php?context=va&aid=23255>.
15. International Atomic Energy Agency, 'The Status of Nuclear Inspections in Iraq: An Update', 7 March 2003 <www.iaea.org>.
16. Michael Dobbs, 'U.S. Had Key Role in Iraq Buildup Trade in Chemical Arms Allowed Despite Their Use on Iranians, Kurds', *Washington Post*, 30 December 2002.
17. Philip Shenon, 'Declaration Lists Companies that Sold Chemicals to Iraq', *New York Times*, 21 December 2002.
18. Dana Milbank and Claudia Deane, 'Hussein Link to 9/11 Lingers in Many Minds', *Washington Post*, 6 September 2003.
19. Dana Milbank, 'Bush Disavows Hussein-Sept. 11 Link', *Washington Post*, 18 September 2003.
20. Downing Street Memo, 2009 <www.downingstreetmemo.com>.
21. Marian Wilkinson, 'AWB Knew Iraq Invasion Plans', *Sydney Morning Herald*, 23 November 2006.
22. Thadeus Herrick, 'US Oil Wants to Work in Iraq, Concerns Discuss How to Raise Output After a Possible War', *Wall Street Journal*, 17 January 2003.
23. Elizabeth Rosenberg, Adam Horowitz and Anthony Alessandrini, 'Iraq Reconstruction Tracker', *Middle East Report*, Summer 2003, pp. 28–9.
24. Paul Bignell, 'Secret Memos Expose Link Between Oil Firms and Invasion of Iraq', *Independent*, 19 April 2011.
25. Michael Moran and Alex Johnson, 'Oil after Saddam: All Bets are in', MSNBC, 7 November 2002.

CHAPTER 17   REGIME CHANGE: THE BREMER ECONOMIC ORDERS

1. Hassan Juma'a Awad, 'Leave Our Country Now', *Guardian*, 17 February 2005.
2. Juhasz, *Bush Agenda*, pp. 190–91.
3. UN Security Council Resolution 1438, 22 May 2003.
4. Donald Rumsfeld, 'Core Principles for a Free Iraq', *Wall Street Journal*, 27 May 2003.
5. Chandrasekaran, *Imperial Life*, pp. 61–2.
6. L. Paul Bremer III, 'Operation Iraqi Prosperity', *Wall Street Journal*, 20 July 2003.
7. Pepe Escobar, 'Bremer's Quick Study in Colony Building', *Asia Times*, 12 July 2004.
8. David Leigh, 'General Sacked by Bush Wanted Early Elections', *Guardian*, 18 March 2004.
9. United Nations, 'The Current Status and Future Prospects for the Transformation and Reconstruction of the Higher Education System in Iraq', UN University Report, 1 May 2005.
10. International Committee of the Red Cross, 'ICRC calls urgently for protection of the civilian population and services and of persons no longer fighting', Press Release, 11 April 2003 <www.icrc.org/eng/resources/documents/misc/5lhjp6.htm>.
11. Robert Fisk, 'Library Books, Letters, and Priceless Documents Are Set Ablaze in Final Chapter of the Sacking of Baghdad', *Independent*, 15 April 2003.
12. Pratap Chatterjee, *Iraq Inc: A Profitable Occupation*, New York: Seven Stories Press, 2004, pp.171, 177–8.

13. Juhasz, *Bush Agenda*, pp. 200–203.
14. Ibid.
15. David Bacon, 'Iraqi Unions Defy Privatisation', *The Progressive*, October 2005.
16. Herbert Docena, 'Silent Battalions of Democracy: How the US is Reconstructing Iraq's State and Society', in *Silent War: The US' Ideological and Economic Occupation of Iraq*, Focus on the Global South Publications, January 2005.
17. Saul Hudson, 'New Iraqi TV Complains of US Censorship', *Reuters*, 13 May 2003.
18. Chandrasekaran, *Imperial Life*, p. 110.
19. Ibid., pp. 110–11.
20. *Economist*, 'Let's All Go to the Yard Sale: Iraq's Economic Liberalization', Editorial, 27 September 2003.
21. Coalition Provisional Authority, 'CPA Regulation Number 39', 21 September 2003. A full list of all CPA Orders is available at <www.casi.org.uk/info/cpa.html>.
22. CPA Order 12.
23. CPA Order 40.
24. *Economist*, 'Let's All Go to the Yard Sale'.
25. Chandrasekaran, *Imperial Life*, pp. 162–3.
26. 'Address by L. Paul Bremer III, Chief Administrator in Iraq', Global Reconciliation Summit, Amman, 23 June 2003.
27. Jeff Madrick, 'An Extreme Plan for Iraq', *New York Times*, 2 October 2003.
28. Neil King Jr, 'Bush Officials Devise a Broad Plan for a Free-Market Economy in Iraq', *Wall Street Journal*, 1 May 2003.
29. *Economist*, 'Let's All Go to the Yard Sale'.
30. Rory McCarthy, 'Foreign Firms to Bid in Huge Iraqi Sale', *Guardian*, 21 September 2003.
31. Joseph Stiglitz, 'Iraq's Next Shock Will be Shock Therapy', Znet, 17 March 2004 <http://www.zcommunications.org/iraqs-next-shock-will-be-shock-therapy-by-joseph-stiglitz>.
32. Ed Vulliamy and Faisal Islam, 'Now For the Really Big Guns', *Observer*, 29 June 2003.
33. 'Moving the Iraqi Economy from Recovery to Sustainable Growth', Statement of Work, BearingPoint, Inc., 21 February 2003 <www.ifg.org/analysis/globalization/ambition.htm>.
34. Antonia Juhasz, 'Ambitions of Empire: the Bush Administration Economic Plan for Iraq (and Beyond)', *Left Turn Magazine*, February/March 2004, and Juhasz, *Bush Agenda*, p. 214.
35. Emad Mekay, 'US on Track for Market Economy', *Inter Press Service*, 11 February 2004.
36. *Middle East Times*, 'US Looks Forward to More Open Iraq Economy', 19 July 2006.
37. Charlie Walsh and P.K. Semier, 'Iraq Government to Restructure and Privatise Some 200 Industrial Companies', *Financial Times*, 7 October 2010.

CHAPTER 18   RECONSTRUCTION AND CORRUPTION: THE NEXT KLONDIKE

1. Mayer, 'What Did the Vice President Do for Halliburton'. Clad is referring to the Klondike Gold Rush, which saw an estimated 100,000 prospectors flock to

the Klondike gold fields in Canada's northwest Yukon region hoping to strike it rich in the late 1890s.

2. Pratap Chatterjee and Herbert Docena, 'Occupation, Inc.', *Southern Exposure*, Winter, 2003–04.
3. David Pallister, 'How the US Sent $12 bn in Cash to Iraq. And Watched It Vanish', *Guardian*, 8 February 2007.
4. Michael Hirsh, 'IRAQ: Breaking the Silence', *Newsweek*, 22 March 2006.
5. Commission on Wartime Contracting, 'Transforming Wartime Contracting: Controlling Costs, Reducing Risks', August 2011 <www.wartimecontracting.gov>.
6. Matt Taibbi, 'The Great Iraq Swindle: How Bush Allowed an Army of For-Profit Contractors to Invade the U.S. Treasury', *Rolling Stone*, September 2007.
7. Chandrasekaran, *Imperial Life*, p. 91.
8. Ariana Cha, 'In Iraq, the Job Opportunity of a Lifetime: Managing a $13 Billion Budget With No Experience', *Washington Post*, 23 May 2004.
9. Michigan State University, 'Peter McPherson Bio' <www.msu.edu/~presofc/vitae.html>.
10. Chandrasekaran, *Imperial Life*, p. 116.
11. Ibid., p. 112.
12. Taibbi, 'Great Iraq Swindle'.
13. Chandrasekaran, *Imperial Life*, pp. 212–17.
14. Ibid., p. 119.
15. Ibid., p. 126.
16. The Hague Resolutions are outlined in Aaron Mate, 'Pillage Is Forbidden: Why the Privatization of Iraq Is Illegal', *The Nation*, 6 November 2003.
17. United Nations, 'UN Security Council Resolution 1438', 22 May 2003.
18. Docena, 'Silent Battalions of Democracy'.
19. Chatterjee, *Iraq Inc.*, p. 182.
20. Chandrasekaran, *Imperial Life*, p. 110.

CHAPTER 19   RECONSTRUCTION AND CORRUPTION: THE HALLIBURTON AND BECHTEL CONTRACTS

1. Mayer, 'What Did the Vice President Do for Halliburton'.
2. Halliburton, 'About Us', 2009 <www.halliburton.com/aboutus>.
3. Paul Krugman, 'Patriots and Profits', *New York Times*, 18 December 2003.
4. Douglas Jehl, 'US Sees Evidence of Overcharging in Iraq Contract', *New York Times*, 12 December 2003.
5. Neil King Jr, 'Halliburton Tells Pentagon Workers Took Kickbacks to Award Projects in Iraq', *Wall Street Journal*, 23 January 2004.
6. CNN, 'Halliburton Over Charges Pentagon $27,000,000 For Troops Meals', 3 February 2004.
7. Krugman, 'Patriots and Profits'.
8. Jehl, 'US Sees Evidence of Overcharging'.
9. Committee on Government Reform, 'Waxman Calls for Congressional Investigation of Halliburton Kickbacks', 24 January 2004 <www.house.gov/reform>.
10. Nicholas Pelham, 'Contractors in Iraq Accused of Importing Labour and Exporting Profit', *Financial Times*, 14 October 2003.

11. Sue Pleming, 'Halliburton Defends Fuel Contract', *Reuter*s, 16 January 2004.
12. Pelham, 'Contractors in Iraq'.
13. Agence France Presse, 'Halliburton Says KBR Unit's Profit, Sales Soar', 30 October 2003.
14. Halliburton's stock price for this period can be traced at Gilead Sciences <www.gilead.com>.
15. Griff Witte, 'Army to End Expansive, Exclusive Halliburton Deal: Logistics Contract to Be Open for Bidding', *Washington Post*, 12 July 2006.
16. Casell Bryan-Low, 'Cheney Cashed In Halliburton Options Worth $35 million', *Wall Street Journal*, 20 September 2000.
17. Center for American Progress, 'Cheney, Halliburton, and the Government', 23 January 2004.
18. Mayer, 'What Did the Vice President Do for Halliburton'.
19. Cheney, 'Defending Liberty in a Global Economy'.
20. Timothy Burger and Adam Zagorin, 'The Paper Trail', *Time* magazine, 30 May 2004.
21. *Washington Post*, 'Firm's Iraq Deal Greater than Cheney Has Said', 23 June 2001.
22. Congressman Henry Waxman, 'Letter to Secretary of Defense Donald Rumsfeld Regarding Halliburton's Ties to Countries that Sponsor Terrorism', 30 April 2003.
23. Institute for Southern Studies, 'Halliburton: Not Just the Oil', Fact Sheet, 2004.
24. Doug Ireland, 'Will the French Indict Cheney?', *The Natio*n, 29 December 2003.
25. Lee Drutman and Charlie Cray, 'Halliburton, Dick Cheney, and Wartime Spoils', Factsheet, Citizen Works, 4 April 2003 <www.citizenworks.org>.
26. Bechtel, 'About Us', 2010 <www.bechtel.com>.
27. Aljazeera, 'Bechtel-Parsons Win Iraq Contracts', 7 January 2004.
28. Corpwatch et al., 'Bechtel: Profiting from Destruction'.
29. Ibid.
30. Dahr Jamail, 'Bechtel Departure Shatters More Iraqi Illusions', *Inter Press Service*, 10 November 2006.
31. Center for Public Integrity, 'Windfalls of War: Fluor Corp.', 2004; see <http://www.iwatchnews.org>.
32. Dena Montague, 'War Profiteers Shell, Bechtel, Fluor Take Record of Terror from Africa to Iraq', *San Francisco Bay View*, 21 May 2003.
33. David Teather, 'Oil Boss Paid $1m a Year by Contract Bidder', *Guardian*, 17 May 2003.

CHAPTER 20   LOCKING DOWN IRAQ: POST SOVEREIGNTY

1. Dexter Filkins, 'A Region Inflamed: Strategy; Tough New Tactics by U.S. Tighten Grip on Iraq Towns', *New York Times*, 7 December 2003.
2. Docena, 'Silent Battalions of Democracy'.
3. Antonia Juhasz, 'Bush's Economic Invasion of Iraq', *Los Angeles Times*, 14 August 2005.
4. Juhasz, *Bush Agenda*, p. 248.
5. Herbert Docena, 'Shock and Awe Therapy: How the United States is Attempting to Control Iraq's Oil and Pry Open Its Economy', Paper presented at World Tribunal on Iraq, Istanbul, June 2005.

6. Transcript of News Conference at National Press Club Afternoon Newsmaker News Conference, Washington, DC, 21 December 2003.

7. Sue Pleming, 'Foreign Forces, Contractors Given Immunity in Iraq', *Reuters*, 29 June 2004.

8. Lisa Giria, 'Immunity for Iraqi Oil Dealings Raises Alarm', *Los Angeles Times*, 8 August 2003.

9. Docena, 'Silent Battalions of Democracy'.

10. Human Rights Watch, 'Violent Response: the U.S. Army in al-Fulluja', June 2003.

11. Dahr Jamail's excellent coverage is from his book, *Beyond the Green Zone*, Chicago, IL: Haymarket, 2007, pp. 138–9; many of his articles from the time are also available on his website <www.dahrjamail.net>. Also see Jo Wilding's 'Inside the Fire', OpenDemocracy, 13 April 2004.

12. Douglas Jehl and Kate Zernike, 'The Reach of War: Abu Ghraib; Scant Evidence Cited in Long Detention of Iraqis', *New York Times*, 30 May 2004.

13. Noam Chomsky, *Failed States: The Abuse of Power and the Assault on Democracy*, New York: Metropolitan Books, 2006, p. 73.

14. Toby Harnden, 'Phantoms Close in on a Ghost Town', *Sunday Telegraph* (UK), 7 November 2004.

15. Rory McCarthy, and Peter Beaumont, 'Civilian Cost of Battle for Falluja Emerges', *Observer*, 14 November 2004.

16. See Chris Doran and Tim Anderson, 'Iraq and the Case for Australian War Crimes Trials', *Crime, Law, Social Change*, vol. 56, no. 3, 2011, pp. 283–99.

17. Donald Rumsfeld, 'Principles for Iraq – Policy Guidelines, May 13, 2003 <www. washingtonpost.com/wp-dyn/content/article/2011/02/14/AR2011021405224. html>.

18. Graham Bradley, 'U.S. to Expand Prison Facilities in Iraq', *Washington Post*, 10 May 2005.

19. Greg Muttitt, *Fuel on the Fire: Oil and Politics in Occupied Iraq*, London: Bodley Head, 2011, pp. 166–7.

20. Ibid., p. 167.

21. Zena Awad, 'Iraqi Trade Unionist Speaks to the Socialist, *The Socialist*, 19 March 2005.

22. Peter Maass, 'The Way of the Commandos', *New York Times Magazine*, 1 May 2005.

23. Max Fuller, 'For Iraq, "The Salvador Option" Becomes Reality', *Global Research*, 2 June 2005 <www.globalresearch.ca/articles/FUL506A.html>.

24. Andrew Buncombe, and Patrick Cockburn, 'Iraq's Death Squads: On the Brink of Civil War', *Independent*, 26 February 2006.

25. Muttitt, *Fuel on the Fire*, p. 179.

26. Ibid , p. 223.

27. Julian Coman, 'CIA Plans New Secret Police Force In Iraq', *Daily Telegraph*, 1 April 2004.

28. Emad Mekay, 'IRAQ: Debt Relief Weighed Down By IMF Burden', *Inter Press Service*, 23 November 2004.

29. Matthew Rothschild, 'IMF Occupies Iraq, Riots Follow', *The Progressive*, 3 January 2006.

30. The Compact can be viewed at <www.uniraq.org/ici.asp>.

31. Iraqi Freedom Congress, 'Iraq: Workers Protest IMF policies', Press Release, 19 October 2008.

CHAPTER 21   IRAQI OIL: A NEW AND IMPROVED SAUDI ARABIA FOR THE TWENTY-FIRST CENTURY

1. David Ivanovich, 'Houston Exec Gets Top Iraq Energy Post', *Houston Chronicle*, 23 September 2003.
2. Herbert Docena, 'What Dreams May Come', *Al Ahram Weekly*, 29 March 2006.
3. Antonia Juhasz, 'Bush's Economic Invasion of Iraq', *Los Angeles Times*, 14 August 2005.
4. Greg Muttitt, 'Crude Designs: The Rip-off of Iraq's Oil Wealth', Report, *Platform*, 22 November 2005 <www.carbonweb.org/documents/crude_designs_large.pdf>.
5. An excellent overview of the oil law is available from Platform and Greg Muttitt: 'The Oil and Gas Law – Signing Away Iraq's Future?', *Platform*, 2007 <www.carbonweb.org/documents/oil_law_briefing.pdf>.
6. Chris Floyd, 'Claiming the Prize: War Escalation Aimed at Securing Iraqi Oil', *Global Research*, 12 January 2007 <www.globalresearch.ca/PrintArticle.php?articleId=4433>.
7. Muttitt, 'The Oil and Gas Law'.
8. 'Iraqi Trade Unions Unite to Oppose Undemocratic Oil Law', Joint Statement by Iraq's five union federations, 14 December 2006.
9. Hassan Juma'a Awad, 'The Iraqi People are the Victims of Investment' <www.niqash.org>, 19 July 2006.
10. Hassan Juma'a Awad, Speech, Basra, 6 February 2007, cited in Muttitt, *Fuel on the Fire*, p. 235.
11. Ewa Jasiewicz, 'SOC Workers Win Their Fight for Higher Wages! Bremer's Orders Defied!', Occupation Watch, 29 January 2004 <http://www.basraoilunion.org/2005/01/soc-workers-win-their-fight-for-higher.html>.
12. Ibid.
13. Ibid.
14. George Bush Jr, Nationally Televised Speech on Iraq, 10 January 2007.
15. Associated Press, 'Al-Maliki Tells Aides U.S. Benchmark Deadline is June 30 or His Ouster Possible', 13 March 2007.
16. Floyd, 'Claiming the Prize'.
17. Muttitt, *Fuel on the Fire*, pp. 253–5.
18. Association of Muslim Scholars, *Fatwa* on Oil Law, 4 July 2007. Cited in Muttitt, *Fuel on the Fire*, p. 263.
19. Institute for Public Accuracy, 'Nobel Peace Laureates Oppose Iraqi Oil Law Imposition', Press Release, 26 June 2007 <http://www.accuracy.org/release/1511-nobel-peace-laureates-oppose-iraqi-oil-law-imposition/>.
20. Kathleen Ridolfo, 'Iraq: Kurds Push Ahead With Oil Contracts', Radio Free Europe, 12 November 2007 <www.rferl.org/content/article/1079118.html>.
21. Hissock, 'Iraq's Oil Industry Looks for OPEC Growth Role'.
22. Muttitt, *Fuel on the Fire*, pp. 324–31.
23. Ibid.
24. Oliver Morgan, 'Iraq May Have to Quit OPEC', *Observer*, 27 April 2004.

CHAPTER 22   THE US MIDDLE EAST FREE TRADE AREA

1. King Jr, 'Iraq: Bush Officials Devise a Broad Plan For Free-Market Economy'.

2. Riad al Khouri, 'EU and U.S. Free Trade Agreements in the Middle East and North Africa', Carnegie Endowment for International Peace, June 2008, p. 22.
3. George Bush Jr, 'Commencement Address to the Graduating Class of the University of South Carolina', 9 May 2003.
4. For a good overview, see Ali Kadri, 'The Right to Development in the Arab World', *Global Research*, 3 March 2011 <www.globalresearch.ca/index.php?context=va&aid=23470>.
5. IMF, *Financial Statements*, quarter ended 31 January 2002.
6. George Abed and Hamid Davoodi, 'Challenges of Growth and Globalization in the Middle East and North Africa', IMF, 2003 <www.imf.org/external/pubs/ft/med/2003/eng/abed.htm>.
7. Juhasz, *Bush Agenda*, pp. 266–7.
8. United States Trade Representative (USTR), 'Middle East Free Trade Area Initiative'. All USTR materials are from its website <www.ustr.gov>.
9. Juhasz, *Bush Agenda*, p. 278.
10. USTR, 'Generalised System of Preferences'.
11. Juhasz, *Bush Agenda*, p. 285.
12. Robert Looney, 'US Middle East Economic Policy: The Use of Free Trade Areas in the War on Terrorism', *Mediterranean Quarterly*, Summer 2005, p. 106.
13. USTR, 'Accession of the Kingdom of Saudi Arabia to the World Trade Organisation', Fact Sheet.
14. Oxford Business Group, 'Speeding Free Trade', *Emirates*, vol. 63, 16 March, 2005.

CHAPTER 23   CASE STUDIES: JORDAN AND MOROCCO

1. USTR, 'Jordan Free Trade Agreement' (Summary).
2. USTR, 'US-Jordan Free Trade Agreement', Final Text.
3. International Labour Organisation (ILO), 'Decent Work Country Programme, Jordan', August 2006 <www.ilo.org/public/english/bureau/program/dwcp/.../jordan.pdf>.
4. Ibid.
5. Ibid.
6. Steven Greenhouse and, Michael Barbaro, 'An Ugly Side of Free Trade: Sweatshops in Jordan', *New York Times*, 3 May 2006.
7. National Labor Committee (NLC), 'US Jordan Free Trade Agreement Descends into Human Trafficking', Report, May 2006 <www.ilo.org/public/english/bureau/program/dwcp/.../jordan.pdf>. The NLC has since been renamed as The Institute for Global Labour and Human Rights.
8. Ibid.
9. USTR, 'Jordan Free Trade Agreement' (Summary).
10. ILO, 'Decent Work Country Programme, Jordan'.
11. Juhasz, *Bush Agenda*, pp. 266–7.
12. Nomi Prins, 'Egyptian Uprising Is a Direct Response to Ruthless Global Capitalism', *Alternet*, 4 February 2011 <www.alternet.org/story/149793/>.
13. Charles Kernaghan, 'Sexual Predators and Serial Rapists Run Wild At Wal-Mart Supplier in Jordan', Report, Institute for Global Labour and Human Rights, June 2011 <www.globallabourrights.org/reports?id=0682>.
14. USTR, 'Jordan Free Trade Agreement' (Summary).
15. Ibid.

16. Dale Gavlak, 'Jordan's king swears in new cabinet after protests', *BBC News*, 10 February 2001.
17. Johnny McDevitt, 'Jordanians protest against soaring food prices', *Guardian*, 15 January 2011.
18. Curtis Ryan, 'Peace, bread and riots: Jordan and the International Monetary Fund', *Middle East Policy*, October 1998, pp. 54–66.
19. USTR, 'Free Trade With Morocco', Fact Sheet, 2 March 2004.
20. Export.gov, 'FAQ: U.S. – Morocco Free Trade Agreement' <www.export.gov>.
21. USTR, 'Free Trade With Morocco', Fact Sheet, 2 March 2004.
22. Laila Lalami, 'Arab Uprisings: What the February 20 Protests Tell Us About Morocco', *The Nation* <www.thenation.com>, 17 February 2011.
23. Ibid.
24. al Khouri, 'EU and US Free Trade Agreements in the Middle East and North Africa', p. 16.
25. USTR, 'Morocco Free Trade Agreement' (Summary).
26. al Khouri, 'EU and US Free Trade Agreements', p. 16.
27. Souhail Karam, 'UPDATE 2-Morocco boosts 2011 subsidies amid regional unrest', *Reuters*, 15 February 2011.

CHAPTER 24   CASE STUDIES: OMAN AND BAHRAIN

1. USTR, 'Statement of U.S. Trade Representative Susan C. Schwab on President George W. Bush's Signing of Legislation to Implement the U.S. – Oman Free Trade Agreement', September 2006.
2. Public Citizen, 'Oman and Labor Rights' <www.citizen.org/trade/oman/labor/>.
3. Ibid.
4. *Kuwait News Agency*, 'Bush signs into law US-Oman Free Trade Agreement', 26 September 2006.
5. Senator Harry Reid, 'Yes to More Free Trade, But No to Forced Labor', *Wall Street Journal*, 15 July 2006.
6. Public Citizen, 'Close Vote on Tiny Oman Free Trade Agreement Exposes Shifts in U.S. Trade Politics', Press Release, 1 August 2006 <www.citizen.org>.
7. Mishaal Al Gergawi, 'Oman – the State of Two Gulfs', *Gulf News*, 6 March 2011.
8. Human Rights Watch, World Report 2011: Bahrain.
9. USTR, 'Bahrain Free Trade Agreement' (Summary).
10. *Export.gov*, 'FAQ: U.S. – Bahrain Free Trade Agreement' <www.export.gov>.
11. USTR, 'Bahrain Free Trade Agreement Fact Sheet'.
12. USTR, 'US Bahrain Free Trade Agreement Final Text'.
13. US Department of State, 'Trafficking in Persons Report', June 2011.
14. Migrant Rights, 'Bahrain Further Restricts Migrant Rights while Publicly Expressing Concern for Migrants', 29 June 2011 <www.bahrainrights.org/en/node/4348>.
15. Finian Cunningham, 'Bahrain: Social Roots of Revolt Against Another US Ally', *Global Research*, 18 February 2011 <www.globalresearch.ca/index.php?context=va&aid=23266>.
16. Ibid.
17. Michael Slackman, and Nadim Audi, 'Protesters in Bahrain Demand More Changes', *New York Times*, 25 Febraty 2011.

18. Finian Cunningham, 'Bahrain: Western Complicity in Saudi-Backed War Crimes', *Global Research*, 6 April 2011 <www.globalresearch.ca/index. php?context=va&aid=24181>.

19. Ibid.

20. Pepe Escobar, 'Exposed: The US-Saudi Libya Deal', *Asia Times*, 2 April 2011.

21. Ibid.

22. Cunningham, 'Bahrain: Social Roots of Revolt'.

23. Matthew Swibel, 'Pumping for Mideast Business', *Forbes.com*, 20 January 2005 <http://www.bilaterals.org/spip.php?article1209>.

24. Emad Mekay, 'US Business Pushing for Middle East FTA', *Inter Press Service*, 7 October 2008; National Foreign Trade Council, 'About Us' <www.nftc.org>, accessed 24 October 2008.

25. Business Council for International Understanding, 'About BCIU' <www.bciu. org>, accessed 24 October 2008.

26. United States-Middle East Free Trade Area Coalition, 'US-Middle East Free Trade Area Coalition Urges Congress to Act Swiftly on US-Bahrain FTA', Press Release, 14 September 2005.

CHAPTER 25 EGYPT AND HOW TO MAKE A FORTUNE FROM HUNGER AND MISERY

1. Clinton made the remarks in March 2009, and was quoted in Jackson Diehl's *Washington Post* story, 'Obama Administration Could Still get it Right on Egypt', 27 January 2011.

2. John Vidal, 'People Die From Hunger While Banks Make a Killing', *Observer*, 22 January 2011.

3. Jon Leyne, 'Egypt: Cairo's Tahrir Square Fills with Protesters', *BBC*, 8 July 2011.

4. Philip Inman, 'Mubarak Family Fortune Could Reach $70bn, Says Expert', *Guardian*, 4 February 2011.

5. Mohamed Elbaradei, 'The Next Step for Egypt's Opposition', *New York Times*, 10 February 2011.

6. Adam Hanieh, 'Debt and "Democracy" in Egypt: The IMF's Deadly Economic Reforms', *Global Research*, 31 May 2011 <www.globalresearch.ca/index. php?context=va&aid=25066>.

7. Prins, 'The Egyptian Uprising Is a Direct Response to Ruthless Global Capitalism'.

8. Ibid.

9. Dr Ali Kadri, 'Egypt's Economy in Crisis', *Global Research*, 18 February 2011 <www.globalresearch.ca/index.php?context=va&aid=23279>.

10. World Bank Data, 'Income share held by fourth 20%', Egypt, 2010 <www. worldbank.org/indicator>.

11. Rami Zurayk, 'Use Your Loaf: Why Food Prices were Crucial in the Arab Spring', *Observer*, 16 July 2011.

12. Tom Engelhardt, 'How Hosni Mubarak Became One of the Richest Men in the World on Our Dime', 13 February 2011 <http://www.alternet.org/story/149901/ how_hosni_mubarak_became_one_of_the_richest_men_in_the_world_on_our_ dime/>.

13. Cohn, 'Egypt was a Common Destination for Torture'.

14. Glenn Greenwald, 'Strong Anti-American Sentiment in Egypt', 26 April 2011 <www.salon.com/2011/04/26/egypt_12/>.
15. IMF, 'Economic Transformation in MENA: Delivering on the Promise of Shared Prosperity', 27 May 2011. prepared for Summit May 27, 2011 Deauville, France <http://www.imf.org/external/np/g8/pdf/052711.pdf>.
16. Eric Walberg, 'Egypt vs IMF: Time to Default?', *Global Research*, 7 July 2011 <www.globalresearch.ca/index.php?context=va&aid=25538>.
17. Hanieh, 'Debt and "Democracy" in Egypt'.
18. al Khouri, 'EU and U.S. Free Agreements', p. 17.
19. Ibid.
20. Robert Looney, 'US Middle East Economic Policy: The Use of Free Trade Areas in the War on Terrorism', *Mediterranean Quarterly*, Summer 2005.
21. Professor Basel Saleh, 'Tunisia: IMF "Economic Medicine" has resulted in Mass Poverty and Unemployment', *Global Research*, 31 December 2010 <www.globalresearch.ca/index.php?context=va&aid=22587>.
22. 'Remarks at the Opening Press Conference', Transcript, World Bank, 14 April 2011.
23. Credit Suisse, 'Emerging Consumer Survey 2011', January 2011 <www.credit-suisse.com/news/doc/media_releases/consumer_survey_0701_small.pdf>.
24. Breakdown of FAO data is from Oxfam, 'Global Food Prices in 2011: Questions and Answers', Oxfam International, February 2011 <www.oxfam.org/en/campaigns/.../food-price-crisis-questions-answers>.
25. Vidal, 'People Die From Hunger While Banks Make a Killing'.
26. Frederick Kaufman, 'How Goldman Sachs Created the Food Crisis', *Foreign Policy in Focus*, 27 April 2011.
27. Ibid.
28. Ibid.
29. Johann Hari, 'How Goldman Sachs Gambled on Starving the World's Poor – And Won', *Independent*, 2 July 2010.
30. Ellen Brown, 'Rising Food Prices and the Egyptian Tinderbox: How Banks and Investors Are Starving the Third World', *Global Research*, 4 February 2011 <www.globalresearch.ca/index.php?context=va&aid=23079>.
31. FAO, 'Poorest Countries' Cereal Bill Continues to Soar, Governments Try to Limit Impact', Press Release, 11 April 2008.
32. *Reuters*, 'Food Price Rises Are Mass Murder: UN Envoy', 20 April 2008.
33. Olivier de Schutter, 'Food Commodities Speculation Food Price Crises', Briefing Note 02-S2010, UN Special Rapporteur on the Right to Food.
34. Vidal, 'People Die From Hunger While Banks Make a Killing'.
35. *Reuters*, 'Obama Signs Sweeping Wall Street Overhaul Into Law', 21 July 2010.

CHAPTER 26   NEOLIBERAL AUTHORITY: IRAQI AGRICULTURE

1. Ghali Hassan, 'Biopiracy and GMOs: The Fate of Iraq's Agriculture', *Global Research*, 12 December 2005 <www.globalresearch.ca/index.php?context=va&aid=1447>.
2. Peter Baker, 'Iraq's Shortage of Medicine May Grow More Severe,' *Washington Post*, 19 December 2002.
3. David Enders, 'Salt of this earth', GRAIN, 13 March 2009 <www.grain.org/article/entries/2250-salt-of-this-earth>.

4. Speaker Biographies, Visions for the Millennium, US Department of Agriculture <www.gipsa.usda.gov>.

5. Jeffrey St Clair, 'The Rat in the Grain: Dan Amstutz and the Looting of Iraqi Agriculture', *Counterpunch*, 4 July 2003 <www.organicconsumers.org/corp/070903_globalization.cfm>.

6. Heather Stewart, 'Fury at Agriculture Post for US Businessman', *Guardian*, 28 April 2003.

7. St Clair, 'The Rat in the Grain'.

8. 'Monsanto's High Level Connections to the Bush Administration', *SourceWatch*, 18 November 2008 <http://sourcewatch.org/index.php?title=Monsanto%27s_High_Level_Connections_to_the_Bush_Administration>.

9. Brendan Nicholson, 'Flugge Received $680,000 from Foreign Aid Funds', *The Age*, 17 February 2006.

10. Marian Wilkinson and David Marr, 'Smoking Gun Drama for PM,' *Sydney Morning Herald*, 17 March 2006.

11. Marc Moncrief, 'Australia Reaps Iraqi Harvest', Corpwatch, 4 April 2006 <http://www.corpwatch.org/article.php?id=13453>.

12. Richard Baker, 'So Which Master was Trevor Flugge Serving While in Iraq?' *The Age*, 9 March, 2006.

13. Leonie Wood and Richard Baker, 'What Howard Didn't See', *The Age*, 13 April, 2006.

14. Ariana Cha, 'Iraqis Face Tough Transition to Market-Based Agriculture', *Washington Post*, 22 January 2004.

15. Juhasz, *Bush Agenda*, p. 204.

16. Moncrief, 'Australia Reaps Iraqi Harvest'.

CHAPTER 27   ORDER 81 AND THE GENETICALLY MODIFIED SEEDS OF DEMOCRACY

1. F. William Engdahl, *Seeds of Destruction: the Hidden Agenda of Genetic Manipulation*, Montreal: Global Research Publishing, 2007, p. 197.

2. CPA Order 81, 26 April 2004.

3. As had the rest of the Middle East.

4. Engdahl, *Seeds of Destruction*, pp. 225–6.

5. Heather Gray, 'Corporate Agribusiness, the Occupation of Iraq and the Dred Scott Decision Home Grown Axis of Evil', *Counterpunch*, 22 July 2005 <http://www.counterpunch.org/gray07222005.html>.

6. Greenpeace, 'All that Glitters is Not Gold: the False Hope of Golden Rice', Briefing, May 2005.

7. George Lerner, 'Activist: Farmer suicides in India linked to debt, globalization', CNN, 5 January 2010.

8. Robert Paarlberg, 'Technology Adoption in Developing Countries: the Case of Genetically Modified Crops', National Intelligence Council Discussion Paper, 23 October 2003.

9. International Service for the Acquisition of Agro-Biotec Applications, 'Global Status of Commercialized Biotech/GM Crops: 2010', ISAAA Brief 42-2010: Executive Summary, February 2010.

10. Ibid.

11. Paarlberg, 'Technology Adoption in Developing Countries'.

12. Center for Food Safety, 'New Report: A Global Citizens Report on the State of GMOs—False Promises, Failed Technologies', Press Release, 13 October 2011.
13. Pew Charitable Trust, 'Genetically Modified Crops in the United States', August 2004.
14. *Reuters*, 'U.N. food envoy questions safety of gene crops', 15 October 2002.
15. Michael Roberts, 'J.E.M. Ag Supply, Inc. v. Pioneer Hi-Bred International, Inc. Its Meaning and Significance for the Agricultural Community', *National Agricultural Law Center*, November 2002 <www.nationalaglawcenter.org/assets/articles/roberts_jem.pdf>.
16. Debi Barker, 'WTO Agreement on Agriculture: Threat to Food Security and Sustainability', International Forum on Globalization, 2003.
17. Engdahl, *Seeds of Destruction*, pp. 221–2.
18. Business Information Center, 'Certification Requirement for Importing Genetically Modified Foodstuffs – Saudi Arabia', November 2002.
19. Barker, 'WTO Agreement on Agriculture'.
20. Zurayk, 'Use Your Loaf'.
21. Engdahl, *Seeds of Destruction*, pp. 268–9.

CHAPTER 28   SEEDS IN THE GROUND

1. As such, Amstutz was technically an 'adviser' to the Ministry of Agriculture.
2. DAI, 'Revitalizing Iraq's agricultural sector', Projects: ARDI <http://tinyurl.com/b739o6>.
3. Ibid.
4. Prairie Grains, 'Seeds of Hope', February 2005 <www.smallgrains.org>.
5. Steve Savage, 'The Cost Of Precaution' <www.Biofortified.com>, 21 May 2011.
6. World Wide Wheat, Company Overview <www.worldwheat.com>.
7. <http://aglifesciences.tamu.edu>.
8. From UN Food and Agriculture Oganisation, FAOSTAT, Country Profiles: Iraq.
9. Inma website <www.inma-iraq.com>. Unless stated otherwise, all Inma materials can be found on this website, and were available as of August 2011.
10. US Department of Agriculture, 'USDA at Work for Agriculture in Iraq', September 2010. Unless stated otherwise, all USDA materials can be found at <www.fas.usda.gov>, and were available as of August 2011.
11. Inma, 'USAID Inma Agribusiness Program and KRG Ministry of Agriculture Discuss Revitalization Opportunities', 10 November 2008.
12. US Embassy Iraq, 'Fact Sheet – USG Agricultural Assistance in Ninewa', 2008 <www.iraq-prt.usembassy.gov>.
13. USDA Foreign Agricultural Services, 'Hybrid Seed Corn Quality Amazes Iraqi Farmers, Expansion in Al Anbar Province Planned', Press Release, 1 February 2010.
14. C. Busby, M. Hamdan and E. Ariabi, 'Cancer, Infant Mortality and Birth Sex-Ratio in Fallujah, Iraq 2005–2009', *International Journal of Environmental Studies and Public Health*, vol. 7, pp. 2828–37, 2010.
15. Enders, 'Salt of this Earth'.
16. Author interview with John Ellerman, US Department of Agriculture adviser, 27 August 2011.
17. Interview with author, 5 August 2011.
18. UN News Centre, 'Rebuilding Iraq's Collapsed Seed Industry', 8 August 2005.
19. Email interview with author, 15 September 2011.

CHAPTER 29 HUNGER AND MISERY: A PROFITABLE OCCUPATION

1. Dahr Jamail and Ali al-Fadhily, 'Now It Is Lack of Food Security', *Inter Press Service*, 19 February 2007.
2. Nayla Razzouk and Kadhim Ajrash, 'Iraq Seeks Foreign Investment in Agriculture to Boost Output' <www.bloomberg.com>, 21 March 2011.
3. UN Office for the Coordination of Humanitarian Affairs, 'Iraq: Interview with Minister of Agriculture', *Humanitarian News and Analysis*, 16 December 2004 <www.irinnews.org>.
4. UN Food and Agriculture Organisation, 'Rebuilding the Plant Genetic Resources Activities in Iraq', 2011 <www.faoiraq.org>.
5. Jamail and al-Fadhily, 'Now It Is Lack of Food Security'.
6. Dahr Jamail and Ali al-Fadhily, 'Farmers in Dire Straights [*sic*]', *Inter Press Service*, 16 November 2006.
7. Jamail and al-Fadhily, 'Now It Is Lack of Food Security'.
8. Ahmed Ali and Dahr Jamail, 'Occupation Strangles Farmers', 1 March 2008 <ipsnews.net/news.asp?idnews=41414>.
9. FAO Country Briefs, Iraq, Updated July 2011 <www.fao.org/countries>.
10. Patrick Cockburn, 'Martyrs of the Iraqi Marshes', *Independent*, 24 April 2009.
11. Ibid.
12. Martin Chulov, 'Iraq Littered With High Levels of Nuclear and Dioxin Contamination, Study Finds', *Guardian*, 22 January 2010.
13. Ibid.
14. USDA, 'USDA at Work for Agriculture in Iraq', September 2010 <www.fas.usda.gov/country/iraq/development/Iraqfactsheet09710.pdf>.
15. Interview with author, 27 August 2011.
16. US Census Bureau Foreign Trade Statistics, 'U.S. Exports to Iraq 2002–2010'.
17. Jamail and al-Fadhily, 'Now It Is Lack of Food Security'.
18. USDA, 'First USDA Agribusiness Trade Mission to Iraq Arrives in Baghdad', Press Release, 7 June 2010.
19. Razzouk and Ajrash, 'Iraq Seeks Foreign Investment in Agriculture'.
20. Layth Mahdi, 'Agricultural Production: Iraq's Best Chance for Restoring Food Security', *Iraq Business News*, 8 June 2011.

CHAPTER 30 THE CORPORATE CAPTURE OF THE DEMOCRATIC STATE

1. Lawrence Summers, 'Office Memorandum: Subject: GEP, the World Bank/IMF MIGA', 12 December 1991.
2. Opinion Research Business, 'More than 1,000,000 Iraqis Murdered', 14 September 2007.
3. UN High Commissioner for Refugees, 'Iraq Refugee Emergency' <www.unrefugee.org>.
4. Harvey, *Brief Introduction to Neoliberalism*, p. 15.
5. Charles Derber, *Regime Change Begins at Home*, San Francisco, CA: Berrett Kohler Publishers, 2004, p. 52.
6. Half in Ten Campaign, 'Restoring Shared Prosperity'; Congressional Budget Office, 'Trends in the Distribution of Household Income', and Hall, 'Strong corporate profits amid weak economy'.

7. Harvey, *Brief Introduction to Neoliberalism*, p. 19.
8. James Richardson, 'World's Richest 1% Own 40% of All Wealth, UN Report Discovers', *Guardian*, 6 December 2006.
9. Arundhati Roy, 'Come September', Speech Given at Lensic Performing Arts Center, Santa Fe, NM, 18 September 2002.
10. Jubilee Debt Campaign, 'How Big is the Debt of Poor Countries?'.
11. Harvey, *Brief Introduction to Neoliberalism*, p. 162.
12. *Business Day*, 'Obama Picks Dynamic Duo to Rescue US', *Business Day*, 24 November 2008.
13. *Forbes*, Henry Paulson Biography <www.forbes.com>.
14. Summers, 'Office Memorandum'.
15. OpenSecrets.org, Barack Obama Top Contributors <http://www.opensecrets. org/politicians/contrib.php?cycle=Career&cid=N00009638>.
16. Milton Friedman, 'The Social Responsibility of Business is to Increase its Profits', *New York Times Magazine*, 13 September 1970.
17. See the coalition of groups involved with Move to Amend <www.movetoamend. org>.

Index